The Structural Representation of Proximity Matrices with MATLAB

To June —

Lay

ASA-SIAM Series on Statistics and Applied Probability

The ASA-SIAM Series on Statistics and Applied Probability is published jointly by the American Statistical Association and the Society for Industrial and Applied Mathematics. The series consists of a broad spectrum of books on topics in statistics and applied probability. The purpose of the series is to provide inexpensive, quality publications of interest to the intersecting membership of the two societies.

Editorial Board

Hubert, L., Arabie, P., and Meulman, J., *The Structural Representation of Proximity Matrices with MATLAB*

Nelson, P. R., Wludyka, P. S., and Copeland, K. A. F., *The Analysis of Means: A Graphical Method for Comparing Means, Rates, and Proportions*

Burdick, R. K., Borror, C. M., and Montgomery, D. C., *Design and Analysis of Gauge R&R Studies: Making Decisions with Confidence Intervals in Random and Mixed ANOVA Models*

Albert, J., Bennett, J., and Cochran, J. J., eds., *Anthology of Statistics in Sports*

Smith, W. F., *Experimental Design for Formulation*

Baglivo, J. A., *Mathematica Laboratories for Mathematical Statistics: Emphasizing Simulation and Computer Intensive Methods*

Lee, H. K. H., *Bayesian Nonparametrics via Neural Networks*

O'Gorman, T. W., *Applied Adaptive Statistical Methods: Tests of Significance and Confidence Intervals*

Ross, T. J., Booker, J. M., and Parkinson, W. J., eds., *Fuzzy Logic and Probability Applications: Bridging the Gap*

Nelson, W. B., *Recurrent Events Data Analysis for Product Repairs, Disease Recurrences, and Other Applications*

Mason, R. L. and Young, J. C., *Multivariate Statistical Process Control with Industrial Applications*

Smith, P. L., *A Primer for Sampling Solids, Liquids, and Gases: Based on the Seven Sampling Errors of Pierre Gy*

Meyer, M. A. and Booker, J. M., *Eliciting and Analyzing Expert Judgment: A Practical Guide*

Latouche, G. and Ramaswami, V., *Introduction to Matrix Analytic Methods in Stochastic Modeling*

Peck, R., Haugh, L., and Goodman, A., *Statistical Case Studies: A Collaboration Between Academe and Industry, Student Edition*

Peck, R., Haugh, L., and Goodman, A., *Statistical Case Studies: A Collaboration Between Academe and Industry*

Barlow, R., *Engineering Reliability*

Czitrom, V. and Spagon, P. D., *Statistical Case Studies for Industrial Process Improvement*

The Structural Representation of Proximity Matrices with MATLAB

Lawrence Hubert

University of Illinois
Champaign, Illinois

Phipps Arabie

Rutgers Business School of Newark and New Brunswick
Newark, New Jersey

Jacqueline Meulman

Leiden University
Leiden, The Netherlands

Society for Industrial and Applied Mathematics
Philadelphia, Pennsylvania

American Statistical Association
Alexandria, Virginia

The correct bibliographic citation for this book is as follows: Hubert, Lawrence, Phipps Arabie, and Jacqueline Meulman, *The Structural Representation of Proximity Matrices with MATLAB*, ASA-SIAM Series on Statistics and Applied Probability, SIAM, Philadelphia, ASA, Alexandria, VA, 2006.

The research reported in this monograph has been partially supported by the National Science Foundation through grant SES-981407 (to Lawrence Hubert) and by the Netherlands Organization for Scientific Research (NWO) through grant 575-67-053 for the "PIONEER" project "Subject Oriented Multivariate Analysis" (to Jacqueline Meulman).

Library of Congress Cataloging-in-Publication Data

Hubert, Lawrence J., 1944-
   The structural representation of proximity matrices with MATLAB / Lawrence Hubert, Phipps Arabie, Jacqueline Meulman.
      p. cm. — (ASA-SIAM series on statistics and applied probability)
   Includes bibliographical references and index.
   ISBN 0-89871-607-1 (pbk.)
   1. Proximity matrices. 2. Functions. 3. Representation of graphs. 4. MATLAB. I. Arabie, Phipps. II. Meulman, Jacqueline. III. Title. IV. Series.

   QA195.H83 2006
   512.9'434—dc22

                                                            2006042210

Dedicated to

Frank B. Baker (by Lawrence Hubert)
Richard C. Atkinson (by Phipps Arabie)
John P. Van de Geer (by Jacqueline Meulman)

Contents

List of Figures

List of Tables

Preface

As the title of this monograph implies, our main goal is to provide and illustrate the use of functions (by way of M-files) within a MATLAB® computational environment to effect a variety of structural representations for proximity information assumed available on a set of objects. The structural representations that will be of interest have been discussed and developed primarily in the applied (behavioral science) statistical literature (e.g., in psychometrics and classification), although interest in these topics has now extended much more widely (for example, to bioinformatics and chemometrics). We subdivide the monograph into three main sections depending on the general class of representations being discussed. Part I develops linear and circular uni- and multidimensional scaling using the city-block metric as the major representational device; Part II is concerned with characterizations based on various graph-theoretic tree structures, specifically with those usually referred to as ultrametrics and additive trees; Part III uses representations defined solely by order properties, particularly to what are called (strongly) anti-Robinson forms. Irrespective of the part of the monograph being discussed, there will generally be two kinds of proximity information analyzed: one-mode and two-mode. One-mode proximity data are defined between the n objects from a *single* set, usually given in the form of a square ($n \times n$) symmetric matrix with a zero main diagonal; two-mode proximity data are defined between the objects from two distinct sets containing, say, n_a and n_b objects, respectively, and given in the form of a rectangular ($n_a \times n_b$) matrix. Also, there will generally be the flexibility to allow the fitting (additively) of multiple structures to either the given one- or two-mode proximity information.

It is not the intent of the monograph to present formal demonstrations of the various assertions we might make along the way, such as for the convergence of a particular algorithm or approach. All of this is generally available in the literature (and much of it by the authors of the current monograph), and the references to this source material are given when appropriate. The primary interest here is to present and demonstrate how to actually find and fit these structures computationally with the help of some sixty-five functions (though M-files) we provide that are usable within a MATLAB computational environment. The usage header information for each of these functions is given in Appendix A (listed alphabetically). The M-files themselves can be downloaded individually from

http://cda.psych.uiuc.edu/srpm_mfiles

Here, the acronym "srpm" stands (obviously) for "structural representation (of) proximity matrices." Also, there is a "zipped" file called srpm_mfiles.zip at this site that includes all of the files, as well as the few small data sets used throughout the monograph to illustrate the results of invoking the various M-files (or, equivalently for us, M-functions); thus, the reader should be able to reproduce all of the examples given in the monograph (assuming, obviously, access to a MATLAB environment). If additional examples are desired, the reader is directed to Michael Lee's web site and the some fifty or so proximity matrices he has collected and made available in the MATLAB MAT-file format (in a "zipped" file called `all.zip`):

```
www.psychology.adelaide.edu.au/
    personalpages/staff/michaellee/homepage
```

The computational approach implemented in the provided M-files for obtaining the sundry representations is, by choice, invariably least-squares and based on what is called the Dykstra–Kaczmarz (DK) method for solving linear inequality constrained least-squares tasks. The latter iterative strategy is reviewed in Chapter 1 (Section 1.4, in particular). All of the representations of concern (over all three monograph parts) can be characterized by explicit linear inequalities; thus, once the latter constraints are known (by, for example, the identification of certain object permutations through secondary optimization problems such as quadratic assignment), the actual representing structure can be obtained by using the iterative DK strategy. Also, as we will see particularly in Part II dealing with graph-theoretic tree structures (ultrametrics and additive trees), the DK approach can even be adopted heuristically to first identify the inequality constraints that we might wish to impose in the first place. And once identified in this exploratory fashion, a second application of DK could then do a confirmatory fitting of the now fixed and identified inequality constraints.

As noted above, our purpose in writing this monograph is to provide an applied documentation source for a collection of M-files that would be of interest to applied statisticians and data analysts but also accessible to a notationally sophisticated but otherwise substantively focused user. Such a person would typically be most interested in analyzing a specific data set by adopting one (or some) of the structural representations we discuss. The background we have tried to assume is at the same level required to follow the documentation for good, commercially available optimization subroutines, such as the Numerical Algorithms Group (NAG) Fortran subroutine library, or at the level of one of the standard texts in applied multivariate analysis usually used for a graduate second-year methodology course in the behavioral and social sciences. An excellent example of the latter would be the widely used text now in its fifth edition by Johnson and Wichern (2002). Draft versions of the current monograph have been used as supplementary material for a course relying on the latter text as the primary reference.

The research reported in this monograph has been partially supported by the National Science Foundation through grant SES-981407 (to Lawrence Hubert) and by the Netherlands Organization for Scientific Research (NWO) through grant 575-67-053 for the "PIONEER" project "Subject Oriented Multivariate Analysis" (to Jacqueline Meulman).

Lawrence Hubert
Phipps Arabie
Jacqueline Meulman

Part I

(Multi- and Unidimensional) City-Block Scaling

Chapter 1

Linear Unidimensional Scaling

The task of linear unidimensional scaling (LUS) can be characterized as a specific data analysis problem: given a set of n objects, $S = \{O_1, \ldots, O_n\}$, and an $n \times n$ symmetric proximity matrix, $\mathbf{P} = \{p_{ij}\}$, arrange the objects along a single dimension such that the induced $n(n-1)/2$ interpoint distances between the objects reflect the proximities in $\mathbf{P}$. The term "proximity" refers to any symmetric numerical measure of relationship between each object pair ($p_{ij} = p_{ji}$ for $1 \leq i, j \leq n$) and for which all self-proximities are considered irrelevant and set equal to zero ($p_{ii} = 0$ for $1 \leq i \leq n$). As a technical convenience, proximities are assumed nonnegative and are given a dissimilarity interpretation, so that large proximities refer to dissimilar objects.

As a starting point to be developed exclusively in this first chapter, we consider the most common formalization of measuring how close the interpoint distances are to the given proximities by the sum of squared discrepancies. Specifically, we wish to find the n coordinates, $x_1, x_2, \ldots, x_n$, such that the least-squares (or L_2) criterion

$$\sum_{i<j} (p_{ij} - |x_j - x_i|)^2 \tag{1.1}$$

is minimized. Although there is some arbitrariness in the selection of this measure of goodness-of-fit for metric scaling, the choice is traditional and has been discussed in some detail in the literature by Guttman (1968), Defays (1978), de Leeuw and Heiser (1977), and Hubert and Arabie (1986), among others. In the various sections that follow, we will develop a particular heuristic strategy for the minimization of (1.1) based on the iterative use of a quadratic assignment improvement technique. Other methods are possible but will not be explicitly discussed here; the reader is referred to Hubert, Arabie, and Meulman (2002) for a comparison among several optimization alternatives for the basic LUS task.

In addition to developing the combinatorial optimization task of actually identifying a best unidimensional scaling, Section 1.3 introduces two additional problems within the LUS context: (a) the confirmatory fitting of a unidimensional scale (through coordinate estimation) based on a fixed (and given) object ordering; (b) the extension to nonmetric unidimensional scaling incorporating an additional optimal monotonic transformation of the proximities. Both these optimization tasks are formulated through the L_2-norm and

3

implemented using applications of what is called the Dykstra–Kaczmarz method of solving linear (in)equality constrained least-squares tasks (Kaczmarz, 1937; Dykstra, 1983). The latter strategy is reviewed briefly in a short addendum (Section 1.4) to this chapter.

1.1   LUS in the L_2-Norm

As a reformulation of the L_2 unidimensional scaling task that will prove crucial as a point of departure in our development of a computational routine, the optimization suggested by (1.1) can be subdivided into two separate problems to be solved simultaneously: find a set of n numbers, $x_1 \leq x_2 \leq \cdots \leq x_n$, *and* a permutation on the first n integers, $\rho(\cdot) \equiv \rho$, for which

$$\sum_{i<j}(p_{\rho(i)\rho(j)} - (x_j - x_i))^2 \tag{1.2}$$

is minimized. Thus, a set of locations (coordinates) is defined along a continuum as represented in ascending order by the sequence $x_1, x_2, \ldots, x_n$; the n objects are allocated to these locations by the permutation ρ, so that object $O_{\rho(i)}$ is placed at location i. Without loss of generality we will impose the one additional constraint that $\sum_i x_i = 0$; i.e., any set of values, $x_1, x_2, \ldots, x_n$, can be replaced by $x_1 - \bar{x}, x_2 - \bar{x}, \ldots, x_n - \bar{x}$, where $\bar{x} = (1/n)\sum_i x_i$, without altering the value of (1.1) or (1.2). Formally, if ρ^* and $x_1^* \leq x_2^* \leq \cdots \leq x_n^*$ define a global minimum of (1.2), and Ω denotes the set of all permutations of the first n integers, then

$$\sum_{i<j}(p_{\rho^*(i)\rho^*(j)} - (x_j^* - x_i^*))^2$$

$$= \min\left[\sum_{i<j}(p_{\rho(i)\rho(j)} - (x_j - x_i))^2 \mid \rho \in \Omega; \; x_1 \leq \cdots \leq x_n; \; \sum_i x_i = 0\right].$$

The measure of loss in (1.2) can be reduced algebraically:

$$\sum_{i<j}p_{ij}^2 + n\left(\sum_i x_i^2 - 2\sum_i x_i t_i^{(\rho)}\right), \tag{1.3}$$

subject to the constraints that $x_1 \leq \cdots \leq x_n$ and $\sum_i x_i = 0$, and letting

$$t_i^{(\rho)} = (u_i^{(\rho)} - v_i^{(\rho)})/n,$$

where

$$u_i^{(\rho)} = \sum_{j=1}^{i-1} p_{\rho(i)\rho(j)} \text{ for } i \geq 2,$$

$$v_i^{(\rho)} = \sum_{j=i+1}^{n} p_{\rho(i)\rho(j)} \text{ for } i < n,$$

and

$$u_1^{(\rho)} = v_n^{(\rho)} = 0.$$

Verbally, $u_i^{(\rho)}$ is the sum of the entries within row $\rho(i)$ of $\{p_{\rho(i)\rho(j)}\}$ from the extreme left up to the main diagonal; $v_i^{(\rho)}$ is the sum from the main diagonal to the extreme right. Or, we might rewrite (1.3) as

$$\sum_{i<j} p_{ij}^2 + n\left(\sum_i (x_i - t_i^{(\rho)})^2 - \sum_i (t_i^{(\rho)})^2\right). \qquad (1.4)$$

In (1.4), the two terms $\sum_i (x_i - t_i^{(\rho)})^2$ and $\sum_i (t_i^{(\rho)})^2$ control the size of the discrepancy index since $\sum_{i<j} p_{ij}^2$ is constant for any given data matrix. Thus, to minimize the original index in (1.2), we should simultaneously minimize $\sum_i (x_i - t_i^{(\rho)})^2$ and maximize $\sum_i (t_i^{(\rho)})^2$. If the equivalent form of (1.3) is considered, our concern would be in minimizing $\sum_i x_i^2$ and maximizing $\sum_i x_i t_i^{(\rho)}$.

As noted first by Defays (1978), the minimization of (1.4) can be carried out directly by the maximization of the single term, $\sum_i (t_i^{(\rho)})^2$ (under the mild regularity condition that all off-diagonal proximities in $\mathbf{P}$ are positive and not merely nonnegative). Explicitly, if ρ^* is a permutation that maximizes $\sum_i (t_i^{(\rho)})^2$, then we can let $x_i = t_i^{(\rho^*)}$, which eliminates the term $\sum_i (x_i - t_i^{(\rho^*)})^2$ from (1.4). In short, because the order induced by $t_1^{(\rho^*)}, \ldots, t_n^{(\rho^*)}$ is consistent with the constraint $x_1 \leq x_2 \leq \cdots \leq x_n$, the minimization of (1.4) reduces to the maximization of the single term $\sum_i (t_i^{(\rho)})^2$, with the coordinate estimation completed as an automatic by-product.

1.1.1 A Data Set for Illustrative Purposes

It is convenient to have a small numerical example available as we discuss optimization strategies in the unidimensional scaling context. Toward this end we list a data file in Table 1.1, called `number.dat`, that contains a dissimilarity matrix taken from Shepard, Kilpatric, and Cunningham (1975). The stimulus domain is the first ten single-digits $\{0, 1, 2, \ldots, 9\}$ considered as abstract concepts; the 10×10 proximity matrix (with an ith row or column corresponding to the $i - 1$ digit) was constructed by averaging dissimilarity ratings for distinct pairs of those integers over a number of subjects and conditions. Given the various analyses of this proximity matrix that have appeared in the literature (e.g., see Hubert, Arabie, and Meulman, 2001), the data reflect two types of very regular patterning based on absolute digit magnitude and the structural characteristics of the digits (e.g., the powers or multiples of 2 or 3, the salience of the two additive/multiplicative identities [0/1], oddness/evenness). These data will be relied on to provide concrete numerical illustrations of the various MATLAB functions we introduce and will be loaded as a proximity matrix (and, importantly, as one that is symmetric and has zero values along the main diagonal) in the MATLAB environment by the command `load number.dat`. As we will see, the dominant single unidimensional scale found for these data is most consistent with digit magnitude.

1.2 L_2 Optimization Methods

This section shows how a well-known combinatorial optimization task, called quadratic assignment, can be used iteratively for LUS in the L_2-norm. Based on the reformulation in

Table 1.1. *The number.dat data file extracted from Shepard, Kilpatric, and Cunningham* (1975).

.000	.421	.584	.709	.684	.804	.788	.909	.821	.850
.421	.000	.284	.346	.646	.588	.758	.630	.791	.625
.584	.284	.000	.354	.059	.671	.421	.796	.367	.808
.709	.346	.354	.000	.413	.429	.300	.592	.804	.263
.684	.646	.059	.413	.000	.409	.388	.742	.246	.683
.804	.588	.671	.429	.409	.000	.396	.400	.671	.592
.788	.758	.421	.300	.388	.396	.000	.417	.350	.296
.909	.630	.796	.592	.742	.400	.417	.000	.400	.459
.821	.791	.367	.804	.246	.671	.350	.400	.000	.392
.850	.625	.808	.263	.683	.592	.296	.459	.392	.000

(1.3), we concentrate on maximizing $\sum_i x_i t_i^{(\rho)}$, with iterative reestimation of the coordinates $x_1, \ldots, x_n$. Various function implementations within MATLAB are given for both the basic quadratic assignment task and how it is used for LUS.

1.2.1   Iterative Quadratic Assignment

Because of the manner in which the discrepancy index for the unidimensional scaling task can be rephrased as in (1.3) and (1.4), the two optimization subproblems to be solved simultaneously of identifying an optimal permutation and a set of coordinates can be separated:

(a) Assuming that an ordering of the objects is known (and denoted, say, as ρ^0 for the moment), find those values $x_1^0 \leq \cdots \leq x_n^0$ to minimize $\sum_i (x_i^0 - t_i^{(\rho^0)})^2$. If the permutation ρ^0 produces a *monotonic* form for the matrix $\{p_{\rho^0(i)\rho^0(j)}\}$ in the sense that $t_1^{(\rho^0)} \leq t_2^{(\rho^0)} \leq \cdots \leq t_n^{(\rho^0)}$, the coordinate estimation is immediate by letting $x_i^0 = t_i^{(\rho^0)}$, in which case $\sum_i (x_i^0 - t_i^{(\rho^0)})^2$ is zero.

(b) Assuming that the locations $x_1^0 \leq \cdots \leq x_n^0$ are known, find the permutation ρ^0 to maximize $\sum_i x_i t_i^{(\rho^0)}$. We note from the work of Hubert and Arabie (1986, p. 189) that any such permutation which even only locally maximizes $\sum_i x_i t_i^{(\rho^0)}$, in the sense that no adjacently placed pair of objects in ρ^0 could be interchanged to increase the index, will produce a monotonic form for the nonnegative matrix $\{p_{\rho^0(i)\rho^0(j)}\}$. Also, the task of finding the permutation ρ^0 to maximize $\sum_i x_i t_i^{(\rho^0)}$ is actually a quadratic assignment (QA) task which has been discussed extensively in the literature of operations research; e.g., see Francis and White (1974), Lawler (1975), and Hubert and Schultz (1976), among others. As usually defined, a QA problem involves two $n \times n$ matrices $\mathbf{A} = \{a_{ij}\}$ and $\mathbf{B} = \{b_{ij}\}$, and we seek a permutation ρ to maximize

$$\Gamma(\rho) = \sum_{i,j} a_{\rho(i)\rho(j)} b_{ij}. \tag{1.5}$$

If we define $b_{ij} = |x_i - x_j|$ and let $a_{ij} = p_{ij}$, then

$$\Gamma(\rho) = \sum_{i,j} p_{\rho(i)\rho(j)} |x_i - x_j| = 2n \sum_i x_i t_i^{(\rho)},$$

and thus the permutation that maximizes $\Gamma(\rho)$ also maximizes $\sum x_i t_i^{(\rho)}$.

The QA optimization task as formulated through (1.5) has an enormous literature attached to it, and the reader is referred to Pardalos and Wolkowicz (1994) for an up-to-date and comprehensive review. For current purposes and as provided in three general M-functions of the next section (pairwiseqa.m, rotateqa.m, and insertqa.m), one might consider the optimization of (1.5) through simple object interchange/rearrangement heuristics. Based on given matrices **A** and **B**, and beginning with some permutation (possibly chosen at random), local interchanges/rearrangements of a particular type are implemented until no improvement in the index can be made. By repeatedly initializing such a process randomly, a distribution over a set of local optima can be achieved. At least within the context of some common data analysis applications, such a distribution may be highly relevant diagnostically for explaining whatever structure might be inherent in the matrix **A**. We give an example of how random starts might be studied for the context of unidimensional scaling toward the end of the current section. This should serve as a general template for other applications (M-files) as well.

In a subsequent subsection below, we introduce the main M-function for unidimensional scaling (uniscalqa.m) based on these earlier QA optimization strategies. In effect, we begin with an equally spaced set of fixed coordinates with their interpoint distances defining the **B** matrix of the general QA index in (1.5) and a random object permutation; a locally optimal permutation is then identified through a collection of local interchanges/rearrangements; the coordinates are reestimated based on this identified permutation; and the whole process is repeated until no change can be made in either the identified permutation or coordinate collection.

The QA interchange/rearrangement heuristics

The three M-functions that carry out general QA interchange/rearrangement heuristics all have the same general usage syntax (note the use of three dots to indicate a statement continuation in MATLAB):

```
[outperm,rawindex,allperms,index] = ...
                    pairwiseqa(prox,targ,inperm)

[outperm,rawindex,allperms,index] = ...
                    rotateqa(prox,targ,inperm,kblock)

[outperm,rawindex,allperms,index] = ...
                    insertqa(prox,targ,inperm,kblock)
```

pairwiseqa.m carries out a QA maximization task using the pairwise interchanges of objects in the current permutation defining the row and column order of the data matrix. *All*

possible such interchanges are generated and considered in turn, and whenever an increase in
the cross-product index would result from a particular interchange, it is made immediately.
The process continues until the current permutation cannot be improved upon by any such
pairwise object interchange; this final locally optimal permutation is OUTPERM. The input
beginning permutation is INPERM (a permutation of the first n integers); PROX is the $n \times n$
input proximity matrix and TARG is the $n \times n$ input target matrix (which are respective
analogues of the matrices **A** and **B** of (1.5)); the final OUTPERM row and column permutation
of PROX has the cross-product index RAWINDEX with respect to TARG; RAWINDEX is
$\Gamma(\rho)$ in (1.5), where ρ is now given as OUTPERM. The cell array ALLPERMS contains
INDEX entries corresponding to all the permutations identified in the optimization, from
ALLPERMS{1} = INPERM to ALLPERMS{INDEX} = OUTPERM. (Note that within
a MATLAB environment, entries of a cell array must be accessed through the curly braces,
{ }.) rotateqa.m carries out a similar iterative QA maximization task but now uses
the rotation (or inversion) of from 2 to KBLOCK (which is less than or equal to $n - 1$)
consecutive objects in the current permutation defining the row and column order of the
data matrix. insertqa.m relies on the reinsertion of from 1 to KBLOCK consecutive
objects somewhere in the permutation defining the current row and column order of the data
matrix.

The function uniscalqa.m

The function M-file uniscalqa.m carries out a unidimensional scaling of a symmetric dissimilarity matrix (with a zero main diagonal) using an iterative QA strategy. We
begin with an equally spaced target, a (random) starting permutation, and use a sequential combination of the pairwise interchange/rotation/insertion heuristics; the target matrix
is reestimated based on the identified (locally optimal) permutation. The whole process
is repeated until no changes can be made in the target or the identified (locally optimal)
permutation. The explicit usage syntax is

```
[outperm,rawindex,allperms,index,coord,diff] = ...
                uniscalqa(prox,targ,inperm,kblock)
```

where all terms are (mostly) present in the three QA heuristic M-functions of the previous subsection. Here, COORD gives the final coordinates achieved, and DIFF provides
the attained value for the least-squares loss function. A recording of a MATLAB session using number.dat follows; note the application of the built-in MATLAB function
randperm(10) to obtain a random input permutation of the first 10 digits, and the use
of the utility M-function, targlin.m (and the command targlin(10)), to generate a
target matrix, targlinear, based on an equally (and unit) spaced set of coordinates. In
the output given below, semicolons are placed after the invocation of the M-functions to
initially suppress the output; transposes (') are then used on the output vectors to conserve
space by using only row (as opposed to column) vectors in the listing.

```
load number.dat
targlinear = targlin(10);
inperm = randperm(10);
kblock = 2;
```

```
[outperm,rawindex,allperms,index,coord,diff] = ...
uniscalqa(number,targlinear,inperm,kblock);

 outperm

outperm =

     1     2     3     5     4     6     7     9    10     8

 coord'

ans =

  Columns 1 through 6

  -0.6570    -0.4247    -0.2608    -0.1492    -0.0566     0.0842

  Columns 7 through 10

   0.1988     0.3258     0.4050     0.5345

 diff

diff =

   1.9599
```

Random restarts for uniscalqa.m

One of our comments indicated that by allowing random starts for some of the routines we would be developing, a possibly diagnostic set of local optima might be generated. To illustrate this in more detail and to provide a template that could be emulated more generally throughout the monograph, we will show how this might be done for the just-introduced unidimensional scaling routine uniscalqa.m. The M-file uniscalqa_montecarlo.m is listed below and takes as input three matrices: PROX, the original input proximity matrix; KBLOCK to control the QA optimization routines; and NSTART to denote the number of random permutations for which uniscalqa.m is to be invoked. As output, there are two cell arrays containing the final permutations and coordinates observed during the random starts (OUTPERMS and COORDS) and three vectors containing the output cross-products, RAWINDICES, the number of permutations visited to obtain the latter, INDICES, and the least-squares loss criterion values, DIFFS.

```
function [outperms,rawindices,indices,coords,diffs] = ...
    uniscalqa_montecarlo(prox,kblock,nstart)

rand('state',sum(100*clock));
```

```
n = size(prox,1);
targ = targlin(n);

for i = 1:nstart
    inperm = randperm(n);
    [outperm,rawindex,allperms,index,coord,diff] = ...
        uniscalqa(prox,targ,inperm,kblock);
    outperms{i} = outperm;
    rawindices(i) = rawindex;
    indices(i) = index;
    coords{i} = coord;
    diffs(i) = diff;
end
```

Note that the state of the random number generator is reset "randomly" at the start of the session (using `rand('state',sum(100clock))`) so the same sequence of random permutations is not obtained; also, the equally spaced target matrix generated from `targlin.m` is automatic input to the call to `uniscalqa.m`.

In the small examples that follow, ten random starts were given for our number data, with only one local optima observed (at an index value of 26.1594); an additional ten random starts for a random proximity matrix (with uniform distribution on [0,1] for the entries constructed with the utility function `randprox.m`) shows two local optima at index values of 24.9350 and 25.1622. Obviously, these types of examples could be extended.

```
 load number.dat
 kblock = 2;
 nstart = 10;
 [outperms,rawindices,indices,coords,diffs] = ...
uniscalqa_montecarlo(number,kblock,nstart);

 rawindices

rawindices =

  Columns 1 through 6

    26.1594    26.1594    26.1594    26.1594    26.1594    26.1594

  Columns 7 through 10

    26.1594    26.1594    26.1594    26.1594

 data = randprox(10);
 data

data =
```

```
Columns 1 through 6

         0    0.8649    0.2503    0.4106    0.8525    0.3221
    0.8649         0    0.4737    0.5080    0.4470    0.9500
    0.2503    0.4737         0    0.5019    0.5958    0.8028
    0.4106    0.5080    0.5019         0    0.1841    0.4619
    0.8525    0.4470    0.5958    0.1841         0    0.8704
    0.3221    0.9500    0.8028    0.4619    0.8704         0
    0.2710    0.7454    0.3279    0.2878    0.3647    0.5435
    0.8550    0.3273    0.1561    0.4915    0.6460    0.9158
    0.6985    0.2331    0.2319    0.9252    0.8957    0.2553
    0.4754    0.3112    0.4829    0.3670    0.5238    0.8076


Columns 7 through 10

    0.2710    0.8550    0.6985    0.4754
    0.7454    0.3273    0.2331    0.3112
    0.3279    0.1561    0.2319    0.4829
    0.2878    0.4915    0.9252    0.3670
    0.3647    0.6460    0.8957    0.5238
    0.5435    0.9158    0.2553    0.8076
         0    0.9291    0.0794    0.8903
    0.9291         0    0.4160    0.0510
    0.0794    0.4160         0    0.2751
    0.8903    0.0510    0.2751         0
```

```
[outperms,rawindices,indices,coords,diffs] = ...
uniscalqa_montecarlo(data,kblock,nstart);
 rawindices


rawindices =

  Columns 1 through 6

   24.9350   25.1622   24.9350   25.1622   25.1622   25.1622

  Columns 7 through 10

   25.1622   24.9350   25.1622   25.1622
```

1.3 Confirmatory and Nonmetric LUS

In developing LUS (as well as other types of) representations for a proximity matrix, it is convenient to have a general mechanism available for solving linear (in)equality constrained least-squares tasks. The two such instances discussed in this section involve (a) the confirmatory fitting of a given object order to a proximity matrix (through an M-file called `linfit.m`) and (b) the construction of an optimal monotonic transformation of a proximity matrix in relation to a given unidimensional ordering (through an M-file called `proxmon.m`). In both these cases, we rely on what can be called the Dykstra–Kaczmarz method. An equality constrained least-squares task may be rephrased as a linear system of equations, with the latter solvable through a strategy of iterative projection as attributed to Kaczmarz (1937; see Bodewig, 1956, pp. 163–164); a more general inequality constrained least-squares task can also be approached through iterative projection as developed by Dykstra (1983). The Kaczmarz and Dykstra strategies are reviewed very briefly in the chapter addendum (Section 1.4) and implemented within the two M-files, `linfit.m` and `proxmon.m`, discussed below.

1.3.1   The Confirmatory Fitting of a Given Order Using linfit.m

The M-function `linfit.m` fits a set of coordinates to a given proximity matrix based on some given input permutation, say, $\rho^{(0)}$. Specifically, we seek $x_1 \leq x_2 \leq \cdots \leq x_n$ such that $\sum_{i<j}(p_{\rho^0(i)\rho^0(j)} - |x_j - x_i|)^2$ is minimized (and where the permutation $\rho^{(0)}$ may not even put the matrix $\{p_{\rho^0(i)\rho^0(j)}\}$ into a monotonic form). Using the syntax

```
[fit,diff,coord] = linfit(prox,inperm)
```

the matrix $\{|x_j - x_i|\}$ is referred to as the fitted matrix (FIT); COORD gives the ordered coordinates; and DIFF is the value of the least-squares criterion. The fitted matrix is found through the Dykstra–Kaczmarz method, where the equality constraints defined by distances along a continuum are imposed to find the fitted matrix; i.e., if $i < j < k$, then $|x_i - x_j| + |x_j - x_k| = |x_i - x_k|$. Once found, the actual ordered coordinates are retrieved by the usual $t_i^{(\rho^0)}$ formula used in (1.3) but computed on FIT.

The example below of the use of `linfit.m` fits two separate orders: the identity permutation, `inperm_identity`, and the one that we know is least-squares optimal, `inperm_optimal` (see Hubert, Arabie, and Meulman, 2002, for an explicit justification of optimality using a dynamic programming routine). We note that, as it should, `diff` is smaller (at a value of 1.9599) using `inperm_optimal` compared to `inperm_identity` (at a value of 2.1046).

```
load number.dat
inperm_identity = [1 2 3 4 5 6 7 8 9 10];
[fit,diff,coord] = linfit(number,inperm_identity);
coord'

ans =

  Columns 1 through 6

    -0.6570    -0.4247    -0.2608    -0.1392    -0.0666     0.0842

  Columns 7 through 10
```

```
    0.1988      0.3627      0.4058      0.4968

 diff

diff =

    2.1046

 inperm_optimal = [1 2 3 5 4 6 7 9 10 8];
 [fit,diff,coord] = linfit(number,inperm_optimal);
 coord'

ans =

  Columns 1 through 6

   -0.6570     -0.4247     -0.2608     -0.1492     -0.0566      0.0842

  Columns 7 through 10

    0.1988      0.3258      0.4050      0.5345

 diff

diff =

    1.9599
```

1.3.2   The Monotonic Transformation of a Proximity Matrix Using proxmon.m

The function proxmon.m provides a monotonically transformed proximity matrix that is closest in a least-squares sense to a given input matrix. The syntax is

```
[monproxpermut,vaf,diff] = proxmon(proxpermut,fitted)
```

Here, PROXPERMUT is the input proximity matrix (which may have been subjected to an initial row/column permutation, hence the suffix PERMUT) and FITTED is a given target matrix; the output matrix MONPROXPERMUT is closest to FITTED in a least-squares sense and obeys the order constraints obtained from each pair of entries in (the upper-triangular portion of) PROXPERMUT (and where the inequality constrained optimization is carried out using the Dykstra–Kaczmarz iterative projection strategy); VAF denotes "variance-accounted-for" and indicates how much variance in MONPROXPERMUT can be accounted for by FITTED; finally, DIFF is the value of the least-squares loss function and is the sum of squared differences between the entries in FITTED and MONPROXPERMUT (actually, DIFF is one-half of such a sum because the loss function in (1.1) is over $i < j$).

In the notation of the previous section when fitting a given order, FITTED would correspond to the matrix $\{|x_j - x_i|\}$, where $x_1 \leq x_2 \leq \cdots \leq x_n$; the input PROXPERMUT would be $\{p_{\rho^0(i)\rho^0(j)}\}$; MONPROXPERMUT would be $\{f(p_{\rho^0(i)\rho^0(j)})\}$, where the function $f(\cdot)$ satisfies the monotonicity constraints; i.e., if $p_{\rho^0(i)\rho^0(j)} < p_{\rho^0(i')\rho^0(j')}$ for $1 \leq i < j \leq n$ and $1 \leq i' < j' \leq n$, then $f(p_{\rho^0(i)\rho^0(j)}) \leq f(p_{\rho^0(i')\rho^0(j')})$. The transformed proximity matrix $\{f(p_{\rho^0(i)\rho^0(j)})\}$ minimizes the least-squares criterion (DIFF) of

$$\sum_{i<j} (f(p_{\rho^0(i)\rho^0(j)}) - |x_j - x_i|)^2$$

over *all* functions $f(\cdot)$ that satisfy the monotonicity constraints. The VAF is a normalization of this loss value by the sum of squared deviations of the transformed proximities from their mean:

$$\text{VAF} = 1 - \frac{\sum_{i<j} (f(p_{\rho^0(i)\rho^0(j)}) - |x_j - x_i|)^2}{\sum_{i<j} (f(p_{\rho^0(i)\rho^0(j)}) - \bar{f})^2},$$

where $\bar{f}$ denotes the mean of the off-diagonal entries in $\{f(p_{\rho^0(i)\rho^0(j)})\}$.

An application incorporating proxmon.m

The script M-file listed below gives an application of proxmon.m using the (globally optimal) permutation found previously for our number.dat matrix. First, linfit.m is invoked to obtain a fitted matrix (fit); proxmon.m then generates the monotonically transformed proximity matrix (monproxpermut) with VAF = .5821 and diff = 1.0623. The strategy is then repeated cyclically (i.e., finding a fitted matrix based on the monotonically transformed proximity matrix, finding a new monotonically transformed matrix, and so on). To avoid degeneracy (where all matrices would converge to zeros), the sum of squares of the fitted matrix is normalized; convergence is based on observing a minimal change (less than 1.0e-006) in the VAF. As indicated in the output below, the final VAF is .6672 with a diff of .9718. (Although the permutation found earlier for number.dat remains the same throughout the construction of the optimal monotonic transformation, in this particular example it would also remain optimal with the same VAF if the unidimensional scaling were repeated with monproxpermut now considered the input proximity matrix. Even though probably rare, other data sets might not have such an invariance, and it may be desirable to initiate an iterative routine that finds a unidimensional scaling (i.e., an object ordering) in addition to monotonically transforming the proximity matrix.)

```
load number.dat
inperm = [8 10 9 7 6 4 5 3 2 1];
[fit diff coord] = linfit(number,inperm);
[monproxpermut vaf diff] = ...
    proxmon(number(inperm,inperm),fit);
sumfitsq = sum(sum(fit.^2));
prevvaf = 2;
while (abs(prevvaf-vaf) >= 1.0e-006)
   prevvaf = vaf;
   [fit diff coord] = linfit(monproxpermut,1:10);
```

```
    sumnewfitsq = sum(sum(fit.^2));
    fit = sqrt(sumfitsq)*(fit/sqrt(sumnewfitsq));
     [monproxpermut vaf diff] = ...
         proxmon(number(inperm,inperm), fit);
end

fit
diff
coord'
monproxpermut
vaf

fit =

  Columns 1 through 6

           0    0.0824    0.1451    0.3257    0.4123    0.5582
      0.0824         0    0.0627    0.2432    0.3298    0.4758
      0.1451    0.0627         0    0.1806    0.2672    0.4131
      0.3257    0.2432    0.1806         0    0.0866    0.2325
      0.4123    0.3298    0.2672    0.0866         0    0.1459
      0.5582    0.4758    0.4131    0.2325    0.1459         0
      0.5834    0.5010    0.4383    0.2578    0.1711    0.0252
      0.7244    0.6419    0.5793    0.3987    0.3121    0.1662
      0.8696    0.7872    0.7245    0.5440    0.4573    0.3114
      1.2231    1.1406    1.0780    0.8974    0.8108    0.6649

  Columns 7 through 10

      0.5834    0.7244    0.8696    1.2231
      0.5010    0.6419    0.7872    1.1406
      0.4383    0.5793    0.7245    1.0780
      0.2578    0.3987    0.5440    0.8974
      0.1711    0.3121    0.4573    0.8108
      0.0252    0.1662    0.3114    0.6649
           0    0.1410    0.2862    0.6397
      0.1410         0    0.1452    0.4987
      0.2862    0.1452         0    0.3535
      0.6397    0.4987    0.3535         0


diff =

      0.9718
```

```
ans =

  Columns 1 through 6

   -0.4558    -0.3795    -0.3215    -0.1544    -0.0742     0.0609

  Columns 7 through 10

    0.0842     0.2147     0.3492     0.6764


monproxpermut =

  Columns 1 through 6

        0      0.2612     0.2458     0.2612     0.2458     0.5116
   0.2612          0      0.2458     0.2458     0.4286     0.2458
   0.2458     0.2458          0      0.2458     0.5116     0.6899
   0.2612     0.2458     0.2458          0      0.2458     0.2458
   0.2458     0.4286     0.5116     0.2458          0      0.2612
   0.5116     0.2458     0.6899     0.2458     0.2612          0
   0.6080     0.5116     0.2458     0.2458     0.2458     0.2458
   0.6899     0.7264     0.2458     0.2612     0.5116     0.2458
   0.5116     0.5116     0.6899     0.6080     0.4286     0.2458
   1.2231     1.1406     1.0780     0.6899     0.7264     0.6080

  Columns 7 through 10

   0.6080     0.6899     0.5116     1.2231
   0.5116     0.7264     0.5116     1.1406
   0.2458     0.2458     0.6899     1.0780
   0.2458     0.2612     0.6080     0.6899
   0.2458     0.5116     0.4286     0.7264
   0.2458     0.2458     0.2458     0.6080
        0      0.1410     0.5116     0.6080
   0.1410          0      0.2458     0.4286
   0.5116     0.2458          0      0.2612
   0.6080     0.4286     0.2612          0


vaf =

    0.6672
```

1.4 The Dykstra–Kaczmarz Method

Kaczmarz's method can be characterized as follows:

Given $\mathbf{A} = \{a_{ij}\}$ of order $m \times n$, $\mathbf{x}' = \{x_1, \ldots, x_n\}$, $\mathbf{b}' = \{b_1, \ldots, b_m\}$, and assuming the linear system $\mathbf{A}\mathbf{x} = \mathbf{b}$ is consistent, define the set $C_i = \{\mathbf{x} \mid \sum_{j=1}^{n} a_{ij}x_j = b_i, 1 \le j \le n\}$, for $1 \le i \le m$. The projection of any $n \times 1$ vector $\mathbf{y}$ onto C_i is simply $\mathbf{y} - (\mathbf{a}_i'\mathbf{y} - b_i)\mathbf{a}_i(\mathbf{a}_i'\mathbf{a}_i)^{-1}$, where $\mathbf{a}_i' = \{a_{i1}, \ldots, a_{in}\}$. Beginning with a vector $\mathbf{x}_0$, and successively projecting $\mathbf{x}_0$ onto C_1, and that result onto C_2, and so on, and cyclically and repeatedly reconsidering projections onto the sets $C_1, \ldots, C_m$, leads at convergence to a vector $\mathbf{x}_0^*$ that is closest to $\mathbf{x}_0$ (in vector 2-norm, so that $\sum_{j=1}^{n}(x_{0j} - x_{0j}^*)^2$ is minimized) and $\mathbf{A}\mathbf{x}_0^* = \mathbf{b}$. In short, Kaczmarz's method iteratively solves least-squares tasks subject to equality restrictions.

Dykstra's method can be characterized as follows:

Given $\mathbf{A} = \{a_{ij}\}$ of order $m \times n$, $\mathbf{x}_0' = \{x_{01}, \ldots, x_{0n}\}$, $\mathbf{b}' = \{b_1, \ldots, b_m\}$, and $\mathbf{w}' = \{w_1, \ldots, w_n\}$, where $w_j > 0$ for all j, find $\mathbf{x}_0^*$ such that $\mathbf{a}_i'\mathbf{x}_0^* \le b_i$ for $1 \le i \le m$ and $\sum_{j=1}^{n} w_j(x_{0j} - x_{0j}^*)^2$ is minimized. Again, (re)define the (closed convex) sets $C_i = \{\mathbf{x} \mid \sum_{j=1}^{n} a_{ij}x_j \le b_i, 1 \le j \le n\}$, and when a vector $\mathbf{y} \notin C_i$, its projection onto C_i (in the metric defined by the weight vector $\mathbf{w}$) is $\mathbf{y} - (\mathbf{a}_i'\mathbf{y} - b_i)\mathbf{a}_i\mathbf{W}^{-1}(\mathbf{a}_i'\mathbf{W}^{-1}\mathbf{a}_i)^{-1}$, where $\mathbf{W}^{-1} = \text{diag}\{w_1^{-1}, \ldots, w_n^{-1}\}$. We again initialize the process with the vector $\mathbf{x}_0$ and each set $C_1, \ldots, C_m$ is considered in turn. If the vector being carried forward to this point when C_i is (re)considered does not satisfy the constraint defining C_i, a projection onto C_i occurs. The sets $C_1, \ldots, C_m$ are cyclically and repeatedly considered but with one difference from the operation of Kaczmarz's method—each time a constraint set C_i is revisited, any changes from the previous time C_i was reached are first "added back." This last process ensures convergence to a (globally) optimal solution $\mathbf{x}_0^*$ (see Dykstra, 1983). Thus, Dykstra's method generalizes the equality restrictions that can be handled by Kaczmarz's strategy to the use of inequality constraints.

Chapter 2

Linear Multidimensional Scaling

Chapter 1 gave an optimization strategy based on iterative quadratic assignment (QA) for the linear unidimensional scaling (LUS) task in the L_2-norm, with all implementations carried out within a MATLAB computational environment. The central LUS task involves arranging the n objects in a set $S = \{O_1, O_2, \ldots, O_n\}$ along a single dimension, defined by coordinates $x_1, x_2, \ldots, x_n$, based on an $n \times n$ symmetric proximity matrix $\mathbf{P} = \{p_{ij}\}$, whose (exclusively nondiagonal) nonnegative entries are given a dissimilarity interpretation ($p_{ij} = p_{ji}$ for $1 \leq i, j \leq n$; $p_{ii} = 0$ for $1 \leq i \leq n$). The L_2 criterion

$$\sum_{i<j}(p_{ij} - |x_j - x_i|)^2 \tag{2.1}$$

is minimized by the choice of the coordinates. The present chapter will give extensions to multidimensional scaling in the city-block metric (see Arabie, 1991, for a review of uses of this metric) for the L_2-norm. The computational routines to be discussed and illustrated are again freely available as MATLAB M-files. We also note that most of the references given in Chapter 1 would also be relevant here as background material on the basic LUS task, but that review will not be repeated. Also, we will not discuss (in this chapter) comparisons to other methods (or strategies) for multidimensional scaling in the city-block metric—for the development of some of these alternatives, see Brusco (2001), Brusco and Stahl (2005), Groenen, Heiser, and Meulman (1999), Hubert, Arabie, and Meulman (1997), and Hubert, Arabie, and Hesson-McInnis (1992).

In the extensions to city-block multidimensional scaling being pursued, a slight generalization to the basic unidimensional task that incorporates an additional additive constant will prove extremely convenient. So, in Section 2.1 we emphasize the more general least-squares loss function of the form

$$\sum_{i<j}(p_{ij} - \{|x_j - x_i| - c\})^2, \tag{2.2}$$

where c is some constant to be estimated along with the coordinates $x_1, \ldots, x_n$. Section 2.2 removes the restriction to fitting only a single unidimensional structure to a symmetric

19

proximity matrix and relies on the type of computational approaches developed in Section 2.1 that include the augmentation by estimated additive constants. Based on these latter strategies, extensions are given to the use of multiple unidimensional structures through a procedure of successive residualization of the original proximity matrix (even though in this process, negative residuals are encountered and have to be fitted). For example, the fitting of two LUS structures to a proximity matrix $\{p_{ij}\}$ could be rephrased as the minimization of an L_2 loss function generalizing (2.2) to the form

$$\sum_{i<j}(p_{ij} - [|x_{j1} - x_{i1}| - c_1] - [|x_{j2} - x_{i2}| - c_2])^2. \qquad (2.3)$$

The attempt to minimize (2.3) could proceed with the fitting of a single LUS structure to $\{p_{ij}\}$, $[|x_{j1} - x_{i1}| - c_1]$, and, once obtained, fitting a second LUS structure, $[|x_{j2} - x_{i2}| - c_2]$, to the residual matrix, $\{p_{ij} - [|x_{j1} - x_{i1}| - c_1]\}$. The process would then cycle by repetitively fitting the residuals from the second linear structure by the first, and the residuals from the first linear structure by the second, until the sequence converges. In any case, obvious extensions would also exist to (2.3) for the inclusion of more than two LUS structures.

The explicit inclusion of two constants, c_1 and c_2, in (2.3), rather than adding these two together and including a single additive constant c, deserves some additional introductory explanation. As would be the case in fitting a single LUS structure using the loss functions in (2.2), two interpretations exist for the role of the additive constant c. We could consider $\{|x_j - x_i|\}$ to be fitted to the translated proximities $\{p_{ij} + c\}$, or alternatively $\{|x_j - x_i| - c\}$ to be fitted to the original proximities $\{p_{ij}\}$, where the constant c becomes part of the actual model. Although these two interpretations do not lead to any algorithmic differences in how we would proceed with minimizing the loss function in (2.2), a consistent use of the second interpretation suggests that we frame extensions to the use of multiple LUS structures as we did in (2.3), where it is explicit that the constants c_1 and c_2 are part of the actual models to be fitted to the (untransformed) proximities $\{p_{ij}\}$. Once c_1 and c_2 are obtained, they could be summed as $c = c_1 + c_2$ and an interpretation made that we have attempted to fit a transformed set of proximities $\{p_{ij} + c\}$ by the sum $\{|x_{j1} - x_{i1}| + |x_{j2} - x_{i2}|\}$ (and in this latter case, a more usual terminology would be one of a two-dimensional scaling (MDS) based on the city-block distance function). However, such a further interpretation is unnecessary and could lead to at least some small terminological confusion in further extensions that we might wish to pursue. For instance, if some type of (optimal nonlinear) transformation, say $f(\cdot)$, of the proximities is also sought (e.g., a monotonic function of some form, as is done in Section 2.3), in addition to fitting multiple LUS structures, and where p_{ij} in (2.3) is replaced by $f(p_{ij})$, and $f(\cdot)$ is to be constructed, the first interpretation would require the use of a "doubly transformed" set of proximities $\{f(p_{ij}) + c\}$ to be fitted by the sum $\{|x_{j1} - x_{i1}| + |x_{j2} - x_{i2}|\}$. In general, it seems best to avoid the need to incorporate the notion of a double transformation in this context and instead merely consider the constants c_1 and c_2 to be part of the models being fitted to a transformed set of proximities $f(p_{ij})$.

2.1 The Incorporation of Additive Constants in LUS

In Section 2.1.1, we present and illustrate an M-function, `linfitac.m`, that fits in L_2 a given single unidimensional scale (by providing the coordinates $x_1, \ldots, x_n$) and the additive constant (c) for some fixed input object ordering along the continuum defined by a permutation $\rho^{(0)}$. This approach directly parallels the M-function given in the previous chapter, called `linfit.m`, but now with an included additive constant estimation. The computational mechanisms implemented in `linfitac.m` are reviewed in Section 2.1.1.

2.1.1 The L_2 Fitting of a Single Unidimensional Scale (with an Additive Constant)

Given a fixed object permutation, $\rho^{(0)}$, we denote the set of all $n \times n$ matrices that are additive translations of the off-diagonal entries in the reordered symmetric proximity matrix $\{p_{\rho^{(0)}(i)\rho^{(0)}(j)}\}$ by $\Delta_{\rho^{(0)}}$, and let Ξ be the set of all $n \times n$ matrices that represent the interpoint distances between all pairs of n coordinate locations along a line. Explicitly,

$$\Delta_{\rho^{(0)}} \equiv \{\{q_{ij}\}\}, \text{ where } q_{ij} = p_{\rho^{(0)}(i)\rho^{(0)}(j)} + c, \text{ for some constant } c, i \neq j; q_{ii} = 0, \text{ for }$$
$1 \leq i, j \leq n;$

$$\Xi \equiv \{\{r_{ij}\}\}, \text{ where } r_{ij} = |x_j - x_i| \text{ for some set of } n \text{ coordinates, } x_1 \leq \cdots \leq x_n;$$
$\sum_i x_i = 0.$

Alternatively, we could define Ξ through a set of linear inequality (for nonnegativity restrictions) and equality constraints (to represent the additive nature of distances along a line, as we did in `linfit.m` in the previous chapter). In either case, both $\Delta_{\rho^{(0)}}$ and Ξ are closed convex sets (in a Hilbert space), and thus, given any $n \times n$ symmetric matrix with a zero main diagonal, its projection onto either $\Delta_{\rho^{(0)}}$ or Ξ exists; i.e., there is a (unique) member of $\Delta_{\rho^{(0)}}$ or Ξ at a closest (Euclidean) distance to the given matrix (e.g., see Cheney and Goldstein, 1959). Moreover, if a procedure of alternating projections onto $\Delta_{\rho^{(0)}}$ and Ξ is carried out (where a given matrix is first projected onto one of the sets, and that result is then projected onto the second, the result of which is in turn projected back onto the first, and so on), the process is convergent and generates members of $\Delta_{\rho^{(0)}}$ and Ξ that are closest to each other (again, this last statement is justified in Cheney and Goldstein, 1959, Theorems 2 and 4).

Given any $n \times n$ symmetric matrix with a main diagonal of all zeros, which we denote arbitrarily as $\mathbf{U} = \{u_{ij}\}$, its projection onto $\Delta_{\rho^{(0)}}$ may be obtained by a simple formula for the sought constant c. Explicitly, the minimum over c of

$$\sum_{i<j} (\{p_{\rho^{(0)}(i)\rho^{(0)}(j)}\} + c - u_{ij})^2$$

is obtained for

$$\hat{c} = (2/n(n-1)) \sum_{i<j} (u_{ij} - p_{\rho^{(0)}(i)\rho^{(0)}(j)}),$$

and thus this last value defines a constant translation of the proximities necessary to generate that member of $\Delta_{\rho^{(0)}}$ closest to $\mathbf{U} = \{u_{ij}\}$. For the second necessary projection and given any $n \times n$ symmetric matrix (again with a main diagonal of all zeros), that we denote arbitrarily as $\mathbf{V} = \{v_{ij}\}$ (but which in our applications will generally have the form $v_{ij} = p_{\rho^{(0)}(i)\rho^{(0)}(j)} + c$

for $i \neq j$ and some constant c), its projection onto Ξ is somewhat more involved and requires minimizing

$$\sum_{i<j}(v_{ij} - r_{ij})^2$$

over r_{ij}, where $\{r_{ij}\}$ is subject to the linear inequality nonnegativity constraints and the linear equality constraints of representing distances along a line (of the set Ξ). Although this is a (classic) quadratic programming problem for which a wide variety of optimization techniques has been published, we adopt (as we did in fitting a LUS without an additive constant in linfit.m) the Dykstra–Kaczmarz iterative projection strategy reviewed in the addendum (Section 1.4) to Chapter 1.

The function linfitac.m

As discussed above, the M-function linfitac.m fits a set of coordinates to a given proximity matrix based on some given input permutation, say, $\rho^{(0)}$, plus an additive constant, c. The usage syntax of

```
[fit,vaf,coord,addcon]  =  linfitac(prox,inperm)
```

is similar to that of linfit.m, except for the inclusion (as output) of the additive constant ADDCON and the replacement of the least-squares criterion of DIFF by the variance-accounted-for (VAF) given by the general formula

$$\text{VAF} = 1 - \frac{\sum_{i<j}(p_{\rho^{(0)}(i)\rho^{(0)}(j)} + c - |x_j - x_i|)^2}{\sum_{i<j}(p_{ij} - \bar{p})^2},$$

where $\bar{p}$ is the mean of the proximity values under consideration.

To illustrate the invariance of VAF to the use of linear transformations of the proximity matrix (although COORD and ADDCON obviously will change depending on the transformation used), we fitted the permutation found optimal to two different matrices: the original proximity matrix for number.dat and one standardized to mean zero and variance one. The latter matrix is obtained with the utility proxstd.m, with usage explained in its M-file header comments given in Appendix A.

In the recording below (as well as earlier in Chapter 1), semicolons are placed after the invocation of the M-functions to suppress the output initially; transposes (') are then used on the output vectors to conserve space by using only row (as opposed to column) vectors in the listing. Note that for the two proximity matrices employed, the VAF values are the same (.5612), but the coordinates and additive constants differ; a listing of the standardized proximity matrix is given in the output to show explicitly how negative proximities pose no problem for the fitting process that allows the incorporation of additive constants within the fitted model.

```
load number.dat
inperm = [1 2 3 5 4 6 7 9 10 8];
[fit,vaf,coord,addcon]  =  linfitac(number,inperm);
vaf
```

```
vaf =

    0.5612

 coord'
ans =

  Columns 1 through 6

   -0.3790    -0.2085    -0.1064    -0.0565    -0.0257     0.0533

  Columns 7 through 10

    0.1061     0.1714     0.1888     0.2565

  addcon

addcon =

   -0.3089

 numberstan = proxstd(number,0.0)

numberstan =

  Columns 1 through 6

         0    -0.5919     0.2105     0.8258     0.7027     1.2934
   -0.5919         0    -1.2663    -0.9611     0.5157     0.2302
    0.2105    -1.2663         0    -0.9217    -2.3739     0.6387
    0.8258    -0.9611    -0.9217         0    -0.6313    -0.5525
    0.7027     0.5157    -2.3739    -0.6313         0    -0.6510
    1.2934     0.2302     0.6387    -0.5525    -0.6510         0
    1.2147     1.0670    -0.5919    -1.1876    -0.7544    -0.7150
    1.8103     0.4369     1.2541     0.2498     0.9882    -0.6953
    1.3771     1.2294    -0.8577     1.2934    -1.4534     0.6387
    1.5199     0.4123     1.3131    -1.3697     0.6978     0.2498

  Columns 7 through 10

    1.2147     1.8103     1.3771     1.5199
    1.0670     0.4369     1.2294     0.4123
   -0.5919     1.2541    -0.8577     1.3131
   -1.1876     0.2498     1.2934    -1.3697
   -0.7544     0.9882    -1.4534     0.6978
   -0.7150    -0.6953     0.6387     0.2498
```

```
        0     -0.6116    -0.9414    -1.2072
   -0.6116          0    -0.6953    -0.4049
   -0.9414    -0.6953          0    -0.7347
   -1.2072    -0.4049    -0.7347          0

[fit,vaf,coord,addcon] = linfitac(numberstan,inperm);
vaf

vaf =

   0.5612

coord'

ans =

  Columns 1 through 6

  -1.8656    -1.0262    -0.5235    -0.2783    -0.1266     0.2624

  Columns 7 through 10

   0.5224     0.8435     0.9292     1.2626

addcon

addcon =

   1.1437
```

2.2   Finding and Fitting Multiple Unidimensional Scales

As reviewed in this chapter's introduction, the fitting of multiple unidimensional structures will be done by (repetitive) successive residualization, along with a reliance on the M-function linfitac.m to fit each separate unidimensional structure, including its associated additive constant. The M-function for this two-dimensional scaling, biscalqa.m, is a bidimensional strategy for the L_2 loss function of (2.3). It has the syntax

```
[outpermone,outpermtwo,coordone,coordtwo,fitone,fittwo, ...
addconone,addcontwo,vaf] = biscalqa(prox, ...
targone,targtwo,inpermone,inpermtwo,kblock,nopt)
```

where the variables are similar to linfitac.m but with a suffix of ONE or TWO to indicate which one of the two unidimensional structures is being referenced. The new variable NOPT controls the confirmatory or exploratory fitting of the two unidimensional scales; a value of NOPT = 0 will fit the two scales indicated by INPERMONE and INPERMTWO in a confirmatory manner; if NOPT = 1, iterative QA is used to locate the better permutations to fit.

In the example given below, the input PROX is the standardized (to a mean of zero and a standard deviation of one) 10×10 proximity matrix based on number.dat (referred to as STANNUMBER); TARGONE and TARGTWO are identical 10×10 equally spaced target matrices; INPERMONE and INPERMTWO are different random permutations of the first 10 integers; KBLOCK is set at 2 (for the iterative QA subfunctions). In the output, OUTPERMONE and OUTPERMTWO refer to the object orders; COORDONE and COORDTWO give the coordinates; FITONE and FITTWO are based on the absolute coordinate differences for the two unidimensional structures; ADDCONONE and ADDCONTWO are the two associated additive constraints; and finally, VAF is the variance-accounted-for in PROX by the two-dimensional structure. (Generally, the VAF in fitting multiple additive structures should be no less than in fitting a single structure. Moreover, one expects an increase in VAF until convergence; this is true throughout the various sections of the monograph.)

```
load number.dat
stannumber = proxstd(number,0.0);
inpermone = randperm(10);
inpermtwo = randperm(10);
kblock = 2;
nopt = 1;
targone = targlin(10);
targtwo = targone;
[outpermone,outpermtwo,coordone,coordtwo,fitone,fittwo,...
addconone,addcontwo,vaf] = biscalqa(stannumber,targone,...
targtwo,inpermone,inpermtwo,kblock,nopt);

outpermone

outpermone =

    10     8     9     7     6     5     4     3     2     1

outpermtwo

outpermtwo =

     6     8     2    10     4     7     1     3     5     9

coordone'

ans =

  Columns 1 through 6
```

```
    -1.4191     -1.0310     -1.0310     -0.6805     -0.0858     -0.0009

  Columns 7 through 10

     0.2915      0.5418      1.2363      2.1786

coordtwo'

ans =

  Columns 1 through 6

    -1.1688     -0.9885     -0.3639     -0.2472     -0.2472      0.1151

  Columns 7 through 10

     0.2629      0.8791      0.8791      0.8791

  addconone

addconone =

     1.3137

  addcontwo

addcontwo =

     0.8803

  vaf

vaf =

     0.8243
```

Although we have used the proximity matrix in number.dat primarily as a convenient numerical example to illustrate our various M-functions, the substantive interpretation
for this particular two-dimensional structure is rather remarkable and worth noting. The
first dimension reflects number magnitude perfectly (in its coordinate order) with two objects (the actual digits 7 8) at the same (tied) coordinate value. The second axis reflects the
structural characteristics perfectly, with the coordinates split into the odd and even numbers
(the digits 6 0 2 4 8 in the second five positions; 5 7 1 9 3 in the first five); there is a
grouping of 2 4 8 at the same coordinates (reflecting powers of 2); there is a grouping of 9
3 6 (reflecting multiples of three) and of 9 3 at the same coordinates (reflecting the powers

of 3); the odd numbers 7 5 that are not powers of 3 are at the extreme two coordinates of this second dimension.

We will not explicitly illustrate its use here, but a tridimensional M-function that we call `triscalqa.m` is an obvious generalization of `biscalqa.m`. Also, the pattern of programming shown could be used directly as a pattern for extensions beyond three unidimensional structures.

2.3   Incorporating Monotonic Transformations of a Proximity Matrix

As a direct extension of the M-function `biscalqa.m` discussed in the last section, the file `bimonscalqa.m` provides an optimal monotonic transformation (by incorporating the use of `proxmon.m` discussed in Chapter 1) of the original proximity matrix given as input in addition to the latter's bidimensional scaling. To prevent degeneracy, the sum-of-squares value for the initial input proximity matrix is maintained in the optimally transformed proximities; the overall strategy is iterative with termination dependent on a change in the VAF being less than 1.0e-005. The usage syntax is almost identical to that of `biscalqa.m`, except for the inclusion of the monotonically transformed proximity matrix MONPROX as an output matrix:

```
[ ... monprox] = bimonscalqa( ... )
```

The ellipses directly above indicate that the same items should be used as in `biscalqa.m`. If `bimonscalqa.m` had been used in the numerical example of the previous section, the same results given would have been output initially plus the results for the optimally transformed proximity matrix. We give this additional output below, which shows that the incorporation of an optimal monotonic transformation provides an increase in the VAF from .8243 to .9362; the orderings on the two dimensions remain the same, as well as the nice substantive explanation of the previous section.

```
outpermone

outpermone =

     1     2     3     4     5     6     7     9     8    10

outpermtwo

outpermtwo =

     9     5     3     1     7     4    10     2     8     6

coordone'

ans =
```

```
   Columns 1 through 6

   -2.3514    -1.3290    -0.6409    -0.3565     0.0775     0.1216

   Columns 7 through 10

    0.5857     1.1342     1.1342     1.6247

coordtwo'

ans =

   Columns 1 through 6

   -0.7793    -0.7793    -0.7793    -0.3891    -0.1196     0.3242

   Columns 7 through 10

    0.3242     0.3480     0.8467     1.0035

 addconone

addconone =

    1.4394

 addcontwo

addcontwo =

    0.7922

 vaf

vaf =

    0.9362

 monprox

monprox =

   Columns 1 through 6

         0    -0.7387    -0.1667     0.5067     0.5067     1.4791
```

```
 -0.7387          0   -0.8218   -0.8218    0.5067   -0.1667
 -0.1667    -0.8218          0   -0.8218   -1.6174    0.5067
  0.5067    -0.8218   -0.8218          0   -0.7387   -0.7387
  0.5067     0.5067   -1.6174   -0.7387          0   -0.7387
  1.4791    -0.1667    0.5067   -0.7387   -0.7387          0
  1.0321     0.5067   -0.7387   -0.8218   -0.8218   -0.8218
  2.6590     0.5067    1.0321   -0.1667    0.5067   -0.8218
  1.7609     1.0321   -0.8218    1.0321   -1.2541    0.5067
  2.6231     0.5067    1.4791   -0.8218    0.5067   -0.0534

Columns  7  through  10

  1.0321     2.6590    1.7609    2.6231
  0.5067     0.5067    1.0321    0.5067
 -0.7387     1.0321   -0.8218    1.4791
 -0.8218    -0.1667    1.0321   -0.8218
 -0.8218     0.5067   -1.2541    0.5067
 -0.8218    -0.8218    0.5067   -0.0534
       0    -0.7387   -0.8218   -0.8218
 -0.7387          0   -0.7387   -0.7387
 -0.8218    -0.7387          0   -0.8218
 -0.8218    -0.7387   -0.8218          0
```

Although we will not provide an example of its use here, `trimonscalqa.m` extends `triscalqa.m` to include an optimal monotonic transformation of whatever is given as the original input proximity matrix.

2.4 Confirmatory Extensions to City-Block Individual Differences Scaling

An obvious conclusion to this chapter is that if one is interested in (nonmetric) city-block scaling in two or three dimensions within L_2, the routines referred to in two dimensions as `biscalqa.m` and `bimonscalqa.m`, or in three dimensions as `triscalqa.m` and `trimonscalqa.m`, would be natural alternatives to consider. One aspect of all of these given M-files that we have not emphasized but will in this chapter's concluding comments is their possible usage in the confirmatory context (by setting the NOPT switch to 0) and fitting various fixed object orderings in multiple dimensions. One possible application of this type of confirmatory fitting would be in an individual differences scaling context. Explicitly, we begin with a collection of, say, K proximity matrices, $\mathbf{P}_1, \ldots, \mathbf{P}_K$, obtained from K separate sources, and through some weighting and averaging process construct a single aggregate proximity matrix, $\mathbf{P}_A$. On the basis of $\mathbf{P}_A$, suppose a two-dimensional city-block scaling is constructed (using, say, `biscalqa.m`); we label the latter the "common space" consistent with what is usually done in the weighted Euclidean model (e.g., see the INDSCAL model of Carroll and Chang, 1970; Arabie, Carroll, and DeSarbo, 1987; Carroll and Arabie, 1998; or the PROXSCAL program in the Categories Module of SPSS—Busing, Commandeur, and Heiser, 1997). Each of the K proximity matrices can then be used in a confirmatory fitting of the object orders along the two axes. Thus, a very general "subject/private space" is generated for each source and where the actual coordinates along both axes are unique to that source, subject only to the object order constraints of the group space. This strategy provides an individual differences model generalization over the usual weighted Euclidean model, where the latter allows only differential axes scaling (stretching or shrinking) in generating the private spaces. These kinds of individual difference generalizations exist both for multiple unidimensional scalings in L_2 as well as for other types of proximity matrix representations such as ultrametrics and additive trees (given in Parts II and III).

Chapter 3

Circular Scaling

This chapter will discuss circular unidimensional scaling (CUS), where the objective is to place the n objects around a closed continuum such that the reconstructed distance between each pair of objects, defined by the minimum length over the two possible paths that join the objects, reflects the given proximities as well as possible. Explicitly, and in analogy with the loss function for linear unidimensional scaling (LUS) in (2.2), we wish to find a set of coordinates, $x_1, \ldots, x_n$, and an $(n+1)$st value, $x_0 \geq |x_j - x_i|$ for all $1 \leq i \neq j \leq n$, minimizing

$$\sum_{i<j} (p_{ij} + c - \min\{|x_j - x_i|, x_0 - |x_j - x_i|\})^2 \tag{3.1}$$

or, equivalently,

$$\sum_{i<j} (p_{ij} - [\min\{|x_j - x_i|, x_0 - |x_j - x_i|\} - c])^2, \tag{3.2}$$

where c is again some constant to be estimated. The value x_0 represents the total length of the closed continuum, and the expression $\min\{|x_j - x_i|, x_0 - |x_j - x_i|\}$ gives the minimum length over the two possible paths joining objects O_i and O_j. In theory, the CUS task could again be solved by complete enumeration of the loss function in (3.1) over a finite but also typically enormous set for even moderate n. Here, we have all possible distinct object orderings around a closed continuum, $(n-1)!/2$, and, for each such ordering, all the possible inflection patterns for where the directionality of the minimum distance calculation changes for the object pairs. These latter inflection points are a necessary condition of using CUS and are one obvious point of departure from LUS. Obviously, for general use and analogous to LUS, some type of search strategy is called for to generate the better orderings and inflection patterns around a closed continuum but with feasible computational effort.

The current chapter is organized around the optimization problems posed by CUS and the two main subtasks of obtaining an appropriate object ordering around a closed continuum and the additional relative placement of the objects according to the directionality of minimum distance calculations. Once these orderings and relative placements have been identified, the estimation of the additive constant in both loss functions (3.1) and (3.2), as well as the identification of the actual coordinates, proceeds through a process of alternating projections onto two closed convex sets. One is defined by the set of all translations of the original proximity values by a constant; the second closed convex set is characterized by the collection of all coordinate structures consistent with the given object ordering and the relative object placement that provides the directionality of minimum distance calculations around the closed continuum. In the specific contexts we consider, the process of alternating projections is convergent (see Cheney and Goldstein, 1959) and generates a final solution defined by two points within the two convex sets that are closest to each other. Although the emphasis in the present chapter is on a single symmetric proximity matrix defined for one set of objects to be fitted by a CUS model, Section 3.2 will also develop a fairly direct extension to the use of sums of such circular structures that can be fitted to a single proximity matrix through successive residualizations of the given matrix (this strategy is analogous to what was done in Chapter 2 for multiple LUS representations).

As a final preliminary note on the data that will be used in this chapter for numerical illustrations, a rather well-known proximity matrix is given in Table 3.1 (and called `morse_digits.dat`). The latter is a 10×10 proximity matrix for the ten Morse code symbols that represent the first ten digits: (0: $- - - - -$; 1: $\bullet - - - -$; 2: $\bullet \bullet - - -$; 3: $\bullet \bullet \bullet - -$; 4: $\bullet \bullet \bullet \bullet -$; 5: $\bullet \bullet \bullet \bullet \bullet$; 6: $- \bullet \bullet \bullet \bullet$; 7: $- - \bullet \bullet \bullet$; 8: $- - - \bullet \bullet$; 9: $- - - - \bullet$). The entries in Table 3.1 have a dissimilarity interpretation and are defined for each object pair by 2.0 minus the sum of the two proportions for a group of subjects used by Rothkopf (1957) representing "same" judgments to the two symbols when given in the two possible presentation orders of the signals. Based on previous multidimensional scalings of the complete data set involving all of the Morse code symbols and in which the data of Table 3.1 are embedded (e.g., see Shepard, 1963; Kruskal and Wish, 1978), it might be expected that the symbols for the digits would form a clear linear unidimensional structure that would be interpretable according to a regular progression in the number of dots to dashes. *It turns out, as discussed in greater detail below, that a circular model (or actually, a sum of circular structures) is probably more consistent with the patterning of the proximities in Table* 3.1 *than are representations based on LUSs.* (For completeness, we might note that the possible usefulness of a circular model for these specific proximities (but not to the consideration of multiple circular structures) has been pointed out before in the literature, most notably in the two-dimensional metric scaling given as an illustrative example by Mardia, Kent, and Bibby (1979, p. 404), or in the combinatorial optimization approach of quadratic assignment (QA) discussed by Hubert and Schultz (1976), which is based on permuting the rows and columns of a proximity matrix to achieve a best fit against a fixed target matrix.)

3.1   The Mechanics of CUS

The CUS task as characterized by the loss function in (3.1) can be considered in two stages as with the presentation of LUS. One subtask is the identification of an ordering of the n objects around a closed continuum that again will be denoted by a permutation of the first n integers, $\varphi(\cdot)$, such that $\varphi(i) = j$ if object O_j is placed at position i; here, position 1 is arbitrarily specified at some point along the closed continuum, and the order of the positions from 1 to n is, for convenience, taken clockwise. In addition to $\varphi(\cdot)$, a set of inflection points must be identified for the n positions to indicate where the minimum distance calculation

Table 3.1. *A proximity matrix, morse_digits.dat, for the ten Morse code symbols representing the first ten digits (data from Rothkopf, 1957).*

0.00	.75	1.69	1.87	1.76	1.77	1.59	1.26	.86	.95
.75	0.00	.82	1.54	1.85	1.72	1.51	1.50	1.45	1.63
1.69	.82	0.00	1.25	1.47	1.33	1.66	1.57	1.83	1.81
1.87	1.54	1.25	0.00	.89	1.32	1.53	1.74	1.85	1.86
1.76	1.85	1.47	.89	0.00	1.41	1.64	1.81	1.90	1.90
1.77	1.72	1.33	1.32	1.41	0.00	.70	1.56	1.84	1.64
1.59	1.51	1.66	1.53	1.64	.70	0.00	.70	1.38	1.70
1.26	1.50	1.57	1.74	1.81	1.56	.70	0.00	.83	1.22
.86	1.45	1.83	1.85	1.90	1.84	1.38	.83	0.00	.41
.95	1.63	1.81	1.86	1.90	1.64	1.70	1.22	.41	0.00

must change direction around the closed continuum. Explicitly, a set of $n - 1$ integers, $1 \leq k_1 \leq \cdots \leq k_{n-1} \leq n$, is sought, where k_i is associated with position i, $1 \leq i \leq n - 1$. For positions $i < j$, the minimum distance is in the clockwise direction when $j \leq k_i$ and in the counterclockwise direction when $j > k_i$ (we note that an integer k_n for position n is unnecessary, and any k_i equal to n merely indicates that for all positions j, for $i < j$, the minimum distance is always in the clockwise direction). The second subtask, once given $\varphi(\cdot)$ and $k_1, \ldots, k_{n-1}$, is the estimation of the set of coordinates and the additive constant c to fit the proximities. We again discuss these two subtasks in the reverse order.

3.1.1 The Estimation of c and $\min\{|x_j - x_i|, x_0 - |x_j - x_i|\}$ for a Fixed Permutation and Set of Inflection Points

For notational convenience, the set of all $n \times n$ matrices that are additive translations of the off-diagonal entries in the reordered proximity matrix, $\{p_{\varphi(i)\varphi(j)}\}$, will again be denoted by Δ_φ (see Section 2.1.1); the set of all $n \times n$ matrices that represent the distances around the closed continuum based on the inflection points $k_1, \ldots, k_{n-1}$ will be more fully denoted by $\Xi(k_1, \ldots, k_{n-1})$ and explicitly defined as follows:

$$\Xi(k_1, \ldots, k_{n-1}) \equiv \{\{r_{ij}\}\},$$

where

$$r_{ij} = |x_j - x_i| \text{ for } i < j \leq k_i;$$
$$r_{ij} = x_0 - |x_j - x_i| \text{ for } i < j \text{ and } j > k_i;$$
$$r_{ji} = r_{ij} \text{ for } 1 \leq i < j \leq n;$$
$$r_{ii} = 0 \text{ for } 1 \leq i \leq n,$$

for some collection of coordinates, $x_1, \ldots, x_n$, and an $(n + 1)$st value, x_0, where

$$x_1 \leq \cdots \leq x_n \leq x_0;$$
$$x_1 \equiv 0.0;$$

$$|x_j - x_i| \leq x_0 - |x_j - x_i| \text{ for } i < j \leq k_i;$$
$$|x_j - x_i| \geq x_0 - |x_j - x_i| \text{ for } i < j \text{ and } j > k_i.$$

As noted in this definition, the first position, x_1, is specified without loss of generality to be 0.0; the value x_0 can be interpreted either as the length of the closed continuum or as a second coordinate value attached to the first position but taken in the clockwise direction. Given Δ_φ and $\Xi(k_1, \ldots, k_{n-1})$ (where the latter can be defined through a set of linear inequality/equality constraints), the process of alternating projections onto Δ_φ and $\Xi(k_1, \ldots, k_{n-1})$ would proceed exactly as in LUS.

3.1.2   Obtaining Object Orderings and Inflection Points around a Closed Continuum

Identifying an object ordering around a closed continuum to be used in the minimization of the loss function in (3.1) follows the same pattern as for LUS. The cross-product statistic in (1.5) is again maximized but with a different $n \times n$ (target) matrix, $T = \{t_{ij}\}$, initially defined by n positions equally spaced around a closed continuum, i.e., $t_{ij} = \min\{|i - j|, n - |i - j|\}$ for $1 \leq i, j \leq n$ (as in LUS, this target could eventually be replaced, now by $t_{ij} = \min\{|x_j - x_i|, x_0 - |x_j - x_i|\}$ based on the outcome of the minimization of (3.1)). Given some best permutation, $\varphi_{K(\cdot)}$, obtained through the initial target and set of local operations on some randomly given initial permutation, a collection of inflection points, $k_1, \ldots, k_{n-1}$, still must be generated before the optimization of (3.1) can continue. This latter task will be approached through a heuristic application of an iterative projection strategy of the same general type developed by Hubert and Arabie (1995b) for the fitting of various graph-theoretic structures to a symmetric proximity matrix.

To attempt an identification of $k_1, \ldots, k_{n-1}$ given the permutation $\varphi_{K(\cdot)}$, we begin with the reordered proximity matrix $\{p_{\varphi_{K(i)}\varphi_{K(j)}}\}$ and initialize a process of iterative projection onto the class of constraints given by the structure $\Xi(k_1, \ldots, k_{n-1})$ but with one exception necessitated by the fact that an appropriate set of values for $k_1, \ldots, k_{n-1}$ is not yet known. Explicitly, when considering a pair of positions, $i < j$ ($2 \leq j - i$), and the two possible constraints that could be imposed, i.e., either $r_{i(i+1)} + \cdots + r_{(j-1)j} = r_{ij}$ or $r - (r_{i(i+1)} + \cdots + r_{(j-1)j}) = r_{ij}$ for $r = r_{12} + \cdots + r_{(n-1)n} + r_{1n}$, we select according to which left side is smaller, based on the current entries in the matrix being carried forward to this point, and impose that specific constraint. Otherwise, the process continues cyclically through the whole set of constraints, and for each time a constraint is reconsidered, any changes that were made the previous time the constraint was encountered are first "undone."

Because of the procedure of redressing the (immediately) previous changes each time a constraint is reconsidered, the process just described may not converge and could eventually oscillate through a finite collection of distinct matrices. If such nonconvergence is observed, and previous changes from that point on are not redressed, the process will then converge to a matrix in $\Xi(k_1, \ldots, k_{n-1})$ for some specific values of $k_1, \ldots, k_{n-1}$. A justification for this last assertion of convergence is given by the general results presented in Hubert and Arabie (1995b); also, that source provides empirical evidence that as a heuristic optimization strategy, it is generally better to begin with the procedure of redressing previous changes until an oscillation is observed, rather than immediately starting without the process of redressing previous changes (which would also produce a matrix in $\Xi(k_1, \ldots, k_{n-1})$ for some specific $k_1, \ldots, k_{n-1}$). It should also be noted that although convergence to some matrix in $\Xi(k_1, \ldots, k_{n-1})$ is guaranteed by the strategy just described, and thus to an identified fixed collection of inflection points, $k_1, \ldots, k_{n-1}$, the latter matrix may now not be optimal for this collection of inflection points in the minimization of (3.1). Specifically, even though the identification of the collection $k_1, \ldots, k_{n-1}$ can proceed by a process of iterative projection and an updating of a matrix $\{r_{ij}\}$ to produce a member of $\Xi(k_1, \ldots, k_{n-1})$, because of the possible nonconvergence noted above and the subsequent lack of redressing previous changes from that point on, the matrix identified in $\Xi(k_1, \ldots, k_{n-1})$ may not be the best achievable even for this particular collection of inflection points (although in our computational experience it is typically very close to being optimal). Thus, as a "polishing" step to ensure that an optimal member of $\Xi(k_1, \ldots, k_{n-1})$ is identified, the collection $k_1, \ldots, k_{n-1}$ and the permutation $\varphi_K(\cdot)$ should be used anew in the optimization of (3.1) to obtain the optimal target matrix, $\{\min\{|x_j - x_i|, x_0 - |x_j - x_i|\}\}$.

3.1.3   The CUS Utilities, cirfit.m and cirfitac.m

The two CUS utilities, that implement the mechanics of fitting the CUS model (including the identification of inflection points), parallel the LUS utilities of `linfit.m` and `linfitac.m`. The M-file `cirfit.m` does a confirmatory fitting of a given order (assumed to be an object ordering around a closed unidimensional structure) using the Dykstra–Kaczmarz iterative projection least-squares method. The usage syntax for `cirfit.m` and `cirfitac.m` is

```
[fit, diff] = cirfit(prox,inperm)

[fit,vaf,addcon] = cirfitac(prox,inperm)
```

where INPERM is the given order and FIT is an $n \times n$ matrix fitted to PROX(INPERM, INPERM) with a least-squares value DIFF. The syntax for the routine `cirfitac.m` is the same, except for the inclusion of an additive constant, ADDCON, and the use of VAF rather than DIFF.

In brief, then, the type of matrix being fitted to the proximity matrix has the form

$$\{\min(|x_{\rho(j)} - x_{\rho(i)}|, x_0 - |x_{\rho(j)} - x_{\rho(i)}|) - c\},$$

where c is an estimated additive constant (assumed equal to zero in `cirfit.m`), $x_{\rho(1)} \leq x_{\rho(2)} \leq \cdots \leq x_{\rho(n)} \leq x_0$, and the last coordinate, x_0, is the circumference of the circular structure. We can obtain these latter coordinates from the adjacent spacings in the output matrix FIT.

As an example, we applied `cirfit.m` to the `morse_digits` proximity matrix with an assumed identity input permutation; the spacings around the circular structure between the placements are as follows: for objects 1 and 2: .5337; 2 and 3: .7534; 3 and 4: .6174; 4 and 5: .1840; 5 and 6: .5747; 6 and 7: .5167; 7 and 8: .3920; 8 and 9: .5467; 9 and 10: .1090; and back around between 10 and 1: .5594 (the sum of all these adjacent spacings is 4.787 and is the circumference (x_0) of the circular structure). For `cirfitac.m` the additive constant was estimated as $-.8031$ with a VAF of .7051; here, the spacings around the circular structure between the placements are as follows: for objects 1 and 2: .2928; 2 and 3: .4322; 3 and 4: .2962; 4 and 5: .0234; 5 and 6: .3338; 6 and 7: .2758; 7 and 8: .2314; 8 and 9: .2800; 9 and 10: .0000; and back around between 10 and 1: .2124 (here, x_0 has a value of 2.378).

```
load morse_digits.dat
[fit,diff] = cirfit(morse_digits,1:10)

fit =

  Columns 1 through 5

           0      0.5337      1.2871      1.9044      2.0884
      0.5337           0      0.7534      1.3707      1.5547
      1.2871      0.7534           0      0.6174      0.8014
      1.9044      1.3707      0.6174           0      0.1840
      2.0884      1.5547      0.8014      0.1840           0
      2.1237      2.1294      1.3761      0.7587      0.5747
      1.6071      2.1407      1.8927      1.2754      1.0914
      1.2151      1.7487      2.2847      1.6674      1.4834
      0.6684      1.2021      1.9554      2.2141      2.0301
      0.5594      1.0931      1.8464      2.3231      2.1391

  Columns 6 through 10

      2.1237      1.6071      1.2151      0.6684      0.5594
      2.1294      2.1407      1.7487      1.2021      1.0931
      1.3761      1.8927      2.2847      1.9554      1.8464
      0.7587      1.2754      1.6674      2.2141      2.3231
      0.5747      1.0914      1.4834      2.0301      2.1391
           0      0.5167      0.9087      1.4554      1.5644
      0.5167           0      0.3920      0.9387      1.0477
      0.9087      0.3920           0      0.5467      0.6557
      1.4554      0.9387      0.5467           0      0.1090
      1.5644      1.0477      0.6557      0.1090           0


diff =

    7.3898

[fit,vaf,addcon] = cirfitac(morse_digits,1:10)

fit =

  Columns 1 through 5
```

0	0.2928	0.7250	1.0212	1.0446
0.2928	0	0.4322	0.7284	0.7518
0.7250	0.4322	0	0.2962	0.3196
1.0212	0.7284	0.2962	0	0.0234
1.0446	0.7518	0.3196	0.0234	0
0.9996	1.0856	0.6534	0.3572	0.3338
0.7238	1.0166	0.9292	0.6330	0.6096
0.4924	0.7852	1.1606	0.8644	0.8410
0.2124	0.5052	0.9374	1.1444	1.1210
0.2124	0.5052	0.9374	1.1444	1.1210

Columns 6 through 10

0.9996	0.7238	0.4924	0.2124	0.2124
1.0856	1.0166	0.7852	0.5052	0.5052
0.6534	0.9292	1.1606	0.9374	0.9374
0.3572	0.6330	0.8644	1.1444	1.1444
0.3338	0.6096	0.8410	1.1210	1.1210
0	0.2758	0.5072	0.7872	0.7872
0.2758	0	0.2314	0.5114	0.5114
0.5072	0.2314	0	0.2800	0.2800
0.7872	0.5114	0.2800	0	0.0000
0.7872	0.5114	0.2800	0.0000	0

```
vaf =

    0.7051
```

```
addcon =

   -0.8031
```

As a variation on `cirfitac.m`, the M-file `cirfitac_ftarg.m` uses an additional fixed target matrix TARG to obtain the inflection points (and therefore TARG should provide a circular ordering). The syntax is otherwise the same as for `cirfitac.m`:

```
[fit,vaf,addcon] = cirfitac_ftarg(prox,inperm,targ)
```

In the example below, an equally (unit-)spaced circular ordering is used for TARG that is obtained from the utility function `targcir.m`; this strategy leads to a (slightly lower compared to `cirfitac.m`) VAF of .6670; here, the spacings around the circular structure between the placements are as follows: for objects 1 and 2: .3294; 2 and 3: .3204; 3 and 4: .2544; 4 and 5: .0344; 5 and 6: .2837; 6 and 7: .2084; 7 and 8: .3124; 8 and 9: .2701; 9 and 10: .0000; and back around between 10 and 1: .2109 (the circumference x_0 is 2.2241).

```
load morse_digits.dat
targcircular = targcir(10)

targcircular =
```

0	1	2	3	4	5	4	3	2	1
1	0	1	2	3	4	5	4	3	2
2	1	0	1	2	3	4	5	4	3
3	2	1	0	1	2	3	4	5	4
4	3	2	1	0	1	2	3	4	5
5	4	3	2	1	0	1	2	3	4
4	5	4	3	2	1	0	1	2	3
3	4	5	4	3	2	1	0	1	2
2	3	4	5	4	3	2	1	0	1
1	2	3	4	5	4	3	2	1	0

```
[fit,vaf,addcon] = cirfitac_ftarg(morse_digits,1:10,...
targcircular)

fit =

  Columns 1 through 6
```

0	0.3294	0.6498	0.9043	0.9387	1.2224
0.3294	0	0.3204	0.5748	0.6093	0.8929
0.6498	0.3204	0	0.2544	0.2888	0.5725
0.9043	0.5748	0.2544	0	0.0344	0.3181
0.9387	0.6093	0.2888	0.0344	0	0.2837
1.2224	0.8929	0.5725	0.3181	0.2837	0
0.7934	1.1014	0.7809	0.5265	0.4921	0.2084
0.4810	0.8104	1.0934	0.8389	0.8045	0.5208
0.2109	0.5403	0.8607	1.1091	1.0747	0.7910
0.2109	0.5403	0.8607	1.1151	1.0747	0.7910

```
  Columns 7 through 10
```

0.7934	0.4810	0.2109	0.2109
1.1014	0.8104	0.5403	0.5403
0.7809	1.0934	0.8607	0.8607
0.5265	0.8389	1.1091	1.1151
0.4921	0.8045	1.0747	1.0747
0.2084	0.5208	0.7910	0.7910
0	0.3124	0.5826	0.5826
0.3124	0	0.2701	0.2701
0.5826	0.2701	0	-0.0000
0.5826	0.2701	-0.0000	0

```
vaf =

    0.6670


addcon =

   -0.8317
```

The use of a fixed circular target matrix in `cirfitac_ftarg.m` (as opposed to finding one internally as is done in `cirfit.m` and `cirfitac.m`) *could* lead to small anomalies in the results, and thus the user should be prepared when using `cirfitac_ftarg.m`. In the example just given, for instance, the (4,10) value (of 1.1151) should probably be 1.1091 to match the (4,9) entry and the fact that 9 and 10 are at tied locations—however, the equally-spaced-circular-target distance from 10 to 4 is shorter clockwise (at a value of 4) than counterclockwise (at a value of 6), and so the (4,10) value of 1.1151 is taken clockwise (as opposed to 1.1091 if taken counterclockwise).

The function unicirac.m

The function M-file `unicirac.m` carries out a CUS of a symmetric dissimilarity matrix (with the estimation of an additive constant) using an iterative QA strategy (and thus is an analogue of `uniscalqa.m` for the LUS task). We begin with an equally spaced circular target constructed using the M-file `targcir.m` (that could be invoked with the command `targcir(10)`), a (random) starting permutation, and then use a sequential combination of the pairwise interchange/rotation/insertion heuristics; the target matrix is reestimated based on the identified (locally optimal) permutation. The whole process is repeated until no changes can be made in the target or the identified (locally optimal) permutation. The explicit usage syntax is

```
[find,vaf,outperm,addcon] = unicirac(prox,inperm,kblock)
```

where the various terms should now be familiar. INPERM is a given starting permutation (assumed to be around the circle) of the first n integers; FIND is the least-squares optimal matrix (with variance-accounted-for of VAF) to PROX having the appropriate circular form for the row and column object ordering given by the final permutation OUTPERM. The spacings between the objects are given by the diagonal entries in FIND (and the extreme $(1, n)$ entry in FIND). KBLOCK defines the block size in the use the iterative QA routine. The additive constant for the model is given by ADDCON.

The problem of local optima is much more severe in CUS than in LUS. The heuristic identification of inflection points and the relevant spacings can vary slightly depending on the "equivalent" orderings identified around a circular structure. The example given below was identified as the best achievable (and for some multiple number of times) over 100 random starting permutations for INPERM; with its VAF of 71.90%, it is apparently the best "attainable." Given the (equivalent to the) identity permutation identified for outperm, the substantive interpretation for this representation is fairly clear—we have a nicely interpretable ordering of the Morse code symbols around a circular structure involving a regular replacement of dashes by dots moving clockwise until the symbol containing all dots is reached and then a subsequent replacement of the dots by dashes until the initial symbol containing all dashes is reached.

```
[find,vaf,outperm,addcon] = ...
unicirac(morse_digits,randperm(10),2)

find =

   Columns 1 through 6

          0     0.0247     0.3620     0.6413     0.9605     1.1581
     0.0247          0     0.3373     0.6165     0.9358     1.1334
     0.3620     0.3373          0     0.2793     0.5985     0.7961
     0.6413     0.6165     0.2793          0     0.3193     0.5169
     0.9605     0.9358     0.5985     0.3193          0     0.1976
     1.1581     1.1334     0.7961     0.5169     0.1976          0
     1.1581     1.1334     0.7961     0.5169     0.1976     0.0000
     1.0358     1.0606     1.0148     0.7355     0.4163     0.2187
     0.7396     0.7643     1.1016     1.0318     0.7125     0.5149
     0.3883     0.4131     0.7503     1.0296     1.0638     0.8662

   Columns 7 through 10

     1.1581     1.0358     0.7396     0.3883
     1.1334     1.0606     0.7643     0.4131
     0.7961     1.0148     1.1016     0.7503
     0.5169     0.7355     1.0318     1.0296
     0.1976     0.4163     0.7125     1.0638
     0.0000     0.2187     0.5149     0.8662
          0     0.2187     0.5149     0.8662
     0.2187          0     0.2963     0.6475
     0.5149     0.2963          0     0.3513
     0.8662     0.6475     0.3513          0


vaf =

     0.7190


outperm =

     4      5      6      7      8      9     10      1      2      3
```

```
addcon =

   -0.7964
```

The plotting function circularplot.m

To assist in the visualization of the results from a CUS, the M-function `circularplot.m` provides the coordinates of a scaling around a circular structure plus a plot of the (labeled) objects around the circle. The usage syntax is

```
[circum,radius,coord,degrees,cumdegrees] = ...
      circularplot(circ,inperm)
```

The coordinates are derived from the $n \times n$ interpoint distance matrix (around a circle) given by `CIRC`; the positions are labeled by the order of objects given in `INPERM`. Output consists of a plot, the circumference of the circle (`CIRCUM`) and radius (`RADIUS`), the coordinates of the plot positions (`COORD`), and the degrees and cumulative degrees induced between the plotted positions (in `DEGREES` and `CUMDEGREES`). The positions around the circle are numbered from 1 (at the "noon" position) to n, moving clockwise around the circular structure.

As an example, Figure 3.1 provides an application of `circularplot.m` to the just given example of `unicirac.m`. The text output also appears below:

```
[circum,radius,coord,degrees,cumdegrees] = ...
circularplot(find,outperm);

 circum

circum =

    2.4126

 radius

radius =

   0.3840

 coord'

ans =

  Columns 1 through 6

        0    0.0247    0.3107    0.3821    0.2293    0.0481
```

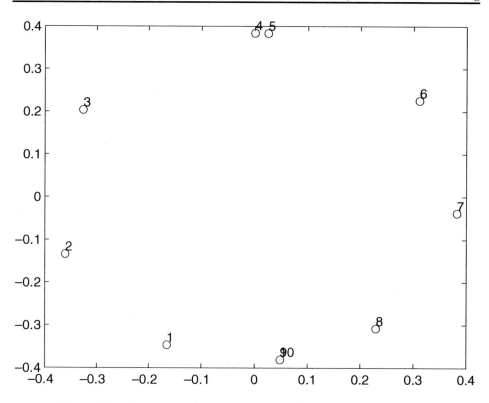

Figure 3.1. *Two-dimensional circular plot for the morse_digits data obtained using circularplot.m.*

```
    0.3840      0.3832      0.2256     -0.0380     -0.3080     -0.3810

Columns 7 through 10

    0.0481     -0.1649     -0.3600     -0.3254
   -0.3810     -0.3468     -0.1336      0.2038

degrees'

ans =

  Columns 1 through 6

    0.0644      0.8783      0.7273      0.8315      0.5146      0.0000

  Columns 7 through 10
```

```
    0.5695      0.7716      0.9148      1.0113

cumdegrees'

ans =

  Columns 1 through 6

    0.0644      0.9428      1.6700      2.5015      3.0161      3.0161

  Columns 7 through 10

    3.5856      4.3571      5.2719      6.2832
```

3.2   Circular Multidimensional Scaling

The discussion in previous sections has been restricted to the fitting of a single circular unidimensional structure to a symmetric proximity matrix. Given the type of computational approach developed for carrying out this task (and, in particular, because of its lack of dependence on the presence of nonnegative proximities), extensions are very direct to the use of multiple unidimensional structures through a process of successive residualization of the original proximity matrix. The fitting of two CUS structures to a proximity matrix generalizes (3.1) to the form

$$\sum_{i<j}(p_{ij} - [\min\{|x_{j1}-x_{i1}|, x_{01} - |x_{j1}-x_{i1}\} - c_1] - [\min\{|x_{j2}-x_{i2}|, x_{02} - |x_{j2}-x_{i2}\} - c_2])^2.$$

$$(3.3)$$

The attempt to minimize (3.3) could proceed with the fitting of a single CUS structure to $\{p_{ij}\}$, $[\min\{|x_{j1}-x_{i1}|, x_{01}-|x_{j1}-x_{i1}\}-c_1]$, using the computational strategy of Section 3.1, and, once obtained, fitting a second CUS structure, $[\min\{|x_{j2}-x_{i2}|, x_{02}-|x_{j2}-x_{i2}|\}-c_2]$, to the residual matrix, $\{p_{ij} - [\min\{|x_{j1}-x_{i1}|, x_{01}-|x_{j1}-x_{i1}|\}]-c_1\}$. The process would then cycle by repetitively fitting the residuals from the second circular structure by the first, and the residuals from the first circular structure by the second, until the sequence converges. In any event, obvious extensions exist for (3.3) to the inclusion of more than two CUS structures or to some mixture of, say, LUS and CUS forms in the spirit of the hybrid models of Carroll and Pruzansky (1975, 1980).

The M-function bicirac.m is a two- (or bi-)dimensional scaling strategy for the L_2 loss function of (3.3) and relies heavily on the M-function unicirac.m to fit each separate circular structure, including its associated additive constant. The syntax is

```
[find,vaf,targone,targtwo,outpermone,outpermtwo, ...
addconone,addcontwo]  =  bicirac(prox,inperm,kblock)
```

where most of the terms should be familiar from previous usage in, say, biscalqa.m. Again, PROX is the input proximity matrix ($n \times n$ with a zero main diagonal and a dissimilarity interpretation); INPERM is a given starting permutation of the first n integers; FIND is the least-squares optimal matrix (with variance-accounted-for of VAF) to PROX and is the sum of the two circular (anti-Robinson) matrices TARGONE and TARGTWO based on the two row and column object orderings given by the final permutations OUTPERMONE and OUTPERMTWO. KBLOCK defines the block size in the use of the iterative QA routine, and ADDCONONE and ADDCONTWO are the two additive constants for the two model components.

As an illustration of the results obtainable from the process just described, using the Morse code data, the MATLAB output below gives the best (according to a VAF of 92.18%) two-CUS representation obtained from 100 random starting permutations for each of the circular components. The two CUS structures have rather clear substantive interpretations: as with our example using unicirac.m, the first shows the regular replacement of dots by dashes moving around the closed continuum; the second provides a perfect ordering around the closed continuum according to ratios of dots to dashes or of dashes to dots and where adjacent pairs of stimuli have dashes and dots exchanged one-for-one; i.e., for the adjacent stimuli pairs moving clockwise, we have

0:5 for $\{- - - - -; \bullet \bullet \bullet \bullet \bullet \bullet\}$ (0,5); 1:4 for $\{\bullet - - - -; - \bullet \bullet \bullet \bullet\}$ (1,6); 2:3 for

$\{\bullet \bullet - - -; - - \bullet \bullet \bullet\}$ (2,7); 3:2 for $\{\bullet \bullet \bullet - -; - - - \bullet \bullet\}$ (3,8); and 1:4 for

$\{- - - - \bullet; \bullet \bullet \bullet \bullet -\}$(9,4).

The two additive constants c_1 and c_2 in (3.3) have values of $-.7002$ and $.3521$, respectively. (As mentioned, the output given below represents the best two-CUS structures obtained for 100 random starting permutations, but as might be expected given the earlier computational results, the same type of local optima were observed here as found in the fitting of a single CUS structure; i.e., several local optima were generated from small differences in the estimation of inflection points and the adjacent object spacings but with the identical object orderings around the closed continua).

```
[find,vaf,targone,targtwo,outpermone,outpermtwo, ...
addconone,addcontwo] = bicirac(morse_digits,randperm(10),2)

find =

   Columns 1 through 6

        0      0.9765   1.4869   1.9626   1.7586   1.7461
   0.9765        0      0.8585   1.5836   1.7815   1.7340
   1.4869   0.8585        0      1.0732   1.4824   1.4414
   1.9626   1.5836   1.0732        0      0.7573   1.3885
   1.7586   1.7815   1.4824   0.7573        0      1.2468
   1.7461   1.7340   1.4414   1.3885   1.2468        0
   1.5637   1.5408   1.6238   1.5709   1.6832   0.7846
   1.4012   1.3783   1.6709   1.7334   1.9374   1.3120
   0.9767   1.4861   1.7787   1.8316   1.8296   1.8771
   0.8569   1.4853   1.8352   1.8882   1.7731   1.8206
```

Columns 7 through 10

```
    1.5637     1.4012     0.9767     0.8569
    1.5408     1.3783     1.4861     1.4853
    1.6238     1.6709     1.7787     1.8352
    1.5709     1.7334     1.8316     1.8882
    1.6832     1.9374     1.8296     1.7731
    0.7846     1.3120     1.8771     1.8206
         0     0.8755     1.4561     1.5759
    0.8755          0     0.9287     1.0485
    1.4561     0.9287          0     0.4679
    1.5759     1.0485     0.4679          0
```

vaf =

    0.9218

targone =

  Columns 1 through 6

```
         0     0.2364     0.2680     0.4852     0.7880     1.1894
    0.2364          0     0.0316     0.2488     0.5516     0.9530
    0.2680     0.0316          0     0.2172     0.5199     0.9214
    0.4852     0.2488     0.2172          0     0.3028     0.7042
    0.7880     0.5516     0.5199     0.3028          0     0.4015
    1.1894     0.9530     0.9214     0.7042     0.4015          0
    1.1826     1.3420     1.3104     1.0933     0.7905     0.3890
    1.0800     1.3164     1.3480     1.1958     0.8931     0.4916
    0.6544     0.8908     0.9224     1.1396     1.3187     0.9172
    0.3450     0.5814     0.6130     0.8302     1.1329     1.2266
```

  Columns 7 through 10

```
    1.1826     1.0800     0.6544     0.3450
    1.3420     1.3164     0.8908     0.5814
    1.3104     1.3480     0.9224     0.6130
    1.0933     1.1958     1.1396     0.8302
    0.7905     0.8931     1.3187     1.1329
    0.3890     0.4916     0.9172     1.2266
         0     0.1026     0.5282     0.8376
    0.1026          0     0.4256     0.7350
    0.5282     0.4256          0     0.3094
    0.8376     0.7350     0.3094          0
```

targtwo =

Columns 1 through 6

```
       0    0.0491    0.1825    0.3852    0.5267    0.6148
  0.0491         0    0.1334    0.3361    0.4776    0.5657
  0.1825    0.1334         0    0.2027    0.3442    0.4324
  0.3852    0.3361    0.2027         0    0.1415    0.2296
  0.5267    0.4776    0.3442    0.1415         0    0.0882
  0.6148    0.5657    0.4324    0.2296    0.0882         0
  0.6001    0.6427    0.5094    0.3066    0.1652    0.0770
  0.3855    0.4346    0.5679    0.5212    0.3798    0.2916
  0.1270    0.1761    0.3095    0.5122    0.6382    0.5500
  0.0598    0.1089    0.2423    0.4450    0.5865    0.6173
```

Columns 7 through 10

```
  0.6001    0.3855    0.1270    0.0598
  0.6427    0.4346    0.1761    0.1089
  0.5094    0.5679    0.3095    0.2423
  0.3066    0.5212    0.5122    0.4450
  0.1652    0.3798    0.6382    0.5865
  0.0770    0.2916    0.5500    0.6173
       0    0.2146    0.4731    0.5403
  0.2146         0    0.2585    0.3257
  0.4731    0.2585         0    0.0672
  0.5403    0.3257    0.0672         0
```

outpermone =

```
     8      9     10      1      2      3      4      5      6      7
```

outpermtwo =

```
     7      3      8      4      9     10      5      1      6      2
```

addconone =

  -0.7002

addcontwo =

   0.3521

Chapter 4

LUS for Two-Mode Proximity Data

The proximity data considered thus far for obtaining some type of structural representation have been assumed to be on one intact set of objects, $S = \{O_1, \ldots, O_n\}$, and complete in the sense that proximity values are present between all object pairs. Suppose now that the available proximity data are two-mode, that is, *between* two distinct object sets, $S_A = \{O_{1A}, \ldots, O_{n_a A}\}$ and $S_B = \{O_{1B}, \ldots, O_{n_b B}\}$, containing n_a and n_b objects, respectively, and defined through an $n_a \times n_b$ proximity matrix $\mathbf{Q} = \{q_{rs}\}$, where again, for convenience, we assume that the entries in $\mathbf{Q}$ are keyed as dissimilarities. We may wish to seek a joint structural representation of the set $S_A \cup S_B$ (considered as a single object set S containing $n_a + n_b = n$ objects) but one that is based only on the available proximities between the sets S_A and S_B.

A two-mode (dissimilarity matrix) data set for illustrative purposes

To provide a specific example that will be used throughout this chapter as an illustration, Table 4.1 presents an 11×9 two-mode proximity matrix $\mathbf{Q}$ on the absorption of light at 9 different wavelengths by 11 different cones (receptors) in goldfish retina (but in a row and column reordered form that will reflect the discussion to follow). These data are from Schiffman and Falkenberg (1968) (and reanalyzed by Schiffman, Reynolds, and Young, 1981, pp. 328–329) and were originally based on an unpublished doctoral dissertation by Marks (1965). The proximities in the table are (200 minus) the heights of ordinates for particular spectral frequencies as labeled by the columns, and thus can be considered dissimilarities reflecting the closeness of a particular receptor to a particular wavelength. Using the original labeling of the rows as given in Schiffman and Falkenberg, the row permutation in Table 4.1 is (3,8,9,2,6,4,1,7,5,11,10); the column permutation is (4,9,6,5,1,7,2,8,3). The latter column permutation in its given order corresponds to wavelengths of (458):blue-indigo, (430):violet, (485):blue, (498):blue-green, (530):green, (540):green, (585):yellow, (610):orange, (660):red.

47

Table 4.1. *The goldfish_receptor.dat data file constructed from Schiffman and Falkenberg (1968).*

47	53	111	143	188	196	200	200	200
48	55	75	100	186	200	200	200	200
46	47	90	125	168	176	177	183	200
99	101	78	60	46	67	107	156	200
122	127	115	79	49	46	91	143	200
115	154	97	73	48	52	84	125	174
198	186	154	148	103	94	63	108	155
135	156	123	127	116	98	49	46	80
141	113	142	148	114	121	61	47	54
173	140	177	176	144	128	64	56	89
200	200	160	161	145	138	80	53	68

4.1　Reordering Two-Mode Proximity Matrices

Given an $n_a \times n_b$ two-mode proximity matrix, $\mathbf{Q}$, defined between the two distinct sets, S_A and S_B, it may be desirable to reorder separately the rows and columns of $\mathbf{Q}$ to display some type of pattern that may be present in its entries or to obtain some joint permutation of the n ($= n_a + n_b$) row and column objects to effect some further type of simplified representation. These kinds of reordering tasks will be approached with a variant of the quadratic assignment (QA) heuristics of the LUS discussion in Chapter 1 applied to a square $(n_a + n_b) \times (n_a + n_b)$ proximity matrix, $\mathbf{P}^{(tm)}$, in which a two-mode matrix $\mathbf{Q}_{(dev)}$ and its transpose (where $\mathbf{Q}_{(dev)}$ is constructed from $\mathbf{Q}$ by deviating its entries from the mean proximity) form the upper-right- and lower-left-hand portions, respectively, with zeros placed elsewhere. (This use of zero in the presence of deviated proximities appears a reasonable choice generally in identifying good reorderings of $\mathbf{P}^{(tm)}$. Without this type of deviation strategy, there would typically be no "mixing" of the row and column objects in the permutations that we would identify for the combined (row and column) object set.) Thus, for $\mathbf{0}$ denoting (an appropriately dimensioned) matrix of all zeros,

$$\mathbf{P}^{(tm)} = \begin{bmatrix} \mathbf{0}_{n_a \times n_a} & \mathbf{Q}_{(dev)n_a \times n_b} \\ \mathbf{Q}'_{(dev)n_b \times n_a} & \mathbf{0}_{n_b \times n_b} \end{bmatrix}$$

is the (square) $n \times n$ proximity matrix subjected to a simultaneous row and column reordering, which in turn will induce separate row and column reorderings for the original two-mode proximity matrix $\mathbf{Q}$.

The M-file `ordertm.m` implements a QA reordering heuristic on the derived matrix $\mathbf{P}^{(tm)}$, with usage

```
[outperm,rawindex,allperms,index,squareprox] = ...
ordertm(proxtm,targ,inperm,kblock)
```

where the two-mode proximity matrix PROXTM (with its entries deviated from the mean proximity within the use of the M-file) forms the upper-right- and lower-left-hand portions of a defined square $(n \times n)$ proximity matrix (SQUAREPROX) with a dissimilarity interpretation, and with zeros placed elsewhere (n = number of rows + number of columns of PROXTM = $n_a + n_b$); three separate local operations are used to permute the rows and columns of the square proximity matrix to maximize the cross-product index with respect to a square target matrix TARG: (a) pairwise interchanges of objects in the permutation defining the row and column order of the square proximity matrix; (b) the insertion of from 1 to KBLOCK (which is less than or equal to $n - 1$) consecutive objects in the permutation defining the row and column order of the data matrix; (c) the rotation of from 2 to KBLOCK (which is less than or equal to $n - 1$) consecutive objects in the permutation defining the row and column order of the data matrix. INPERM is the beginning input permutation (a permutation of the first n integers); PROXTM is the two-mode $n_a \times n_b$ input proximity matrix; TARG is the $n \times n$ input target matrix. OUTPERM is the final permutation of SQUAREPROX with the cross-product index RAWINDEX with respect to TARG. ALLPERMS is a cell array containing INDEX entries corresponding to all the permutations identified in the optimization from ALLPERMS{1} = INPERM to ALLPERMS{INDEX} = OUTPERM.

In the example to follow, ordertm.m is used on the dissimilarity matrix of Table 4.1. The square equally spaced target matrix is obtained from the LUS utility targlin.m. A listing of the (reordered) matrix, squareprox(outperm,outperm), if given, would show clearly the unidimensional pattern for a two-mode data matrix that will be explicitly fitted in the next section of this chapter.

```
load goldfish_receptor.dat
[outperm,rawindex,allperms,index,squareprox] = ...
ordertm(goldfish_receptor,targlin(20),randperm(20),2);
outperm
```

outperm =

  Columns 1 through 10

    20   11   10   19   9   18   8   7   17   16

  Columns 11 through 20

     6   5   4   15   14   13   3   12   2   1

4.2   Fitting a Two-Mode Unidimensional Scale

It is possible to fit, through iterative projection, best-fitting (in the L_2-norm) unidimensional scales to two-mode proximity data based on a given permutation of the combined row and column object set. Specifically, if $\rho(\cdot)$ denotes some given permutation of the first n integers (where the first n_a integers denote row objects, labeled $1, 2, \ldots, n_a$, and the remaining n_b integers denote column objects, labeled $n_a + 1, n_a + 2, \ldots, n_a + n_b(= n)$), we seek a set of coordinates, $x_1 \leq x_2 \leq \cdots \leq x_n$, such that using the reordered square proximity matrix,

$\mathbf{P}_{\rho_0}^{(tm)} = \{p_{\rho_0(i)\rho_0(j)}^{(tm)}\}$, the least-squares criterion

$$\sum_{i,j=1}^{n} w_{\rho_0(i)\rho_0(j)}(p_{\rho_0(i)\rho_0(j)}^{(tm)} - |x_j - x_i|)^2$$

is minimized, where $w_{\rho_0(i)\rho_0(j)} = 0$ if $\rho_0(i)$ and $\rho_0(j)$ are both row or both column objects, and $= 1$ otherwise. The entries in the matrix fitted to $\mathbf{P}_{\rho_0}^{(tm)}$ are based on the absolute coordinate differences (which correspond to nonzero values of the weight function $w_{\rho_0(i)\rho_0(j)}$), and thus satisfy certain linear inequality constraints generated from how the row and column objects are intermixed by the given permutation $\rho_0(\cdot)$. To give a schematic representation of how these constraints are generated, suppose r_1 and r_2 (c_1 and c_2) denote two arbitrary row (column) objects, and suppose the following 2×2 matrix represents what is to be fitted to the four proximity values present between r_1, r_2 and c_1, c_2:

	c_1	c_2
r_1	a	b
r_2	c	d

Depending on how these four objects are ordered (and intermixed) by the permutation $\rho_0(\cdot)$, certain constraints must be satisfied by the entries $a, b, c,$ and d. The representative constraints are given schematically below according to the types of intermixing that might be present:

(a) $r_1 \prec r_2 \prec c_1 \prec c_2$ implies $a + d = b + c$;
(b) $r_1 \prec c_1 \prec r_2 \prec c_2$ implies $a + c + d = b$;
(c) $r_1 \prec c_1 \prec c_2 \prec r_2$ implies $a + c = b + d$;
(d) $r_1 \prec r_2 \prec c_1$ implies $c \leq a$;
(e) $r_1 \prec c_1 \prec c_2$ implies $a \leq b$.

The confirmatory unidimensional scaling of a two-mode proximity matrix (based on iterative projection using a given permutation of the row and column objects) is carried out with the M-file `linfittm`, with usage

```
[fit,diff,rowperm,colperm,coord] = linfittm(proxtm,inperm)
```

Here, PROXTM is the two-mode proximity matrix, and INPERM is the given ordering of the row and column objects pooled together; FIT is an $n_a \times n_b$ matrix of absolute coordinate differences fitted to PROXTM(ROWPERM, COLPERM), with DIFF being the (least-squares criterion) sum of squared discrepancies between FIT and PROXTM(ROWPERM, COLMEAN); ROWPERM and COLPERM are the row and column object orderings derived from INPERM. The $(n_a + n_b) = n$ coordinates (ordered with the smallest such coordinate set at a value of zero) are given in COORD.

The example given below uses a permutation obtained from `ordertm.m` on the data matrix `goldfish_receptor.dat`.

```
[fit,diff,rowperm,colperm,coord] = ...
linfittm(goldfish_receptor,outperm);
 fit
```

```
fit =

  Columns 1 through 6

     27.7467     19.6170     49.8824    105.1624    113.7988    174.4352
     38.8578      8.5059     38.7712     94.0513    102.6877    163.3241
     64.4133     17.0497     13.2157     68.4958     77.1321    137.7685
     82.0890     34.7253      4.4600     50.8201     59.4565    120.0928
     84.6355     37.2719      7.0065     48.2735     56.9099    117.5463
    151.4133    104.0497     73.7843     18.5042      9.8679     50.7685
    156.0800    108.7163     78.4510     23.1709     14.5345     46.1018
    172.9689    125.6052     95.3399     40.0598     31.4234     29.2129
    259.6356    212.2720    182.0066    126.7265    118.0901     57.4538
    286.9689    239.6052    209.3399    154.0598    145.4234     84.7871
    295.1911    247.8275    217.5621    162.2820    153.6456     93.0093

  Columns 7 through 9

    189.5261    212.4352    231.8897
    178.4150    201.3241    220.7786
    152.8594    175.7685    195.2230
    135.1837    158.0928    177.5473
    132.6372    155.5463    175.0008
     65.8594     88.7685    108.2230
     61.1927     84.1018    103.5563
     44.3039     67.2129     86.6674
     42.3629     19.4538      0.0007
     69.6961     46.7871     27.3326
     77.9184     55.0093     35.5548

  diff

diff =

  1.4372e+005

 rowperm'

ans =

  Columns 1 through 10

     11     10      9      8      7      6      5      4      3      2

  Column 11
```

```
        1

  colperm'

ans =

      9       8       7       6       5       4       3       2       1

  coord'

ans =

  Columns 1 through 6

            0    27.7467    38.8578    47.3636    64.4133    77.6290

  Columns 7 through 12

    82.0890    84.6355   132.9091   141.5455   151.4133   156.0800

  Columns 13 through 18

  172.9689   202.1818   217.2727   240.1818   259.6356   259.6363

  Columns 19 through 20

  286.9689   295.1911
```

In complete analogy with the LUS discussion (where the M-file `linfitac.m` generalizes `linfit.m` by fitting an additive constant along with the absolute coordinate differences), the more general unidimensional scaling model can be fitted with an additive constant using the M-file `linfittmac.m`. Specifically, we now seek a set of coordinates, $x_1 \leq x_2 \leq \cdots \leq x_n$, and an additive constant c, such that using the reordered square proximity matrix, $\mathbf{P}_{\rho_0}^{(tm)} = \{p_{\rho_0(i)\rho_0(j)}^{(tm)}\}$, the least-squares criterion

$$\sum_{i,j=1}^{n} w_{\rho_0(i)\rho_0(j)} (p_{\rho_0(i)\rho_0(j)}^{(tm)} + c - |x_j - x_i|)^2$$

is minimized, where again $w_{\rho_0(i)\rho_0(j)} = 0$ if $\rho_0(i)$ and $\rho_0(j)$ are both row or both column objects, and $= 1$ otherwise. The M-file usage is

```
[fit,vaf,rowperm,colperm,addcon,coord] = ...
    linfittmac(proxtm,inperm)
```

and does a confirmatory two-mode fitting of a given unidimensional ordering of the row and column objects of a two-mode proximity matrix PROXTM using the Dykstra–Kaczmarz iterative projection least-squares method. In comparison, the M-file `linfittmac.m` differs from linfittm.m by including the estimation of an additive constant, and thus allow-ing VAF to be legitimately given as the goodness-of-fit index (as opposed to just DIFF as we did in linfittm.m). Again, INPERM is the given ordering of the row and col-umn objects together; FIT is an n_a (number of rows) $\times$ n_b (number of columns) matrix of absolute coordinate differences fitted to PROXTM(ROWPERM, COLPERM); ROWPERM and COLPERM are the row and column object orderings derived from INPERM. The esti-mated additive constant ADDCON can be interpreted as being added to PROXTM (or, alter-natively, subtracted from the fitted matrix FIT).

The same exemplar permutation is used below (as was used for linfittm.m); following the MATLAB output that now includes the additive constant of -55.0512 and the VAF of .8072, the two unidimensional scalings (in their coordinate forms) are provided in Table 4.2 with an explicit indication of what is a row object (R) and what is a column object (C).

```
[fit,vaf,rowperm,colperm,addcon,coord] = ...
linfittmac(goldfish_receptor,outperm);
 vaf

vaf =

    0.8072

 rowperm'

ans =

  Columns 1 through 10

     11     10      9      8      7      6      5      4      3      2

  Column 11

      1

 colperm'

ans =

      9      8      7      6      5      4      3      2      1

 addcon

addcon =

  -55.0512
```

```
coord'

ans =

  Columns 1 through 6

        0    16.7584    27.1305    27.9496    41.1914    46.4762

  Columns 7 through 12

   47.9363    49.2521    82.8626    91.1532    91.9133    96.1573

  Columns 13 through 18

  113.0462   122.1074   137.1983   160.1074   166.6057   166.6124

  Columns 19 through 20

  178.1118   186.3341
```

4.3   Multiple LUS Reorderings and Fittings

Two M-files are provided that put together the (QA) reordering of a two-mode rectangular proximity matrix with the fitting of the unidimensional scale(s). The first, uniscaltmac.m, combines the use of ordertm.m and linfittmac.m along with (re)estimations of the (originally equally spaced) target matrix using the coordinates obtained until the identified permutation stabilizes. The usage includes the same terms as for the encompassing M-files:

```
[find, vaf, outperm, rowperm, colperm, addcon, coord] = ...
uniscaltmac(proxtm, inperm, kblock)
```

The second M-file, biscaltmac.m, finds and fits, through successive residualization, the sum of two linear unidimensional scales using iterative projection to a two-mode proximity matrix in the L_2-norm based on permutations identified through the use of iterative QA. The usage has the form

```
[find,vaf,targone,targtwo,outpermone,outpermtwo, ...
  rowpermone,colpermone,rowpermtwo,colpermtwo,addconone, ...
  addcontwo,coordone,coordtwo,axes] = ...
biscaltmac(proxtm,inpermone,inpermtwo,kblock,nopt)
```

Most of the terms should be obvious from earlier usage statements; the $n \times 2$ matrix, AXES, gives the two-dimensional plotting coordinates for the combined row and column object set. As was allowed in the bidimensional scaling routine biscalqa.m, the variable NOPT controls the confirmatory or exploratory fitting of the unidimensional scales; a value of

Table 4.2. *The two unidimensional scalings of the goldfish_receptor data.*

Color	Number	R or C	No constant	With constant
red (660)	20	C	0.0	0.0
	11	R	27.7467	16.7584
	10	R	38.8578	27.1305
orange (610)	19	C	47.3636	27.9496
	9	R	64.4133	41.1914
yellow (585)	18	C	77.6290	46.4762
	8	R	82.0890	47.9363
	7	R	84.6355	49.2521
green (540)	17	C	132.9091	82.8626
green (530)	16	C	141.5455	91.1532
	6	R	151.4133	91.9133
	5	R	156.0800	96.1573
	4	R	172.9689	113.0462
blue-green (490)	15	C	202.1818	122.1074
blue (485)	14	C	217.2727	137.1983
violet (430)	13	C	240.1818	160.1074
	3	R	259.6356	166.6057
blue-indigo (458)	12	C	259.6363	166.6124
	2	R	286.9689	178.1118
	1	R	295.1911	186.3341

NOPT = 0 will fit in a confirmatory mode the two scales indicated by INPERMONE and INPERMTWO; a value of NOPT = 1 uses iterative QA to locate the better permutations to fit.

An example of using biscaltmac.m follows, leading to a two-dimensional scaling of the goldfish_receptor data with a VAF of .9620. A two-dimensional graphical representation of the coordinates will be given in the next section after the necessary plotting utility, biplottm.m, is introduced.

```
load goldfish_receptor.dat
 [find,vaf,targone,targtwo,outpermone,outpermtwo,...
rowpermone,colpermone,rowpermtwo,colpermtwo,addconone,...
addcontwo,coordone,coordtwo,axes] = ...
biscaltmac(goldfish_receptor,randperm(20),randperm(20),2,1);
 vaf

vaf =

    0.9620

outpermone
```

```
outpermone =

  Columns 1 through 10

    20    11    10    19     9    18     8     7    17    16

  Columns 11 through 20

     6     5     4    15    14    13     3    12     2     1

 coordone'

ans =

  Columns 1 through 6

         0    5.3813   29.6923   29.6923   47.3362   47.3362

  Columns 7 through 12

   47.3362   47.3362   80.1506   88.7578   91.1164  100.5008

  Columns 13 through 18

  115.5844  131.4868  141.7676  149.8850  160.3825  160.3825

  Columns 19 through 20

  173.7454  181.0428

 outpermtwo

outpermtwo =

  Columns 1 through 10

     3    20     1     2    13    10     9    19    12     8

  Columns 11 through 20

    14    11    18     6    15     4     5    16    17     7

 coordtwo'

ans =
```

```
Columns 1 through 6

        0     6.7276     6.7277     7.8975    14.0132    14.0891

Columns 7 through 12

   14.0891    27.5247    27.5247    30.1025    40.4679    40.4710

Columns 13 through 18

   49.4002    58.0796    58.0796    66.8364    72.2495    72.7100

Columns 19 through 20

   72.8142    90.6794

 axes

axes =

   181.0428     6.7277
   173.7454     7.8975
   160.3825          0
   115.5844    66.8364
   100.5008    72.2495
    91.1164    58.0796
    47.3362    90.6794
    47.3362    30.1025
    47.3362    14.0891
    29.6923    14.0891
     5.3813    40.4710
   160.3825    27.5247
   149.8850    14.0132
   141.7676    40.4679
   131.4868    58.0796
    88.7578    72.7100
    80.1506    72.8142
    47.3362    49.4002
    29.6923    27.5247
         0     6.7276
```

4.4   Some Useful Two-Mode Utilities

This section gives several miscellaneous M-functions that carry out various operations on a two-mode proximity matrix and for which no other section of this monograph seemed appropriate. The first two, `proxstdtm.m` and `proxrandtm.m`, are very simple and provide standardized and randomly (entry-)permuted two-mode proximity matrices, respectively, that might be useful, for example, in testing the various M-functions we give. The syntax

```
[stanproxtm,stanproxmulttm] = proxstdtm(proxtm,mean)
```

is intended to suggest that STANPROXTM provides a linear transformation of the entries in PROXTM to a standard deviation of one and a mean of MEAN; STANPROXMULTTM is a multiplicative transformation so that the entries in this $n_a \times n_b$ matrix have a sum-of-squares of $n_a n_b$. For the second utility M-function

```
[randproxtm] = proxrandtm(proxtm)
```

implies that the two-mode matrix RANDPROXTM has its entries as a random permutation of the entries in PROXTM.

A third utility function, `proxmontm.m`, provides a monotonically transformed two-mode proximity matrix that is close in a least-squares sense to a given input two-mode matrix. The syntax is

```
[monproxpermuttm, vaf, diff] = ...
   proxmontm(proxpermuttm,fittedtm)
```

Here, PROXPERMUTTM is the original input two-mode proximity matrix (which may have been subjected to initial row and column permutations, hence the suffix PERMUTTM), and FITTEDTM is a given two-mode target matrix; the output matrix MONPROXPERMUTTM is closest to FITTEDTM in a least-squares sense and obeys the order constraints obtained from each pair of entries in PROXPERMUTTM (and where the inequality constrained optimization is carried out using the Dykstra–Kaczmarz iterative projection strategy); as usual, VAF indicates how much variance in MONPROXPERMUTTM can be accounted for by FITTEDTM; finally, DIFF is the value of the least-squares loss function and is the sum of squared differences between the entries in MONPROXPERMUTTM and FITTEDTM. We will give an application of an M-file incorporating `proxmontm.m` when we suggest in Section 4.5 a way of implementing two-dimensional, two-mode nonmetric multidimensional scaling.

A final utility function, `biplottm.m`, plots the combined row and column object set using the coordinates given in, for example, the $n \times 2$ output matrix AXES as output from the M-file of the last section, `biscaltmac.m`. The usage syntax is

```
biplottm(axes,nrow,ncol)
```

Here, the number of rows (columns) is NROW (NCOL), and n is the sum of NROW and NCOL. The first NROW rows of the $n \times 2$ matrix AXES give the row object coordinates; the last NCOL rows of AXES give the column object coordinates. The plotting symbol for rows is a circle (o); for columns it is an asterisk (*). The labels for rows are from 1 to NROW; those for columns are from 1 to NCOL. (It should be noted that Release 14 for MATLAB and of the Statistics Toolbox (5.0) includes a somewhat similar M-function called `biplot.m`. Our

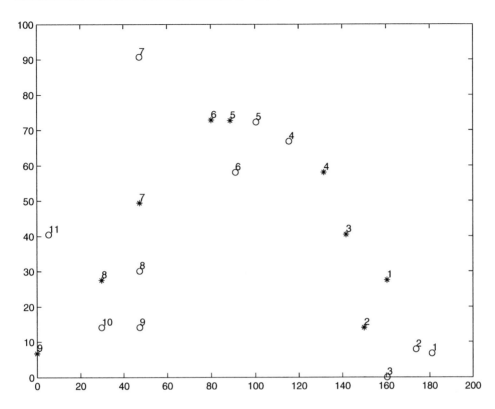

Figure 4.1. *Two-dimensional joint biplot for the goldfish_receptor data obtained using biplottm.m.*

biplottm.m routine is tailored to the two-mode context we have been discussing, and therefore may be the preferred plotting strategy within this chapter.)

Figure 4.1 give an application of biplottm.m for the AXES matrix of the last example given in Section 4.3 (for the goldfish_receptor data). Again, the appropriate colors appear close to the relevant cones.

4.5 Two-Mode Nonmetric Bidimensional Scaling

By uniting the utility function proxmon.m with biscaltmac.m, we can construct an M-file, bimonscaltmac.m, that carries out a nonmetric bidimensional scaling of a two-mode proximity matrix in the city-block metric. The usage is the same as that of biscaltmac.m in Section 4.3, except for the additional output matrix MONPROXTM that is a monotonic transformation of the original two-mode proximity matrix PROXTM:

```
[..., monproxtm] = bimonscaltmac(...)
```

We give an example below using the same goldfish_receptor.dat matrix; the VAF has increased (slightly) to .9772. The joint plot of the row and column object set is given

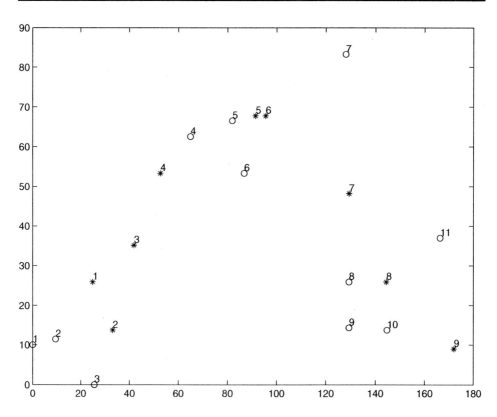

Figure 4.2. *Two-dimensional joint biplot for the goldfish_receptor data obtained using bimonscaltmac.m and biplottm.m.*

in Figure 4.2 and closely resembles Figure 4.1 obtained without the use of a monotonic transformation.

```
[find,vaf,targone,targtwo,outpermone,outpermtwo,...
rowpermone,colpermone,rowpermtwo,colpermtwo,addconone,...
addcontwo,coordone,coordtwo,axes,monproxtm] = ...
bimonscaltmac(goldfish_receptor,1:20,1:20,1,1);

 vaf

vaf =

    0.9772

 outpermone

outpermone =
```

```
Columns 1 through 10

   1      2     12      3     13     14     15      4      5      6

Columns 11 through 20

  16     17      7      8     18      9     19     10     11     20

outpermtwo

outpermtwo =

Columns 1 through 10

   3     20      1      2     13     10      9     19      8     12

Columns 11 through 20

  14     11     18      6     15      4      5     16     17      7

coordone'

ans =

Columns 1 through 6

        0    9.3971   24.9145   25.6090   33.0810   41.8175

Columns 7 through 12

  52.5796   64.9000   81.8939   86.7370   91.3614   95.4814

Columns 13 through 18

 128.0062  129.3501  129.3501  129.3501  144.3894  144.6789

Columns 19 through 20

 166.2783  172.0484

coordtwo'

ans =

Columns 1 through 6
```

```
        0     9.0068   10.0288   11.4579   13.7505   13.7515

Columns 7 through 12

  14.3479   25.9193   25.9193   25.9193   35.1740   37.0213

Columns 13 through 18

  48.2031   53.3228   53.3228   62.5256   66.5361   67.7899

Columns 19 through 20

  67.7899   83.2680
```

monproxtm

monproxtm =

```
Columns 1 through 6

   58.7038    63.2885   108.3069   141.6262   189.0671   189.0671
   58.7038    63.2885    82.1362   108.3069   181.2299   189.0671
   58.7038    58.7038    85.7059   124.9383   167.7111   167.7111
  108.3069   108.3069    82.1362    63.2885    58.7038    72.2093
  124.9383   136.7608   120.4397    82.1362    58.7038    48.4205
  120.4397   141.6262    97.3034    72.2093    58.7038    58.7038
  189.0671   189.0671   154.9866   141.6262   108.3069    91.1332
  138.5167   154.9866   124.9383   138.5167   120.4397   108.3069
  141.6262   120.4397   141.6262   141.6262   120.4397   121.7048
  167.7111   141.6262   167.7111   167.7111   141.6262   138.5167
  189.1641   193.2795   162.2199   166.2670   141.6262   138.5167

Columns 7 through 9

  203.9042   196.9665   208.6756
  192.8095   189.0671   200.9956
  181.2299   181.2299   191.5023
  108.3069   154.9866   197.4823
   91.1332   141.6262   189.0671
   82.1362   124.9383   167.7111
   70.2554   108.3069   154.9866
   58.7038    48.4214    82.1362
   67.2074    58.7038    63.2885
   72.2093    63.2885    82.1362
   82.1262    63.2885    72.2093
```

Part II

The Representation of Proximity Matrices by Tree Structures

Introduction to Graph-Theoretic Representational Structures

Various methods of data representation based on graph-theoretic structures have been developed over the last several decades for explaining the pattern of information potentially present in a single (or possibly in a collection of) numerically given proximity matri(ces), each defined between pairs of objects from a single set or, in some cases, between the objects from several distinct sets (for example, see Carroll, 1976; Carroll, Clark, and De-Sarbo, 1984; Carroll and Pruzansky, 1980; De Soete, 1983, 1984a,b,c; De Soete, Carroll, and DeSarbo, 1987; De Soete et al., 1984; Hutchinson, 1989; Klauer and Carroll, 1989, 1991; Hubert and Arabie, 1995b). Typically, a specific class of graph-theoretic structures is assumed capable of representing the proximity information, and the proposed method seeks a member from the class producing a reconstructed set of proximities that are as close as possible to the original. The most prominent graph-theoretic structures used are those usually referred to as ultrametrics and additive trees, and these will be the primary emphasis here as well.

Although a variety of strategies have been proposed for locating good exemplars from whatever class of graph-theoretic structures is being considered, one approach has been to adopt a least-squares criterion in which the class exemplar is identified by attempting to minimize the sum of squared discrepancies between the original proximities and their reconstructions obtained through the use of the particular structure selected by the data analyst. One common implementation of the least-squares optimization strategy has been defined by the usual least-squares criterion but augmented by some collection of penalty functions that seek to impose whatever constraints are mandated by the structural representation being sought. Then, through the use of some unconstrained optimization scheme (e.g., steepest descent, conjugate gradients), an attempt is made to find both (a) the particular constraints that should be imposed to define the specific structure from the class and (b) the reconstructed proximities based on the structure finally identified. The resulting optimization strategy is heuristic in the sense that there is no guarantee of global optimality for the final structural representation identified even within the chosen graph-theoretic class, because the particular constraints defining the selected structure were located by a possibly reasonable but not verifiably optimal search strategy that was (implicitly) implemented in the course of the process of optimization. A second implementation of the least-squares optimization approach, and the one that we will concentrate on exclusively, is based on the type of iterative projection strategy already illustrated in conjunction with linear unidimensional scaling (LUS) (see the addendum (Section 1.4) on solving linear inequality constrained least-squares tasks) and developed in detail for the graph-theoretic context by Hubert and Arabie (1995b). In its nonheuristic form, iterative projection allows the reconstruction of a set of proximities based on a fixed collection of constraints implied by whatever specific graph-theoretic structure has been selected for their representation. As in LUS, successive (or iterative) projections onto closed convex sets are carried out that are defined by the collection of given constraints implied by the structural representation chosen. Thus, the need for penalty terms is avoided and there is no explicit use of gradients in the attendant optimization strategy; also, it is fairly straightforward to incorporate a variety of different types of constraints that may be auxiliary to those generated from the given structural representation but nonetheless of interest to impose on the reconstruction.

As a least-squares optimization strategy (in a nonheuristic form), iterative projection assumes that whatever constraint set is to be applied is completely known prior to its application. However, just as the various penalty-function and gradient-optimization techniques have been turned into heuristic search strategies for the particular structures of interest by allowing the collection of constraints to vary over the course of the optimization process, we attempt the same in using iterative projection to find the better-fitting ultrametrics and additive trees for a given proximity matrix. Thus, in addition to carrying out a least-squares task subject to given structural constraints, iterative projection will be considered as one possible heuristic search strategy (and an alternative to those heuristic methods that have been suggested in the literature and based exclusively on the use of some type of penalty function) for locating the actual constraints to impose, and therefore to identify the specific form of the structural representation sought.

The various least-squares optimization tasks entailing both the identification of the specific form of the structural representation to adopt and the subsequent least-squares fitting itself generally fall into the class of NP-hard problems (e.g., for ultrametric and additive trees, see Day, 1987, 1996; Křivánek, 1986; Křivánek and Morávek, 1986); thus, the best we can hope for is a heuristic extension of the iterative projection strategy leading to good but not necessarily optimal final structural representations within the general class of representations desired. As is standard with a reliance on such heuristic optimization methods, the use of multiple starting points will hopefully determine a set of local optima characterizing the better solutions attainable for a given data set. The presence of local optima in the use of any heuristic and combinatorially based optimization strategy is unavoidable, given the NP-hardness of the basic optimization tasks of interest and the general inability of (partial) enumeration methods (when available) to be computationally feasible for use on even moderate-sized data sets. The number of and variation in the local optima observable for any specific situation will obviously depend on the given data, the structural representation sought, and the heuristic search strategy used. But whenever present, local optima may actually be diagnostic for the structure(s) potentially appropriate for characterizing a particular data set. Thus, their identification may even be valuable in explaining the patterning of the data and/or in noting the difficulties with adopting a specific representational form to help discern underlying structure.

Chapter 5

Ultrametrics for Symmetric Proximity Data

The task of hierarchical clustering can be characterized as a specific data analysis problem: given a set of n objects, $S = \{O_1, \ldots, O_n\}$, and an $n \times n$ symmetric proximity matrix $\mathbf{P} = \{p_{ij}\}$ (nonnegative and with a dissimilarity interpretation), find a sequence of partitions of S, denoted as $\mathcal{P}_1, \mathcal{P}_2, \ldots, \mathcal{P}_n$, satisfying the following:

(a) $\mathcal{P}_1$ is the (trivial) partition where all n objects from S are placed into n separate classes;

(b) $\mathcal{P}_n$ is the (also trivial) partition where a single subset contains all n objects;

(c) $\mathcal{P}_k$ is obtained from $\mathcal{P}_{k-1}$ by uniting some pair of classes present in $\mathcal{P}_{k-1}$;

(d) the minimum levels at which object pairs first appear together within the same class should reflect the proximities in $\mathcal{P}$. Or more formally, if we define $\mathbf{U}^0 = \{u_{ij}^0\} = \min\{k - 1 \mid \text{objects } O_i \text{ and } O_j \text{ appear within the same class in } \mathcal{P}_k\}$, then if the partition hierarchy is representing the given proximities well, the entries in $\mathbf{U}^0$ and $\mathbf{P}$ should be, for example, similarly ordered. We discuss the properties of matrices such as $\mathbf{U}^0$ in more detail below.

To give an example, we performed a complete-link hierarchical clustering (using SYSTAT) on the number.dat proximity matrix used extensively in Part I and obtained the following partitions of the object indices from 1 to 10 (remembering that these correspond to the digits 0 to 9):

$\mathcal{P}_1$: {{1},{2},{3},{4},{5},{6},{7},{8},{9},{10}}
$\mathcal{P}_2$: {{3,5},{1},{2},{4},{6},{7},{8},{9},{10}}
$\mathcal{P}_3$: {{3,5},{4,10},{1},{2},{6},{7},{8},{9}}
$\mathcal{P}_4$: {{3,5},{4,7,10},{1},{2},{6},{8},{9}}
$\mathcal{P}_5$: {{3,5,9},{4,7,10},{1},{2},{6},{8}}
$\mathcal{P}_6$: {{3,5,9},{4,7,10},{6,8},{1},{2}}
$\mathcal{P}_7$: {{3,5,9},{4,7,10},{6,8},{1,2}}
$\mathcal{P}_8$: {{3,5,9},{4,6,7,8,10},{1,2}}
$\mathcal{P}_9$: {{3,4,5,6,7,8,9,10},{1,2}}
$\mathcal{P}_{10}$: {{1,2,3,4,5,6,7,8,9,10}}

The matrix $\mathbf{U}^0$ was constructed and saved as a 10×10 matrix in the file numcltarg.dat, which will be used later in an example:

```
0 6 9 9 9 9 9 9 9 9
6 0 9 9 9 9 9 9 9 9
9 9 0 8 1 8 8 8 4 8
9 9 8 0 8 7 3 7 8 2
9 9 1 8 0 8 8 8 4 8
9 9 8 7 8 0 7 5 8 7
9 9 8 3 8 7 0 7 8 3
9 9 8 7 8 5 7 0 8 7
9 9 4 8 4 8 8 8 0 8
9 9 8 2 8 7 3 7 8 0
```

We note that this same hierarchical clustering could have been obtained alternatively with the cluster.m routine from the Statistics Toolbox for MATLAB, allowing the user to remain completely within a MATLAB environment (assuming, obviously, that the Statistics Toolbox is available).

A concept routinely encountered in discussions of hierarchical clustering is that of an ultrametric, which can be characterized here as any nonnegative symmetric dissimilarity matrix for the objects in S, denoted generically by $\mathbf{U} = \{u_{ij}\}$, where $u_{ij} = 0$ if and only if $i = j$, and $u_{ij} \leq \max[u_{ik}, u_{jk}]$ for all $1 \leq i, j, k \leq n$ (this last inequality, called the three-point or three-object condition, is equivalent to the statement that for any distinct triple of subscripts, i, j, and k, the largest two proximities among u_{ij}, u_{ik}, and u_{jk} are equal and (therefore) not less than the third). Any ultrametric can be associated with the specific partition hierarchy it induces, having the form $\mathcal{P}_1, \mathcal{P}_2, \ldots, \mathcal{P}_T$, where $\mathcal{P}_1$ and $\mathcal{P}_T$ are now the two trivial partitions that, respectively, contain all objects in separate classes and all objects in the same class, and $\mathcal{P}_k$ is formed from $\mathcal{P}_{k-1}$ ($2 \leq k \leq T$) by (agglomeratively) uniting certain (and possibly more than two) subsets in $\mathcal{P}_{k-1}$. For those subsets merged in $\mathcal{P}_{k-1}$ to form $\mathcal{P}_k$, all between-subset ultrametric values must be equal and no less than any other ultrametric value associated with an object pair within a class in $\mathcal{P}_{k-1}$. Thus, individual partitions in the hierarchy can be identified by merely increasing a threshold variable starting at zero and observing that $\mathcal{P}_k$ for $1 \leq k \leq T$ is defined by a set of subsets in which all within-subset ultrametric values are less than or equal to some specific threshold value, and all ultrametric values between subsets are strictly greater. Conversely, any partition hierarchy of the form $\mathcal{P}_1, \ldots, \mathcal{P}_T$ can be identified with the equivalence class of all ultrametric matrices that induce it. We note that if only a *single* pair of subsets can be united in $\mathcal{P}_{k-1}$ to form $\mathcal{P}_k$ for $2 \leq k \leq T$, then $T = n$, and we could then revert to the characterization of a full partition hierarchy $\mathcal{P}_1, \ldots, \mathcal{P}_n$ used earlier.

Given some fixed partition hierarchy $\mathcal{P}_1, \ldots, \mathcal{P}_T$, there are an infinite number of ultrametric matrices that induce it, but all can be generated by (restricted) monotonic functions of what might be called the basic ultrametric matrix $\mathbf{U}^0$ defined earlier. Explicitly, any ultrametric in the equivalence class whose members induce the same fixed hierarchy, $\mathcal{P}_1, \ldots, \mathcal{P}_T$, can be obtained by a strictly increasing monotonic function of the entries in $\mathbf{U}^0$, where the function maps zero to zero. Moreover, because u_{ij}^0 for $i \neq j$ can be only one of the integer values from 1 to $T - 1$, each ultrametric in the equivalence class that generates the fixed hierarchy may be defined by one of $T - 1$ distinct values. When these $T - 1$ values are ordered from the smallest to the largest, the $(k-1)$st smallest value corresponds to the partition $\mathcal{P}_k$ in the partition hierarchy $\mathcal{P}_1, \ldots, \mathcal{P}_T$ and implicitly to all object pairs that appear together for the first time within a subset in $\mathcal{P}_k$.

To provide an alternative interpretation, the basic ultrametric matrix can also be characterized as defining a collection of linear equality and inequality constraints that any ultrametric in a specific equivalence class must satisfy. Specifically, for each object triple there
is (a) a specification of which ultrametric values among the three must be equal plus two
additional inequality constraints so that the third is not greater; (b) an inequality or equality
constraint for every pair of ultrametric values based on their order relationship in the basic
ultrametric matrix; and (c) an equality constraint of zero for the main diagonal entries in **U**.
In any case, given these fixed equality and inequality constraints, standard L_p regression
methods (such as those given in Späth, 1991) could be adapted to generate a best-fitting
ultrametric, say $\mathbf{U}^* = \{u_{ij}^*\}$, to the given proximity matrix $\mathbf{P} = \{p_{ij}\}$. Concretely, we might
find $\mathbf{U}^*$ by minimizing

$$\sum_{i<j}(p_{ij} - u_{ij})^2, \ \sum_{i<j} \mid p_{ij} - u_{ij} \mid, \ \text{or possibly } \max_{i<j} \mid p_{ij} - u_{ij} \mid .$$

(As a convenience here and later, it is assumed that $p_{ij} > 0$ for all $i \neq j$, to avoid the
technicality of possibly locating best-fitting "ultrametrics" that could violate the condition
that $u_{ij} = 0$ if and only if $i = j$.)

5.1 Fitting a Given Ultrametric in the L_2-Norm

The function `ultrafit.m` with usage

```
[fit,vaf] = ultrafit(prox,targ)
```

generates (using iterative projection based on the linear (in)equality constraints obtained
from the fixed ultrametric—see Section 1.4) the best-fitting ultrametric in the L_2-norm
(FIT) within the same equivalence class as that of a given ultrametric matrix TARG. The
matrix PROX contains the symmetric input proximities and VAF is the variance-accounted-
for (defined, as usual, by normalizing the obtained L_2-norm loss value):

$$\text{VAF} = 1 - \frac{\sum_{i<j}(p_{ij} - u_{ij}^*)^2}{\sum_{i<j}(p_{ij} - \bar{p})^2},$$

where $\bar{p}$ is the mean off-diagonal proximity in **P**, and $\mathbf{U}^* = \{u_{ij}^*\}$ is the best-fitting ultrametric.

   In the example below, the target matrix is `numcltarg` obtained from the complete-
link hierarchical clustering of `number`; the VAF generated by these ultrametric constraints
is .4781. Comparing the target matrix `numcltarg` and `fit`, the particular monotonic
function, say $f(\cdot)$, of the entries in the basic ultrametric matrix that generates the fitted
matrix are $f(1) = .0590$, $f(2) = .2630$, $f(3) = .2980$, $f(4) = .3065$, $f(5) = .4000$,
$f(6) = .4210$, $f(7) = .4808$, $f(8) = .5535$, $f(9) = .6761$.

```
load number.dat
load numcltarg.dat
[fit,vaf] = ultrafit(number,numcltarg)

fit =
```

```
Columns 1 through 6

        0    0.4210    0.6761    0.6761    0.6761    0.6761
   0.4210         0    0.6761    0.6761    0.6761    0.6761
   0.6761    0.6761         0    0.5535    0.0590    0.5535
   0.6761    0.6761    0.5535         0    0.5535    0.4808
   0.6761    0.6761    0.0590    0.5535         0    0.5535
   0.6761    0.6761    0.5535    0.4808    0.5535         0
   0.6761    0.6761    0.5535    0.2980    0.5535    0.4808
   0.6761    0.6761    0.5535    0.4808    0.5535    0.4000
   0.6761    0.6761    0.3065    0.5535    0.3065    0.5535
   0.6761    0.6761    0.5535    0.2630    0.5535    0.4808

Columns 7 through 10

   0.6761    0.6761    0.6761    0.6761
   0.6761    0.6761    0.6761    0.6761
   0.5535    0.5535    0.3065    0.5535
   0.2980    0.4808    0.5535    0.2630
   0.5535    0.5535    0.3065    0.5535
   0.4808    0.4000    0.5535    0.4808
        0    0.4808    0.5535    0.2980
   0.4808         0    0.5535    0.4808
   0.5535    0.5535         0    0.5535
   0.2980    0.4808    0.5535         0


vaf =

   0.4781
```

5.2   Finding an Ultrametric in the L_2-Norm

The M-file ultrafnd.m implements a heuristic search strategy using iterative projection to locate a best-fitting ultrametric in the L_2-norm. The method used is from Hubert and Arabie (1995b), which should be consulted for the explicit algorithmic details implemented in ultrafnd.m (as well as for many of the other M-files to be presented). The M-file usage has the form

```
[find,vaf] = ultrafnd(prox,inperm)
```

where FIND is the ultrametric identified having variance-accounted-for VAF. The matrix PROX contains the symmetric input proximities; INPERM is a permutation that defines an order in which the constraints are considered over all object triples. In the example below, for instance, INPERM is simply set as the MATLAB built-in random permutation function randperm(n) (using the size $n = 10$ explicitly for the number illustration). Thus, the search can be rerun with the same specification but now using many different random starting sequences. Two such searches are shown below leading to VAFs of .4941 and .4781 (the latter is the same as obtained from fitting the best ultrametric in Section 5.1 using numcltarg for a fixed set of constraints; the former provides a slightly different and better-fitting ultrametric).

```
[find,vaf] = ultrafnd(number,randperm(10))

find =

  Columns 1 through 6

        0    0.7300    0.7300    0.7300    0.7300    0.7300
   0.7300         0    0.5835    0.5835    0.5835    0.5835
   0.7300    0.5835         0    0.5535    0.0590    0.5535
   0.7300    0.5835    0.5535         0    0.5535    0.4808
   0.7300    0.5835    0.0590    0.5535         0    0.5535
   0.7300    0.5835    0.5535    0.4808    0.5535         0
   0.7300    0.5835    0.5535    0.2980    0.5535    0.4808
   0.7300    0.5835    0.5535    0.4808    0.5535    0.4000
   0.7300    0.5835    0.3065    0.5535    0.3065    0.5535
   0.7300    0.5835    0.5535    0.2630    0.5535    0.4808

  Columns 7 through 10

   0.7300    0.7300    0.7300    0.7300
   0.5835    0.5835    0.5835    0.5835
   0.5535    0.5535    0.3065    0.5535
   0.2980    0.4808    0.5535    0.2630
   0.5535    0.5535    0.3065    0.5535
   0.4808    0.4000    0.5535    0.4808
        0    0.4808    0.5535    0.2980
   0.4808         0    0.5535    0.4808
   0.5535    0.5535         0    0.5535
   0.2980    0.4808    0.5535         0


vaf =

   0.4941

[find,vaf] = ultrafnd(number,randperm(10))

find =
```

```
Columns 1 through 6

         0      0.4210     0.6761     0.6761     0.6761     0.6761
    0.4210          0      0.6761     0.6761     0.6761     0.6761
    0.6761     0.6761          0      0.5535     0.0590     0.5535
    0.6761     0.6761     0.5535          0      0.5535     0.4808
    0.6761     0.6761     0.0590     0.5535          0      0.5535
    0.6761     0.6761     0.5535     0.4808     0.5535          0
    0.6761     0.6761     0.5535     0.2980     0.5535     0.4808
    0.6761     0.6761     0.5535     0.4808     0.5535     0.4000
    0.6761     0.6761     0.3065     0.5535     0.3065     0.5535
    0.6761     0.6761     0.5535     0.2630     0.5535     0.4808

Columns 7 through 10

    0.6761     0.6761     0.6761     0.6761
    0.6761     0.6761     0.6761     0.6761
    0.5535     0.5535     0.3065     0.5535
    0.2980     0.4808     0.5535     0.2630
    0.5535     0.5535     0.3065     0.5535
    0.4808     0.4000     0.5535     0.4808
         0      0.4808     0.5535     0.2980
    0.4808          0      0.5535     0.4808
    0.5535     0.5535          0      0.5535
    0.2980     0.4808     0.5535          0


vaf =

    0.4781
```

5.3   Graphically Representing an Ultrametric

Once an ultrametric matrix has been identified, there are two common ways in which the information within the matrix might be displayed. The first is to perform a simple reordering of the rows and columns of the given matrix to make apparent the sequence of partitions being induced by the ultrametric. The form desired is typically called anti-Robinson (see, for example, Hubert and Arabie, 1994 (or Part III of this text), for a very complete discussion of using and fitting such matrix orderings). When a matrix is in anti-Robinson form, the entries within each row (and column) are nondecreasing moving away from the main diagonal in either direction. As the example given below will show, any ultrametric matrix can be put into such a form easily (but nonuniquely). The second strategy for representing an ultrametric relies on the graphical form of an inverted tree (or as it is typically called in the classification literature, a dendrogram), where one can read the values of the ultrametric directly from the displayed structure. We give an example of such a tree below (and provide at the end of this Chapter the LATEX code (within the `picture` environment) to generate this particular graphical structure).

To give the illustration of reordering an ultrametric matrix to display its anti-Robinson form, the example found in Section 5.2 with a VAF of .4941 will be used, along with a short M-file, `ultraorder.m`. This function implements a simple mechanism of first generating a unidimensional equally spaced target matrix from the utility M-file `targlin.m` and then reorders heuristically the given ultrametric matrix against this given target with the quadratic assignment functions `pairwiseqa.m` and `insertqa.m` (the latter uses the maximum block size of $n - 1$ for `kblock`). The explicit usage is

```
[orderprox,orderperm] = ultraorder(prox)
```

where PROX is assumed to be an ultrametric matrix; ORDERPERM is a permutation used to display the anti-Robinson form in ORDERPROX, where

```
    orderprox = prox(orderperm,orderperm).
```

```
load number.dat
[find,vaf] = ultrafnd(number,randperm(10));

[orderprox,orderperm] = ultraorder(find)

orderprox =

  Columns 1 through 6

          0      0.7300      0.7300      0.7300      0.7300      0.7300
     0.7300           0      0.3065      0.3065      0.5535      0.5535
     0.7300      0.3065           0      0.0590      0.5535      0.5535
     0.7300      0.3065      0.0590           0      0.5535      0.5535
     0.7300      0.5535      0.5535      0.5535           0      0.2630
     0.7300      0.5535      0.5535      0.5535      0.2630           0
     0.7300      0.5535      0.5535      0.5535      0.2980      0.2980
     0.7300      0.5535      0.5535      0.5535      0.4808      0.4808
     0.7300      0.5535      0.5535      0.5535      0.4808      0.4808
     0.7300      0.5835      0.5835      0.5835      0.5835      0.5835

  Columns 7 through 10

     0.7300      0.7300      0.7300      0.7300
     0.5535      0.5535      0.5535      0.5835
     0.5535      0.5535      0.5535      0.5835
     0.5535      0.5535      0.5535      0.5835
     0.2980      0.4808      0.4808      0.5835
     0.2980      0.4808      0.4808      0.5835
          0      0.4808      0.4808      0.5835
     0.4808           0      0.4000      0.5835
```

```
      0.4808      0.4000            0      0.5835
      0.5835      0.5835      0.5835            0
```

`orderperm =`

```
      1      9      3      5      10      4      7      8      6      2
```

The reordered matrix using the row and column order of $0 \prec 8 \prec 2 \prec 4 \prec 9 \prec 3 \prec 6 \prec 7 \prec 5 \prec 1$ is given below; here the blocks of equal-valued entries are highlighted, indicating the partition hierarchy (also given below) induced by the ultrametric.

	0	8	2	4	9	3	6	7	5	1
0	x	.73	.73	.73	.73	.73	.73	.73	.73	.73
8	.73	x	.31	.31	.55	.55	.55	.55	.55	.58
2	.73	.31	x	.06	.55	.55	.55	.55	.55	.58
4	.73	.31	.06	x	.55	.55	.55	.55	.55	.58
9	.73	.55	.55	.55	x	.26	.30	.48	.48	.58
3	.73	.55	.55	.55	.26	x	.30	.48	.48	.58
6	.73	.55	.55	.55	.30	.30	x	.48	.48	.58
7	.73	.55	.55	.55	.48	.48	.48	x	.40	.58
5	.73	.55	.55	.55	.48	.48	.48	.40	x	.58
1	.73	.58	.58	.58	.58	.58	.58	.58	.58	x

Partition	Level Formed
{{0,8,2,4,9,3,6,7,5,1}}	.73
{{0},{8,2,4,9,3,6,7,5,1}}	.58
{{0},{8,2,4,9,3,6,7,5},{1}}	.55
{{0},{8,2,4},{9,3,6,7,5},{1}}	.48
{{0},{8,2,4},{9,3,6},{7,5},{1}}	.40
{{0},{8,2,4},{9,3,6},{7},{5},{1}}	.31
{{0},{8},{2,4},{9,3,6},{7},{5},{1}}	.30
{{0},{8},{2,4},{9,3},{6},{7},{5},{1}}	.26
{{0},{8},{2,4},{9},{3},{6},{7},{5},{1}}	.06
{{0},{8},{2},{4},{9},{3},{6},{7},{5},{1}}	—

For the partition hierarchy just given, the alternative structure of a dendrogram (or tree) for its representation is given in Figure 5.1. The terminal "nodes" of this structure, indicated by open circles, correspond to the ten digits; the filled circles are internal "nodes" reflecting the level at which certain new classes in a partition hierarchy are constructed. For instance, using the calibration given on the long vertical line at the left, a new class consisting of the digits {9,3,6,7,5} is formed at level .48 by uniting the two classes {9,3,6} and {7,5}. Thus, in the ultrametric matrix given earlier, the values between the entries in these two classes are all a constant .48.

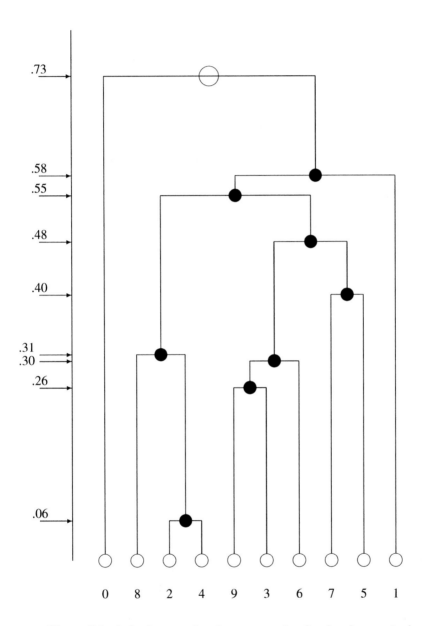

Figure 5.1. *A dendrogram (tree) representation for the ultrametric described in the text having VAF of .4941.*

The dendrogram just given can be modified (at least in how it should be interpreted) to motivate the representational form of an additive tree to be introduced in Chapter 6: (a) the values in the calibration along the long vertical axis need to be halved; (b) all horizontal lines are now to be understood as having no interpretable length and are present only for graphical convenience; (c) a spot on the dendrogram is indicated (here by a large open circle), called the "root." A crucial characterization feature of an ultrametric is that the root is equidistant from all terminal nodes. Given these interpretive changes, the ultrametric values for each object pair can now be reconstructed by the length of the path in the tree connecting the two relevant objects. Thus, an ultrametric is reconstructed from the lengths of paths between objects in a tree; the special form of a tree for an ultrametric is one in which there exists a root that is equidistant from all terminal nodes. In the generalization to an additive tree of Chapter 6, the condition of requiring the existence of an equidistant root is removed, thus allowing the branches attached to the terminal nodes to be stretched or shrunk at will.

5.3.1   LaTeX Code for the Dendrogram of Figure 5.1

```
\begin{figure}

\caption{A dendrogram (tree) representation for the
ultrametric described in the text having VAF of .4941}

\setlength{\unitlength}{.5pt}

\begin{picture}(500,1000)

\put(50,0){\makebox(0,0){0}}
\put(100,0){\makebox(0,0){8}}
\put(150,0){\makebox(0,0){2}}
\put(200,0){\makebox(0,0){4}}
\put(250,0){\makebox(0,0){9}}
\put(300,0){\makebox(0,0){3}}
\put(350,0){\makebox(0,0){6}}
\put(400,0){\makebox(0,0){7}}
\put(450,0){\makebox(0,0){5}}
\put(500,0){\makebox(0,0){1}}


\put(50,50){\circle{20}}
\put(100,50){\circle{20}}
\put(150,50){\circle{20}}
\put(200,50){\circle{20}}
\put(250,50){\circle{20}}
\put(300,50){\circle{20}}
\put(350,50){\circle{20}}
```

```
\put(400,50){\circle{20}}
\put(450,50){\circle{20}}
\put(500,50){\circle{20}}

\put(175,110){\circle*{20}}
\put(275,310){\circle*{20}}
\put(312.5,350){\circle*{20}}
\put(137.5,360){\circle*{20}}
\put(425,450){\circle*{20}}
\put(368.75,530){\circle*{20}}
\put(253.125,600){\circle*{20}}
\put(376.5625,630){\circle*{20}}
\put(213.28125,780){\circle{30}}

\put(0,50){\line(0,1){800}}
\put(50,60){\line(0,1){720}}
\put(100,60){\line(0,1){300}}
\put(150,60){\line(0,1){50}}
\put(200,60){\line(0,1){50}}
\put(250,60){\line(0,1){250}}
\put(300,60){\line(0,1){250}}
\put(350,60){\line(0,1){290}}
\put(400,60){\line(0,1){390}}
\put(450,60){\line(0,1){390}}
\put(500,60){\line(0,1){570}}
\put(175,110){\line(0,1){250}}
\put(275,310){\line(0,1){40}}
\put(312.5,350){\line(0,1){180}}
\put(425,450){\line(0,1){80}}
\put(368.75,530){\line(0,1){70}}
\put(137.5,360){\line(0,1){240}}
\put(253.125,600){\line(0,1){30}}
\put(376.5625,630){\line(0,1){150}}

\put(150,110){\line(1,0){50}}
\put(250,310){\line(1,0){50}}
\put(275,350){\line(1,0){75}}
\put(100,360){\line(1,0){75}}
\put(400,450){\line(1,0){50}}
\put(312.5,530){\line(1,0){112.5}}
\put(137.5,600){\line(1,0){231.25}}
\put(253.125,630){\line(1,0){246.875}}
\put(50,780){\line(1,0){326.5625}}

\put(-50,110){\vector(1,0){50}}
\put(-50,115){\makebox(0,0)[b]{.06}}
```

```
\put(-50,310){\vector(1,0){50}}
\put(-50,315){\makebox(0,0)[b]{.26}}
\put(-50,350){\vector(1,0){50}}
\put(-70,345){\makebox(0,0)[b]{.30}}
\put(-50,360){\vector(1,0){50}}
\put(-70,365){\makebox(0,0)[b]{.31}}
\put(-50,450){\vector(1,0){50}}
\put(-50,455){\makebox(0,0)[b]{.40}}
\put(-50,530){\vector(1,0){50}}
\put(-50,535){\makebox(0,0)[b]{.48}}
\put(-50,600){\vector(1,0){50}}
\put(-50,605){\makebox(0,0)[b]{.55}}
\put(-50,630){\vector(1,0){50}}
\put(-50,635){\makebox(0,0)[b]{.58}}
\put(-50,780){\vector(1,0){50}}
\put(-50,785){\makebox(0,0)[b]{.73}}
\put(-50,110){\vector(1,0){50}}
\put(-50,115){\makebox(0,0)[b]{.06}}

\end{picture}
\end{figure}
```

5.3.2   Plotting the Dendrogram with ultraplot.m

The M-file `ultraplot.m` uses two of the routines (`dendrogram.m` and `linkage.m`) from the Statistics Toolbox for MATLAB to plot the dendrogram associated with an ultrametric matrix. Because the input matrix is assumed perfectly ultrametric in form, without loss of generality, `linkage.m` is invoked within `ultraplot.m` with the complete(-link) option; the resulting output matrix is then used immediately to obtain the final plot by a call to `dendrogram.m`.

So, if the user has the Statistics Toolbox available, a graphical representation of the ultrametric can be generated directly with the syntax

```
ultraplot(ultra)
```

where ULTRA is the ultrametric matrix. A figure window opens in MATLAB displaying the appropriate tree, which can then be saved in one of the common graphics file formats and included in a printed document (we have typically used the encapsulated postscript form (*.eps)). Figure 5.2 shows the tree obtained from `number.dat` and `ultrafnd.m`.

```
load number.dat
[find,vaf] = ultrafnd(number,randperm(10));
```

```
vaf =
```

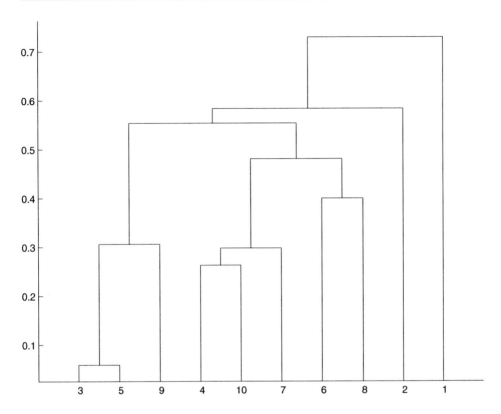

Figure 5.2. *Dendrogram plot for the number data obtained using ultraplot.m.*

```
0.4941

ultraplot(find)

additive_constant =

    0
```

If there are any negative values in the input matrix `ultra` (as obtained, for example, when fitting multiple ultrametrics to a single proximity matrix), an additive constant equal to the negative of the minimum value in `ultra` is added to the off-diagonal entries in `ultra` before the plot is carried out.

Chapter 6

Additive Trees for Symmetric Proximity Data

A currently popular alternative to the use of a simple ultrametric in classification, and one which might be considered a natural extension of the notion of an ultrametric, is that of an additive tree; comprehensive discussions can be found in Mirkin (1996, Chapter 7) or throughout Barthélemy and Guénoche (1991). Generalizing the earlier characterization of an ultrametric, an $n \times n$ matrix $\mathbf{A} = \{a_{ij}\}$ can be called an additive tree (metric or matrix) if the three-object (or three-point) ultrametric condition is replaced by a four-object (or four-point) condition: $a_{ij} + a_{kl} \leq \max\{a_{ik} + a_{jl}, a_{il} + a_{jk}\}$ for $1 \leq i, j, k, l \leq n$; equivalently, for any object quadruple O_i, O_j, O_k, and O_l, the largest two values among the sums $a_{ij} + a_{kl}$, $a_{ik} + a_{jl}$, and $a_{il} + a_{jk}$ must be equal.

   Any additive tree matrix $\mathbf{A}$ can be represented (in many ways) as a sum of two matrices, say $\mathbf{U} = \{u_{ij}\}$ and $\mathbf{C} = \{c_{ij}\}$, where $\mathbf{U}$ is an ultrametric matrix, and $c_{ij} = g_i + g_j$ for $1 \leq i \neq j \leq n$ and $c_{ii} = 0$ for $1 \leq i \leq n$, based on some set of values $g_1, \ldots, g_n$ (Carroll, Clark, and DeSarbo, 1984, pp. 71–72). The multiplicity of such possible decompositions results from the choice of where essentially to place the root in the type of graphical tree representation we will use. Generally, for us, the root will be placed halfway along the longest path in the tree, generating a decomposition of the matrix $\mathbf{A}$ using a procedure from Barthélemy and Guénoche (1991, Section 3.3.3):

   (a) Given $\mathbf{A}$, let O_{i*}, $O_{j*} \in S$ denote the two objects between which the longest path is defined in the tree; i.e., the pair of objects O_{i*} and O_{j*} is associated with the largest entry in $\mathbf{A}$, say a_{i*j*}.

   (b) Define $\mathbf{U}$ by letting

$$u_{ij} = a_{ij} - (g_i + g_j), \text{ where } g_i = \max\{a_{ii*}, a_{jj*}\} - M,$$

with M chosen so that $u_{ij} > 0$ for $i \neq j$. The matrix $\mathbf{C} = \{c_{ij}\}$ is then constructed by letting $c_{ii} = 0$ for $1 \leq i \leq n$, and $c_{ij} = g_i + g_j$ for $1 \leq i \neq j \leq n$. (If M is set equal to the largest entry a_{i*j*}, the values in $\mathbf{U}$ would have to be positive, and two values among $g_1, \ldots, g_n$ would be zero with the remainder less than or equal to zero. Thus, a value for M less than a_{i*j*} is usually found by trial and error that will give positive entries within $\mathbf{U}$ and as many positive values as possible for $g_1, \ldots, g_n$.)

To construct the type of graphical additive tree representation we will give below, the process followed is first to graph the dendrogram induced by **U**, where (as for any ultrametric) the chosen root is equidistant from all terminal nodes. The branches connecting the terminal nodes are then lengthened or shortened depending on the signs and absolute magnitudes of $g_1, \ldots, g_n$. If one were willing to consider the (arbitrary) inclusion of a sufficiently large additive constant to the entries of **A**, the values of $g_1, \ldots, g_n$ could be assumed nonnegative. In this case, the matrix **C** would represent what is now commonly called a centroid metric (see, for example, the usage in Barthélemy and Guénoche, 1991, Chapter 3); although having some advantages (particularly for some of the graphical representations we give in avoiding the issue of presenting negative branch lengths), such a restriction is not absolutely necessary for what we do in the remaining sections and chapters of Part II. In fact, even though some of the entries among $g_1, \ldots, g_n$ may be negative, for convenience we will still routinely refer to a centroid metric (component) even though some of the defined "distances" may actually be negative.

6.1　Fitting a Given Additive Tree in the L_2-Norm

The function `atreefit.m` with usage

```
[fit,vaf] = atreefit(prox,targ)
```

parallels that of `ultrafit.m` of Section 5.1 and generates (again using iterative projection based on the linear (in)equality constraints obtained from a fixed additive tree—see Section 1.4) the best-fitting additive tree in the L_2-norm (`FIT`) within the same equivalence class as that of a given additive tree matrix `TARG`. Thus, both `FIT` and `TARG` satisfy the exact same set of four-point conditions. The matrix `PROX` contains the symmetric input proximities and `VAF` is the variance-accounted-for.

In the example below, the target matrix is again `numcltarg` obtained from the complete-link hierarchical clustering of `number.dat`; the `VAF` generated by these (now considered as additive tree) constraints is .6249 (and, as to be expected, is a value larger than for the corresponding best-fitting ultrametric value of .4781).

```
[fit,vaf] = atreefit(number,numcltarg)

fit =

  Columns 1 through 6

        0     0.4210     0.7185     0.7371     0.7092     0.8188
   0.4210          0     0.5334     0.5520     0.5241     0.6337
   0.7185     0.5334          0     0.4882     0.0590     0.5700
   0.7371     0.5520     0.4882          0     0.4790     0.4337
   0.7092     0.5241     0.0590     0.4790          0     0.5607
   0.8188     0.6337     0.5700     0.4337     0.5607          0
   0.7116     0.5265     0.4627     0.2506     0.4535     0.4082
   0.8670     0.6818     0.6181     0.4818     0.6089     0.4000
```

```
    0.7549      0.5698      0.3111      0.5247      0.3019      0.6064
    0.8318      0.6467      0.5830      0.2630      0.5737      0.5284

Columns 7 through 10

    0.7116      0.8670      0.7549      0.8318
    0.5265      0.6818      0.5698      0.6467
    0.4627      0.6181      0.3111      0.5830
    0.2506      0.4818      0.5247      0.2630
    0.4535      0.6089      0.3019      0.5737
    0.4082      0.4000      0.6064      0.5284
         0      0.4563      0.4992      0.3454
    0.4563           0      0.6546      0.5766
    0.4992      0.6546           0      0.6194
    0.3454      0.5766      0.6194           0

vaf =

    0.6249
```

6.2   Finding an Additive Tree in the L_2-Norm

Analogous to the M-file `ultrafnd.m` from Section 5.2 for identifying best-fitting ultrametrics, `atreefnd.m` implements the heuristic search strategy of Hubert and Arabie (1995b) using iterative projection but now for constructing the best-fitting additive trees in the L_2-norm. The usage has the form

```
[find,vaf] = atreefnd(prox,inperm)
```

where FIND is the identified additive tree having variance-accounted-for, VAF. Again, the matrix PROX contains the symmetric input proximities, and INPERM is a permutation that defines an order in which the constraints are considered over all object quadruples. In the example below, two such searches are shown starting with random permutations (through the use of `randperm(10)`) that give VAFs of .6359 and .6249.

```
[find,vaf] = atreefnd(number,randperm(10))

find =

  Columns 1 through 6

         0      0.4210      0.6467      0.6448      0.6374      0.8049
    0.4210           0      0.4616      0.4596      0.4523      0.6198
    0.6467      0.4616           0      0.3634      0.0590      0.5235
    0.6448      0.4596      0.3634           0      0.3542      0.4385
    0.6374      0.4523      0.0590      0.3542           0      0.5143
```

```
     0.8049        0.6198        0.5235        0.4385        0.5143             0
     0.7523        0.5671        0.4709        0.3858        0.4617        0.4132
     0.9263        0.7412        0.6449        0.5599        0.6357        0.5872
     0.8634        0.6783        0.5820        0.4970        0.5728        0.5244
     0.8733        0.6881        0.5919        0.5068        0.5827        0.5342

  Columns 7 through 10

     0.7523        0.9263        0.8634        0.8733
     0.5671        0.7412        0.6783        0.6881
     0.4709        0.6449        0.5820        0.5919
     0.3858        0.5599        0.4970        0.5068
     0.4617        0.6357        0.5728        0.5827
     0.4132        0.5872        0.5244        0.5342
          0        0.3930        0.3301        0.3400
     0.3930             0        0.4000        0.4569
     0.3301        0.4000             0        0.3941
     0.3400        0.4569        0.3941             0

vaf =

     0.6359

[find,vaf] = atreefnd(number,randperm(10))

find =

  Columns 1 through 6

          0        0.4210        0.7185        0.7371        0.7092        0.8188
     0.4210             0        0.5334        0.5520        0.5241        0.6337
     0.7185        0.5334             0        0.4882        0.0590        0.5700
     0.7371        0.5520        0.4882             0        0.4790        0.4337
     0.7092        0.5241        0.0590        0.4790             0        0.5607
     0.8188        0.6337        0.5700        0.4337        0.5607             0
     0.7116        0.5265        0.4627        0.2506        0.4535        0.4082
     0.8670        0.6818        0.6181        0.4818        0.6089        0.4000
     0.7549        0.5698        0.3111        0.5247        0.3019        0.6064
     0.8318        0.6467        0.5830        0.2630        0.5737        0.5284

  Columns 7 through 10

     0.7116        0.8670        0.7549        0.8318
     0.5265        0.6818        0.5698        0.6467
     0.4627        0.6181        0.3111        0.5830
     0.2506        0.4818        0.5247        0.2630
```

```
      0.4535      0.6089      0.3019      0.5737
      0.4082      0.4000      0.6064      0.5284
           0      0.4563      0.4992      0.3454
      0.4563           0      0.6546      0.5766
      0.4992      0.6546           0      0.6194
      0.3454      0.5766      0.6194           0
```

vaf =

    0.6249

6.3   Decomposing an Additive Tree

The M-file atreedec.m decomposes a given additive tree matrix into an ultrametric and a centroid metric matrix (where the root is halfway along the longest path). The form of the usage is

```
[ulmetric,ctmetric] = atreedec(prox,constant)
```

where PROX is the input (additive tree) proximity matrix (with a zero main diagonal and a dissimilarity interpretation); CONSTANT is a nonnegative number (less than or equal to the maximum proximity value) that controls the positivity of the constructed ultrametric values; ULMETRIC is the ultrametric component of the decomposition; CTMETRIC is the centroid metric component (given by values $g_1, \ldots, g_n$ assigned to each of the objects, some of which may actually be negative depending on the input proximity matrix used). In the example below, the additive tree matrix identified earlier with a VAF of .6359 is decomposed using a value of .70 for the constant to control the positivity of the ultrametric values.

```
[find,vaf] = atreefnd(number,randperm(10));
[ulmetric,ctmetric] = atreedec(find,.70);
ulmetric
```

ulmetric =

  Columns 1 through 6

```
           0      0.1536      0.4737      0.4737      0.4737      0.4737
      0.1536           0      0.4737      0.4737      0.4737      0.4737
      0.4737      0.4737           0      0.4720      0.1749      0.4720
      0.4737      0.4737      0.4720           0      0.4720      0.3888
      0.4737      0.4737      0.1749      0.4720           0      0.4720
      0.4737      0.4737      0.4720      0.3888      0.4720           0
      0.4737      0.4737      0.4720      0.3888      0.4720      0.2560
      0.4737      0.4737      0.4720      0.3888      0.4720      0.2560
```

```
   0.4737      0.4737      0.4720      0.3888      0.4720      0.2560
   0.4737      0.4737      0.4720      0.3888      0.4720      0.2560

Columns 7 through 10

   0.4737      0.4737      0.4737      0.4737
   0.4737      0.4737      0.4737      0.4737
   0.4720      0.4720      0.4720      0.4720
   0.3888      0.3888      0.3888      0.3888
   0.4720      0.4720      0.4720      0.4720
   0.2560      0.2560      0.2560      0.2560
        0      0.1144      0.1144      0.1144
   0.1144           0      0.0103      0.0574
   0.1144      0.0103           0      0.0574
   0.1144      0.0574      0.0574           0

ctmetric'

ans =

Columns 1 through 6

   0.2263      0.0412     -0.0533     -0.0552     -0.0626      0.1049

Columns 7 through 10

   0.0523      0.2263      0.1634      0.1733

[orderprox,orderperm] = ultraorder(ulmetric)


orderprox =

Columns 1 through 6

        0      0.1536      0.4737      0.4737      0.4737      0.4737
   0.1536           0      0.4737      0.4737      0.4737      0.4737
   0.4737      0.4737           0      0.1749      0.4720      0.4720
   0.4737      0.4737      0.1749           0      0.4720      0.4720
   0.4737      0.4737      0.4720      0.4720           0      0.2560
   0.4737      0.4737      0.4720      0.4720      0.2560           0
   0.4737      0.4737      0.4720      0.4720      0.2560      0.1144
   0.4737      0.4737      0.4720      0.4720      0.2560      0.1144
   0.4737      0.4737      0.4720      0.4720      0.2560      0.1144
   0.4737      0.4737      0.4720      0.4720      0.3888      0.3888
```

```
Columns 7 through 10

     0.4737       0.4737       0.4737       0.4737
     0.4737       0.4737       0.4737       0.4737
     0.4720       0.4720       0.4720       0.4720
     0.4720       0.4720       0.4720       0.4720
     0.2560       0.2560       0.2560       0.3888
     0.1144       0.1144       0.1144       0.3888
          0       0.0574       0.0574       0.3888
     0.0574            0       0.0103       0.3888
     0.0574       0.0103            0       0.3888
     0.3888       0.3888       0.3888            0


orderperm =

     2     1     3     5     6     7    10     9     8     4
```

6.4 Graphically Representing an Additive Tree

The information present in an additive tree can be provided in several ways. First, given the decomposition into an ultrametric and a centroid metric, the partition hierarchy induced by the ultrametric could be given explicitly, along with the levels at which the various new subsets in the partitions are formed. The fitted additive tree values could then be identified as a sum of (a) the level at which an object pair, say O_i and O_j, first appear together within a common subset of the hierarchy and (b) the sum of g_i and g_j for the pair from the centroid metric component. As an illustration using the example just given in Section 6.3, the partition hierarchy has the following form:

Partition	Level Formed
{{1,0,2,4,5,6,9,8,7,3}}	.47
{{1,0},{2,4},{5,6,9,8,7,3}}	.39
{{1,0},{2,4},{5,6,9,8,7},{3}}	.26
{{1,0},{2,4},{5},{6,9,8,7},{3}}	.17
{{1,0},{2},{4},{5},{6,9,8,7},{3}}	.15
{{1},{0},{2},{4},{5},{6,9,8,7},{3}}	.11
{{1},{0},{2},{4},{5},{6},{9,8,7},{3}}	.06
{{1},{0},{2},{4},{5},{6},{9},{8,7},{3}}	.01
{{1},{0},{2},{4},{5},{6},{9},{8},{7},{3}}	.00

with centroid metric values of

digit	g_i
0	.23
1	.04
2	−.05
3	−.06
4	−.06
5	.10
6	.05
7	.23
8	.16
9	.17

Thus, the additive tree value for the digit pair (3,6) of .39 [.3858] is formed from the level .39 [.3888] at which 3 and 6 first appear together in the hierarchy plus the sum of the g_i's for the two digits of −.06 [−.0552] and .05 [.0523]. A dendrogram representation for the partition hierarchy is given in Figure 6.1.

A graphical representation for the additive tree is given in Figure 6.2, which was obtained from the dendrogram of Figure 6.1 by stretching and shrinking the branches attached to the terminal nodes by the g_i values (and cutting the vertical scale given in the dendrogram by half). Thus, the length of a path in the tree from one terminal node to another (ignoring all horizontal lines as having uninterpretable lengths) would generate the values given in the additive tree matrix.

6.5   An Alternative for Finding an Additive Tree in the L_2-Norm (Based on Combining a Centroid Metric and an Ultrametric)

If the four-point condition characterizing an additive tree is strengthened so that all the sums in the defining conditions for all object quadruples are equal (and not only for the largest two such sums), the additive tree matrix so obtained has entries representable as $g_i + g_j$ for a collection of values $g_1, \ldots, g_n$. This specially constrained additive tree is usually referred to as a centroid metric and, as noted by Carroll and Pruzansky (1980) and De Soete et al. (1984), can be fitted to a proximity matrix in the L_2-norm through closed-form expressions. Specifically, if **P** denotes the proximity matrix, then g_i can be given as the ith row sum of **P** excluding the diagonal entry, divided by $n − 2$, minus the total off-diagonal sum divided by $2(n − 1)(n − 2)$.

The M-file `centfit.m` for obtaining the best-fitting centroid metric in the L_2-norm, has usage

```
[fit,vaf,lengths] = centfit(prox)
```

where PROX is the usual input proximity matrix (with a zero main diagonal and a dissimilarity interpretation); the n values that define the approximating sums, $g_i + g_j$, present in

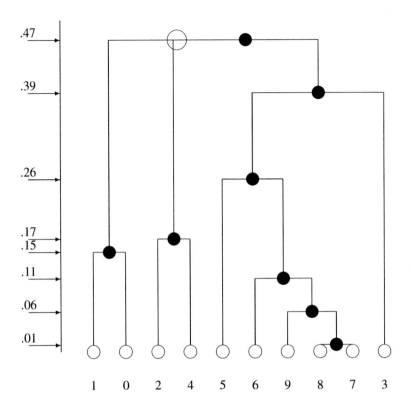

Figure 6.1. *A dendrogram (tree) representation for the ultrametric component of the additive tree described in the text having VAF of .6359.*

the fitted matrix FIT, are given in the vector LENGTHS of size $n \times 1$. The example below uses centfit.m with the number.dat data set, leading to an additive tree with VAF of .3248; this tree could be represented graphically as a "star" tree with one internal node and spokes having the lengths given in the output vector LENGTHS.

```
load number.dat
[fit,vaf,lengths] = centfit(number)

fit =

  Columns 1 through 6

         0    0.7808    0.6877    0.6709    0.6784    0.7647
    0.7808         0    0.5026    0.4858    0.4933    0.5796
    0.6877    0.5026         0    0.3927    0.4002    0.4864
    0.6709    0.4858    0.3927         0    0.3834    0.4697
    0.6784    0.4933    0.4002    0.3834         0    0.4772
```

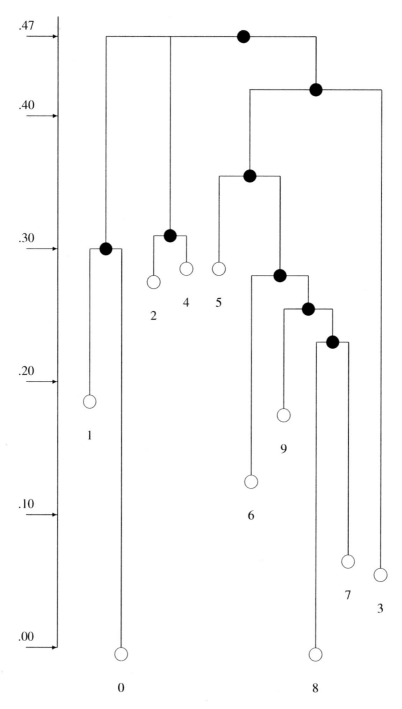

Figure 6.2. *A graph-theoretic representation for the additive tree described in the text having VAF of .6359.*

```
    0.7647      0.5796      0.4864      0.4697      0.4772           0
    0.6589      0.4738      0.3807      0.3639      0.3714      0.4577
    0.8128      0.6277      0.5346      0.5178      0.5253      0.6116
    0.7499      0.5648      0.4717      0.4549      0.4624      0.5487
    0.7657      0.5806      0.4874      0.4707      0.4782      0.5644

Columns 7 through 10

    0.6589      0.8128      0.7499      0.7657
    0.4738      0.6277      0.5648      0.5806
    0.3807      0.5346      0.4717      0.4874
    0.3639      0.5178      0.4549      0.4707
    0.3714      0.5253      0.4624      0.4782
    0.4577      0.6116      0.5487      0.5644
         0      0.5058      0.4429      0.4587
    0.5058           0      0.5968      0.6126
    0.4429      0.5968           0      0.5497
    0.4587      0.6126      0.5497           0

vaf =

    0.3248

lengths =

  Columns 1 through 6

    0.4830      0.2978      0.2047      0.1880      0.1955      0.2817

  Columns 7 through 10

    0.1760      0.3298      0.2670      0.2827
```

An alternative strategy for identifying good-fitting additive trees (and one that will be used in a slightly different form on two-mode proximity data in Section 8.2) relies on the possible decomposition of an additive tree into an ultrametric and centroid metric. The M-file atreectul.m first fits a centroid metric in closed form; an ultrametric is then identified on the residual matrix. The sum of these two matrices is an additive tree. The usage would follow that of atreefnd.m:

[find,vaf] = atreectul(prox,inperm)

where FIND is the identified additive tree with variance-accounted-for, VAF. Again, the matrix PROX contains the symmetric input proximities, and INPERM is a permutation that defines an order in which the constraints are considered over all object triples in the identification of the ultrametric component. In the example below, one search is shown starting with a random permutation (through the use of `randperm(10)`) that gives the same additive tree identified earlier with a VAF of .6249.

```
[find,vaf] = atreectul(number,randperm(10));
vaf
```

```
vaf =

   0.6249
```

Chapter 7

Fitting Multiple Tree Structures to a Symmetric Proximity Matrix

The use of multiple structures, whether they be ultrametrics or additive trees, to represent additively a given proximity matrix proceeds directly through successive residualization and iteration. We restrict ourselves to the fitting of two such structures, but the same process would apply for any such number. Initially, a first matrix is fitted to a given proximity matrix and a first residual matrix obtained; a second structure is then fitted to these first residuals, producing a second residual matrix. Iterating, the second fitted matrix is now subtracted from the original proximity matrix and a first (re)fitted matrix obtained; this first (re)fitted matrix in turn is subtracted from the original proximity matrix and a new second matrix (re)fitted. This process continues until the VAF by the sum of both fitted matrices no longer changes by a set amount (the value of 1.0e-006 is used in the M-files of the next two sections).

7.1 Multiple Ultrametrics

The M-file `biultrafnd.m` fits (additively) two ultrametric matrices in the L_2-norm. The explicit usage is

```
[find,vaf,targone,targtwo] = biultrafnd(prox,inperm)
```

where PROX is the given input proximity matrix (with a zero main diagonal and a dissimilarity interpretation); INPERM is a permutation that determines the order in which the inequality constraints are considered (and thus can be made random to search for different locally optimal representations); FIND is the obtained least-squares matrix (with variance-accounted-for of VAF) to PROX and is the sum of the two ultrametric matrices TARGONE and TARGTWO.

In the example to follow, a VAF of .8001 was achieved for the two identified ultrametrics (and where one needs to add an (arbitrary) constant (e.g., a value of .40 would suffice in this case, but other examples might require different additive constants) to the entries in TARGTWO to satisfy the technical requirement here that ultrametric values should be nonnegative). It might be noted substantively that the first ultrametric matrix (in TARGONE) reflects the structural properties of the digits; the second ultrametric matrix (in TARGTWO) is completely consistent with digit magnitude. This result is a very nice mixture of ultrametric structures with a convenient substantive interpretation for both components.

```
[find,vaf,targone,targtwo] = ...
    biultrafnd(number,randperm(10));

vaf

vaf =

   0.8001

[orderproxone,orderpermone] = ultraorder(targone)

orderproxone =

  Columns 1 through 6

           0     0.7796     0.7796     0.7796     0.7796     0.7796
      0.7796          0     0.2168     0.2168     0.5512     0.5512
      0.7796     0.2168          0     0.0701     0.5512     0.5512
      0.7796     0.2168     0.0701          0     0.5512     0.5512
      0.7796     0.5512     0.5512     0.5512          0     0.1733
      0.7796     0.5512     0.5512     0.5512     0.1733          0
      0.7796     0.5512     0.5512     0.5512     0.2772     0.2772
      0.7796     0.5512     0.5512     0.5512     0.4622     0.4622
      0.7796     0.5512     0.5512     0.5512     0.4622     0.4622
      0.7796     0.5945     0.5945     0.5945     0.5945     0.5945

  Columns 7 through 10

      0.7796     0.7796     0.7796     0.7796
      0.5512     0.5512     0.5512     0.5945
      0.5512     0.5512     0.5512     0.5945
      0.5512     0.5512     0.5512     0.5945
      0.2772     0.4622     0.4622     0.5945
      0.2772     0.4622     0.4622     0.5945
           0     0.4622     0.4622     0.5945
      0.4622          0     0.3103     0.5945
      0.4622     0.3103          0     0.5945
      0.5945     0.5945     0.5945          0


orderpermone =

      1     9     3     5     10     4     7     8     6     2
```

```
[orderproxtwo,orderpermtwo] = ultraorder(targtwo)

orderproxtwo =

  Columns 1 through 6

        0   -0.3586   -0.2531   -0.1721   -0.0111   -0.0111
  -0.3586        0   -0.2531   -0.1721   -0.0111   -0.0111
  -0.2531   -0.2531        0   -0.1721   -0.0111   -0.0111
  -0.1721   -0.1721   -0.1721        0   -0.0111   -0.0111
  -0.0111   -0.0111   -0.0111   -0.0111        0   -0.1422
  -0.0111   -0.0111   -0.0111   -0.0111   -0.1422        0
   0.0897    0.0897    0.0897    0.0897    0.0897    0.0897
   0.0897    0.0897    0.0897    0.0897    0.0897    0.0897
   0.0897    0.0897    0.0897    0.0897    0.0897    0.0897
   0.0897    0.0897    0.0897    0.0897    0.0897    0.0897

  Columns 7 through 10

   0.0897    0.0897    0.0897    0.0897
   0.0897    0.0897    0.0897    0.0897
   0.0897    0.0897    0.0897    0.0897
   0.0897    0.0897    0.0897    0.0897
   0.0897    0.0897    0.0897    0.0897
   0.0897    0.0897    0.0897    0.0897
        0   -0.0982   -0.0982   -0.0479
  -0.0982        0   -0.2012   -0.0479
  -0.0982   -0.2012        0   -0.0479
  -0.0479   -0.0479   -0.0479        0


orderpermtwo =

     1     2     3     4     5     6     8     7     9    10
```

7.2 Multiple Additive Trees

The M-file biatreefnd.m fits (additively) two additive tree matrices in the L_2-norm. The explicit usage is

```
[find,vaf,targone,targtwo] = biatreefnd(prox,inperm)
```

where PROX is the given input proximity matrix (with a zero main diagonal and a dissimilarity interpretation); INPERM is a permutation that determines the order in which the inequality constraints are considered (and thus can be made random to search for different locally optimal representations); FIND is the found least-squares matrix (with variance-accounted-for of VAF) to PROX and is the sum of the two additive tree matrices TARGONE and TARGTWO.

In the example to follow, a VAF of .9003 was achieved for the two identified additive trees. Here one needs, as in the multiple ultrametric case, to add an (arbitrary) constant to the entries in TARGTWO to satisfy the technical requirement here that additive tree values should be nonnegative; also, sufficiently large additive constants would need to be imposed on the two ultrametric components to ensure nonnegativity of the resulting values. These additive constants do not affect the achieved VAF or the resulting representations in any material way.) Similarly, as in the interpretation of the example in the last section, it might be noted substantively that the second additive tree matrix (in TARGTWO) reflects the structural properties of the digits; the first matrix (in TARGONE) is completely consistent with digit magnitude. Thus, again we have a very nice mixture of structures with convenient substantive interpretations for both components.

```
[find,vaf,targone,targtwo] = ...
    biatreefnd(number,randperm(10));

vaf

vaf =

    0.9003

[ulmetricone,ctmetricone] = atreedec(targone,0.0);
[ulmetrictwo,ctmetrictwo] = atreedec(targtwo,0.0);
ctmetricone'

ans =

  Columns 1 through 6

    0.9652    0.7801    0.6716    0.6164    0.7114    0.7976

  Columns 7 through 10

    0.7699    0.9652    0.9023    0.9051

ctmetrictwo'

ans =

  Columns 1 through 6

    0.0373    0.0994    0.1256    0.1256    0.1256    0.1129
```

```
Columns 7 through 10

    0.0267     0.1129     0.1105     0.1256

[orderproxone,orderpermone] = ultraorder(ulmetricone)

orderproxone =

  Columns 1 through 6

         0    -1.1786    -1.1786    -0.9652    -0.9652    -0.9652
   -1.1786          0    -1.3014    -0.9652    -0.9652    -0.9652
   -1.1786    -1.3014          0    -0.9652    -0.9652    -0.9652
   -0.9652    -0.9652    -0.9652          0    -1.2128    -1.1030
   -0.9652    -0.9652    -0.9652    -1.2128          0    -1.1030
   -0.9652    -0.9652    -0.9652    -1.1030    -1.1030          0
   -0.9652    -0.9652    -0.9652    -1.1030    -1.1030    -1.4617
   -0.9652    -0.9652    -0.9652    -1.1030    -1.1030    -1.4617
   -0.9652    -0.9652    -0.9652    -1.1030    -1.1030    -1.3477
   -0.9652    -0.9652    -0.9652    -0.9850    -0.9850    -0.9850

  Columns 7 through 10

   -0.9652    -0.9652    -0.9652    -0.9652
   -0.9652    -0.9652    -0.9652    -0.9652
   -0.9652    -0.9652    -0.9652    -0.9652
   -1.1030    -1.1030    -1.1030    -0.9850
   -1.1030    -1.1030    -1.1030    -0.9850
   -1.4617    -1.4617    -1.3477    -0.9850
         0    -1.5653    -1.3477    -0.9850
   -1.5653          0    -1.3477    -0.9850
   -1.3477    -1.3477          0    -0.9850
   -0.9850    -0.9850    -0.9850          0


orderpermone =

     3     2     1     5     6    10     9     8     7     4

[orderproxtwo,orderpermtwo] = ultraorder(ulmetrictwo)

orderproxtwo =

  Columns 1 through 6

         0    -0.1539    -0.1539    -0.1539    -0.1256    -0.1256
```

```
  -0.1539           0   -0.4893   -0.4893   -0.1256   -0.1256
  -0.1539     -0.4893         0   -0.6099   -0.1256   -0.1256
  -0.1539     -0.4893   -0.6099         0   -0.1256   -0.1256
  -0.1256     -0.1256   -0.1256   -0.1256         0   -0.4855
  -0.1256     -0.1256   -0.1256   -0.1256   -0.4855         0
  -0.1256     -0.1256   -0.1256   -0.1256   -0.2524   -0.2524
  -0.1256     -0.1256   -0.1256   -0.1256   -0.2524   -0.2524
  -0.1256     -0.1256   -0.1256   -0.1256   -0.2524   -0.2524
  -0.1256     -0.1256   -0.1256   -0.1256   -0.1596   -0.1596
```

Columns 7 through 10

```
  -0.1256     -0.1256   -0.1256   -0.1256
  -0.1256     -0.1256   -0.1256   -0.1256
  -0.1256     -0.1256   -0.1256   -0.1256
  -0.1256     -0.1256   -0.1256   -0.1256
  -0.2524     -0.2524   -0.2524   -0.1596
  -0.2524     -0.2524   -0.2524   -0.1596
        0     -0.5246   -0.3151   -0.1596
  -0.5246           0   -0.3151   -0.1596
  -0.3151     -0.3151         0   -0.1596
  -0.1596     -0.1596   -0.1596         0
```

orderpermtwo =

```
     7        9        5        3        8        6       10        4        2        1
```

Chapter 8

Ultrametrics and Additive Trees for Two-Mode (Rectangular) Proximity Data

Thus far in Part II, the proximity data considered for obtaining some type of structure, such as an ultrametric or an additive tree, have been assumed to be on one intact set of objects, $S = \{O_1, \ldots, O_n\}$, and complete in the sense that proximity values are present between all object pairs. Just as linear unidimensional scaling (LUS) was generalized for two-mode proximity data in Chapter 4, suppose now that the available proximity data are two-mode and *between* two distinct object sets, $S_A = \{O_{1A}, \ldots, O_{n_aA}\}$ and $S_B = \{O_{1B}, \ldots, O_{n_bB}\}$, containing n_a and n_b objects, respectively, given by an $n_a \times n_b$ proximity matrix $\mathbf{Q} = \{q_{rs}\}$. Again, we assume that the entries in $\mathbf{Q}$ are keyed as dissimilarities, and a joint structural representation is desired for the set $S_A \cup S_B$.

Conditions have been proposed in the literature for when the entries in a matrix fitted to $\mathbf{Q}$ characterize an ultrametric or an additive tree representation. In particular, suppose an $n_a \times n_b$ matrix $\mathbf{F} = \{f_{rs}\}$ is fitted to $\mathbf{Q}$ through least-squares subject to the constraints that follow:

Ultrametric (Furnas, 1980):

for all distinct object quadruples, $O_{rA}, O_{sA}, O_{rB}, O_{sB}$, where $O_{rA}, O_{sA} \in S_A$ and $O_{rB}, O_{sB} \in S_B$, and considering the entries in $\mathbf{F}$ corresponding to the pairs (O_{rA}, O_{rB}), (O_{rA}, O_{sB}), $(O_{sA}\ O_{rB})$, and (O_{sA}, O_{sB}), say $f_{r_Ar_B}, f_{r_As_B}, f_{s_Ar_B}, f_{s_As_B}$, respectively, the largest two must be equal.

Additive trees (Brossier, 1987):

for all distinct object sextuples, $O_{rA}, O_{sA}, O_{tA}, O_{rB}, O_{sB}, O_{tB}$, where $O_{rA}, O_{sA}, O_{tA} \in S_A$ and $O_{rB}, O_{sB}, O_{tB} \in S_B$, and considering the entries in $\mathbf{F}$ corresponding to the pairs (O_{rA}, O_{rB}), (O_{rA}, O_{sB}), (O_{rA}, O_{tB}), (O_{sA}, O_{rB}), (O_{sA}, O_{sB}), (O_{sA}, O_{tB}), (O_{tA}, O_{rB}), (O_{tA}, O_{sB}), and (O_{tA}, O_{tB}), say $f_{r_Ar_B}, f_{r_As_B}, f_{r_At_B}, f_{s_Ar_B}, f_{s_As_B}, f_{s_At_B}, f_{t_Ar_B}, f_{t_As_B}, f_{t_At_B}$, respectively, the largest two of the following sums must be equal:

$$f_{r_Ar_B} + f_{s_As_B} + f_{t_At_B};$$
$$f_{r_Ar_B} + f_{s_At_B} + f_{t_As_B};$$
$$f_{r_As_B} + f_{s_Ar_B} + f_{t_At_B};$$
$$f_{r_As_B} + f_{s_At_B} + f_{t_Ar_B};$$

$$f_{r_A t_B} + f_{s_A r_B} + f_{t_A s_B};$$
$$f_{r_A t_B} + f_{s_A s_B} + f_{t_A r_B}.$$

In both cases of ultrametric and additive trees for two-mode proximity data, the necessary constraints characterizing a solution are linear and define closed convex sets in which a solution must lie. Thus, the application of iterative projection as a heuristic search strategy for the best-fitting solutions is fairly direct, and an example of an ultrametric found and fitted to a two-mode matrix will be given in Section 8.1. We will not, however, give a comparable example of fitting the additive tree constraints to such a proximity matrix; the (scratch) storage requirements necessitated by iterative projection in directly using the additive tree constraints given above and keeping track of the various augmentations made can become rather onerous for moderate-sized data matrices in the course of the heuristic search. For general use, an alternative approach to the fitting of additive trees is preferable, one that again uses iterative projection but with the ultrametric conditions in conjunction with a secondary centroid metric; this strategy avoids any major (scratch) storage difficulties and will be reviewed and illustrated in Section 8.2. We might note that the process of fitting two-mode proximity data by additive trees or ultrametrics using iterative projection heuristics may generate a rather large number of distinct locally optimal solutions with differing VAF values, particularly in contrast to the situation usually observed for symmetric proximity data. Although this abundance is not inevitably the case and obviously depends on the particular data set being considered, it is not unusual and should be expected by a user.

8.1   Fitting and Finding Two-Mode Ultrametrics

To illustrate the fitting of a given two-mode ultrametric, a two-mode target is generated by the upper-right 6×4 portion of the 10×10 ultrametric target matrix, numcltarg, used in Section 5.1. This file will be called numcltarg6x4.dat and has contents as follows:

```
9  9  9  9
9  9  9  9
8  8  4  8
3  7  8  2
8  8  4  8
7  5  8  7
```

The six rows correspond to the digits 0, 1, 2, 3, 4, and 5; the four columns to 6, 7, 8, and 9. As the two-mode 6×4 proximity matrix, the appropriate upper-right portion of the number proximity matrix will be used in the fitting process; the corresponding file is called number6x4.dat, with the following contents:

```
.788  .909  .821  .850
.758  .630  .791  .625
.421  .796  .367  .808
.300  .592  .804  .263
.388  .742  .246  .683
.396  .400  .671  .592
```

The M-file `ultrafittm.m` fits a given ultrametric to a two-mode proximity matrix (using iterative projection in the L_2-norm) and has usage

```
[fit,vaf] = ultrafittm(proxtm,targ)
```

where PROXTM is the two-mode (rectangular) input proximity matrix (with a dissimilarity interpretation); TARG is an ultrametric matrix of the same size as PROXTM; FIT is the least-squares optimal matrix (with variance-accounted-for of VAF) to PROXTM satisfying the two-mode ultrametric constraints implicit in TARG. An example follows using `numcltarg6x4` for TARG and `number6x4` as PROXTM:

```
load number6x4.dat
load numcltarg6x4.dat
[fit,vaf] = ultrafittm(number6x4,numcltarg6x4)

fit =

    0.7715    0.7715    0.7715    0.7715
    0.7715    0.7715    0.7715    0.7715
    0.6641    0.6641    0.3065    0.6641
    0.3000    0.5267    0.6641    0.2630
    0.6641    0.6641    0.3065    0.6641
    0.5267    0.4000    0.6641    0.5267


vaf =

    0.6978
```

A VAF of .6978 was obtained for the fitted ultrametric; we give the hierarchy below with indications of when the partitions were formed in the L_2-norm fitted ultrametric (in FIT) and in the original target (in `numcltarg6x4`):

Partition	Level Formed (L_2)	Level Formed (Target)
{{0,1,2,4,8,3,9,6,5,7}}	.7715	9
{{0},{1},{2,4,8,3,9,6,5,7}}	.6641	8
{{0},{1},{2,4,8},{3,9,6,5,7}}	.5267	7
{{0},{1},{2,4,8},{3,9,6},{5,7}}	.4000	5
{{0},{1},{2,4,8},{3,9,6},{5},{7}}	.3065	4
{{0},{1},{2},{4},{8},{3,9,6},{5},{7}}	.3000	3
{{0},{1},{2},{4},{8},{3,9},{6},{5},{7}}	.2630	2
{{0},{1},{2},{4},{8},{3},{9},{6},{5},{7}}	—	—

The M-file `ultrafndtm.m` relies on iterative projection heuristically to locate a best-fitting two-mode ultrametric. The usage is

```
[find,vaf] = ultrafndtm(proxtm,inpermrow,inpermcol)
```

where PROXTM is the two-mode input proximity matrix (with a dissimilarity interpretation); INPERMROW and INPERMCOL are permutations for the row and column objects that determine the order in which the inequality constraints are considered; FIND is the found least-squares matrix (with variance-accounted-for of VAF) to PROXTM satisfying the ultrametric constraints. The example below for the `number6x4` two-mode data (using random permutations for INPERMROW and INPERMCOL) finds an ultrametric with VAF of .7448.

```
[find,vaf] = ultrafndtm(number6x4,randperm(6),randperm(4))

find =

    0.8420    0.8420    0.8420    0.8420
    0.7010    0.7010    0.7010    0.7010
    0.6641    0.6641    0.3670    0.6641
    0.3000    0.5267    0.6641    0.2630
    0.6641    0.6641    0.2460    0.6641
    0.5267    0.4000    0.6641    0.5267


vaf =
    0.7448
```

The partition hierarchy identified is similar to that found for the target `numcltarg6x4`, although there is some minor variation in how the digits 0 and 1 are treated:

Partition	Level Formed (L_2)
{{0,1,2,4,8,3,9,6,5,7}}	.8420
{{0},{1,2,4,8,3,9,6,5,7}}	.7010
{{0},{1},{2,4,8,3,9,6,5,7}}	.6641
{{0},{1},{2,4,8},{3,9,6,5,7}}	.5267
{{0},{1},{2,4,8},{3,9,6},{5,7}}	.4000
{{0},{1},{2,4,8},{3,9,6},{5},{7}}	.3670
{{0},{1},{2},{4,8},{3,9,6},{5},{7}}	.3000
{{0},{1},{2},{4,8},{3,9},{6},{5},{7}}	.2630
{{0},{1},{2},{4,8},{3},{9},{6},{5},{7}}	.2460
{{0},{1},{2},{4},{8},{3},{9},{6},{5},{7}}	—

8.2   Finding Two-Mode Additive Trees

As noted in the introductory material in this chapter, the identification of a best-fitting two-mode additive tree will be done somewhat differently (because of storage considerations) than for a two-mode ultrametric representation. Specifically, a (two-mode) centroid metric and a (two-mode) ultrametric matrix will be identified so that their sum is a good-fitting two-mode additive tree. Because a centroid metric can be obtained in closed form, we first illustrate the fitting of just a centroid metric to a two-mode proximity matrix with the M-file `centfittm.m`. Its usage is of the form

```
[fit,vaf,lengths] = centfittm(proxtm)
```

which gives the least-squares fitted two-mode centroid metric (FIT) to PROXTM, the two-mode rectangular input proximity matrix (with a dissimilarity interpretation). The n values (where n = number of rows(n_a) + number of columns(n_b)) serve to define the approximating sums, $u_r + v_s$, where the u_r are for the n_a rows and the v_s for the n_b columns; these u_r and v_s values are given in the vector LENGTHS of size $n \times 1$, with row values first followed by the column values. The closed-form formula used for u_r (or v_s) can be given simply as the rth row (or sth column) mean of PROXTM minus one-half the grand mean (see Carroll and Pruzansky, 1980, and De Soete et al., 1984, for a further discussion). In the example given below using the two-mode matrix `number6x4`, a two-mode centroid metric by itself has a VAF of .4737.

```
    [fit,vaf,lengths] = centfittm(number6x4);
    fit

fit =

        0.7405       0.9101       0.8486       0.8688
        0.5995       0.7691       0.7076       0.7278
        0.4965       0.6661       0.6046       0.6248
        0.3882       0.5579       0.4964       0.5165
        0.4132       0.5829       0.5214       0.5415
        0.4132       0.5829       0.5214       0.5415

    vaf

vaf =

        0.4737

    lengths'

ans =

    Columns 1 through 6

        0.5370       0.3960       0.2930       0.1847       0.2097       0.2097

    Columns 7 through 10

        0.2035       0.3731       0.3116       0.3318
```

The finding of a two-mode additive tree with the M-file `atreefndtm.m` proceeds iteratively. A two-mode centroid metric is first found and the original two-mode proximity matrix residualized; a two-mode ultrametric is then identified for the residual matrix. The process repeats with the centroid and ultrametric components alternatingly being refit until a small change in the overall VAF occurs (a value less than 1.0e-006 is used). The M-file has the explicit usage

```
[find,vaf,ultra,lengths] = ...
     atreefndtm(proxtm,inpermrow,inpermcol)
```

and, as noted above, relies on iterative projection heuristically to find a two-mode ultrametric component that is added to a two-mode centroid metric to produce a two-mode additive tree. Here, PROXTM is the rectangular input proximity matrix (with a dissimilarity interpretation); INPERMROW and INPERMCOL are permutations for the row and column objects that determine the order in which the inequality constraints are considered; FIND is the found least-squares matrix (with variance-accounted-for of VAF) to PROXTM satisfying the two-mode additive tree constraints. The vector LENGTHS contains the row followed by column values for the two-mode centroid metric component; ULTRA is the ultrametric component. In the example given below, the identified two-mode additive tree for `number6x4` has a VAF of .9053, with a nice structural interpretation of the digits along with some indication now of odd and even digit groupings. The partition hierarchy is reported below the MATLAB output along with an indication of when the various partitions are formed.

```
   [find,vaf,ultra,lengths] = ...
atreefndtm(number6x4,randperm(6),randperm(4))

   find

find =

       0.6992     0.9029     0.9104     0.8561
       0.6298     0.6300     0.8411     0.7029
       0.4398     0.8160     0.3670     0.7692
       0.4549     0.5748     0.6661     0.2630
       0.3692     0.7453     0.2460     0.6985
       0.4582     0.4000     0.6694     0.5313

   vaf

vaf =

       0.9053

   ultra

ultra =

       0.1083     0.0520     0.1083     0.0520
```

```
    0.1083    -0.1516     0.1083    -0.0318
   -0.0078     0.1083    -0.2919     0.1083
    0.1083    -0.0318     0.1083    -0.2968
   -0.0078     0.1083    -0.3422     0.1083
    0.1083    -0.2099     0.1083    -0.0318
```

lengths'

ans =

Columns 1 through 6

```
    0.4570     0.3876     0.3138     0.2127     0.2431     0.2160
```

Columns 7 through 10

```
    0.1339     0.3939     0.3451     0.3471
```

Partition	Level Formed
{{6,4,8,2,9,3,5,7,1,0}}	.1083
{{6,4,8,2},{9,3,5,7,1,0}}	.0520
{{6,4,8,2},{9,3,5,7,1},{0}}	−.0078
{{6},{4,8,2},{9,3,5,7,1},{0}}	−.0318
{{6},{4,8,2},{9,3},{5,7,1},{0}}	−.1516
{{6},{4,8,2},{9,3},{5,7},{1},{0}}	−.2099
{{6},{4,8,2},{9,3},{5},{7},{1},{0}}	−.2919
{{6},{4,8},{2},{9,3},{5},{7},{1},{0}}	−.2968
{{6},{4,8},{2},{9},{3},{5},{7},{1},{0}}	−.3422
{{6},{4},{8},{2},{9},{3},{5},{7},{1},{0}}	—

8.3 Completing a Two-Mode Ultrametric to One Defined on $S_A \cup S_B$

Instead of relying only on our general intuition (and problem-solving skills) to transform a fitted two-mode ultrametric to one we could interpret directly as a sequence of partitions for the joint set $S_A \cup S_B$, the M-file ultracomptm.m provides the explicit completion of a given two-mode ultrametric matrix to a symmetric proximity matrix (defined on $S_A \cup S_B$ and satisfying the usual ultrametric constraints). Thus, this completion, in effect, estimates the (missing) ultrametric values that must be present between objects from the same cluster but from the different modes. The general syntax has the form

```
[ultracomp] = ultracomptm(ultraproxtm)
```

where ULTRAPROXTM is the $n_a \times n_b$ fitted two-mode ultrametric matrix; ULTRACOMPTM is the completed $n \times n$ proximity matrix having the usual ultrametric pattern for the complete object set of size $n = n_a + n_b$. As seen in the examples below, the use of `ultrafndtm.m` plus `ultracomptm.m` on the `number6x4` data and the subsequent application of the `ultraorder.m` routine leads directly to the partition hierarchy we identified earlier:

```
load number6x4.dat
[find,vaf] = ultrafndtm(number6x4,randperm(6),randperm(4));
vaf
```

```
vaf =

   0.7448
```

```
[ultracomp] = ultracomptm(find)
```

```
ultracomp =
```

Columns 1 through 6

0	0.8420	0.8420	0.8420	0.8420	0.8420
0.8420	0	0.7010	0.7010	0.7010	0.7010
0.8420	0.7010	0	0.6641	0.3670	0.6641
0.8420	0.7010	0.6641	0	0.6641	0.5267
0.8420	0.7010	0.3670	0.6641	0	0.6641
0.8420	0.7010	0.6641	0.5267	0.6641	0
0.8420	0.7010	0.6641	0.3000	0.6641	0.5267
0.8420	0.7010	0.6641	0.5267	0.6641	0.4000
0.8420	0.7010	0.3670	0.6641	0.2460	0.6641
0.8420	0.7010	0.6641	0.2630	0.6641	0.5267

Columns 7 through 10

0.8420	0.8420	0.8420	0.8420
0.7010	0.7010	0.7010	0.7010
0.6641	0.6641	0.3670	0.6641
0.3000	0.5267	0.6641	0.2630
0.6641	0.6641	0.2460	0.6641
0.5267	0.4000	0.6641	0.5267
0	0.5267	0.6641	0.3000
0.5267	0	0.6641	0.5267
0.6641	0.6641	0	0.6641
0.3000	0.5267	0.6641	0

```
[orderprox,orderperm] = ultraorder(ultracomp)
```

```
orderprox =
```

```
Columns 1 through 6
```

0	0.8420	0.8420	0.8420	0.8420	0.8420
0.8420	0	0.2460	0.3670	0.6641	0.6641
0.8420	0.2460	0	0.3670	0.6641	0.6641
0.8420	0.3670	0.3670	0	0.6641	0.6641
0.8420	0.6641	0.6641	0.6641	0	0.3000
0.8420	0.6641	0.6641	0.6641	0.3000	0
0.8420	0.6641	0.6641	0.6641	0.3000	0.2630
0.8420	0.6641	0.6641	0.6641	0.5267	0.5267
0.8420	0.6641	0.6641	0.6641	0.5267	0.5267
0.8420	0.7010	0.7010	0.7010	0.7010	0.7010

```
Columns 7 through 10
```

0.8420	0.8420	0.8420	0.8420
0.6641	0.6641	0.6641	0.7010
0.6641	0.6641	0.6641	0.7010
0.6641	0.6641	0.6641	0.7010
0.3000	0.5267	0.5267	0.7010
0.2630	0.5267	0.5267	0.7010
0	0.5267	0.5267	0.7010
0.5267	0	0.4000	0.7010
0.5267	0.4000	0	0.7010
0.7010	0.7010	0.7010	0

```
orderperm =

     1     9     5     3     7    10     4     8     6     2
```

Similarly, for the two-mode additive tree example, we have the partition hierarchy we gave initially and what was retrieved immediately from the use of ultracomptm.m and ultraorder.m on the output ultrametric matrix, ultra:

```
[find,vaf,ultra,lengths] = ...
atreefndtm(number6x4,randperm(6),randperm(4));

  vaf

vaf =

    0.9053

[ultracomp] = ultracomptm(ultra)
```

```
ultracomp =

  Columns 1 through 6

          0      0.0520      0.1083      0.0520      0.1083      0.0520
     0.0520           0      0.1083     -0.0318      0.1083     -0.1516
     0.1083      0.1083           0      0.1083     -0.2919      0.1083
     0.0520     -0.0318      0.1083           0      0.1083     -0.0318
     0.1083      0.1083     -0.2919      0.1083           0      0.1083
     0.0520     -0.1516      0.1083     -0.0318      0.1083           0
     0.1083      0.1083     -0.0078      0.1083     -0.0078      0.1083
     0.0520     -0.1516      0.1083     -0.0318      0.1083     -0.2099
     0.1083      0.1083     -0.2919      0.1083     -0.3422      0.1083
     0.0520     -0.0318      0.1083     -0.2968      0.1083     -0.0318

  Columns 7 through 10

     0.1083      0.0520      0.1083      0.0520
     0.1083     -0.1516      0.1083     -0.0318
    -0.0078      0.1083     -0.2919      0.1083
     0.1083     -0.0318      0.1083     -0.2968
    -0.0078      0.1083     -0.3422      0.1083
     0.1083     -0.2099      0.1083     -0.0318
          0      0.1083     -0.0078      0.1083
     0.1083           0      0.1083     -0.0318
    -0.0078      0.1083           0      0.1083
     0.1083     -0.0318      0.1083           0

  [orderprox,orderperm] = ultraorder(ultracomp)

orderprox =

  Columns 1 through 6

          0     -0.0078     -0.0078     -0.0078      0.1083      0.1083
    -0.0078           0     -0.3422     -0.2919      0.1083      0.1083
    -0.0078     -0.3422           0     -0.2919      0.1083      0.1083
    -0.0078     -0.2919     -0.2919           0      0.1083      0.1083
     0.1083      0.1083      0.1083      0.1083           0     -0.2968
     0.1083      0.1083      0.1083      0.1083     -0.2968           0
     0.1083      0.1083      0.1083      0.1083     -0.0318     -0.0318
     0.1083      0.1083      0.1083      0.1083     -0.0318     -0.0318
     0.1083      0.1083      0.1083      0.1083     -0.0318     -0.0318
     0.1083      0.1083      0.1083      0.1083      0.0520      0.0520
```

```
Columns 7 through 10

   0.1083      0.1083      0.1083      0.1083
   0.1083      0.1083      0.1083      0.1083
   0.1083      0.1083      0.1083      0.1083
   0.1083      0.1083      0.1083      0.1083
  -0.0318     -0.0318     -0.0318      0.0520
  -0.0318     -0.0318     -0.0318      0.0520
        0     -0.1516     -0.1516      0.0520
  -0.1516           0     -0.2099      0.0520
  -0.1516     -0.2099           0      0.0520
   0.0520      0.0520      0.0520           0


orderperm =

    7    9    5    3   10    4    2    6    8    1
```

8.3.1 The goldfish_receptor Data

We could also illustrate the results of using our various M-files from this chapter on the two-mode `goldfish_receptor` data, but given the extensiveness of the output, we provide just the commands we would use and leave the reader to provide the output. The VAF value for the best ultrametric found was .6209; the best additive tree had VAF .8663. As to be expected, the various colors are associated with the appropriate cones.

```
load goldfish_receptor.dat
[find,vaf] = ultrafndtm(goldfish_receptor,...
    randperm(11),randperm(9));


vaf =

   0.6209

[ultracomp] = ultracomptm(find);
[orderprox,orderperm] = ultraorder(ultracomp);

[find,vaf,ultra,lengths] = ...
atreefndtm(goldfish_receptor,randperm(11),randperm(9));

vaf =

   0.8663


[ultracomp] = ultracomptm(ultra);
```

Part III

The Representation of Proximity Matrices by Structures Dependent on Order (Only)

An Introduction to
Order-Theoretic
Representational Structures

Nonmetric multidimensional scaling (NMDS) as developed by Shepard (1962a,b) and Kruskal (1964a,b) has become a very familiar method in the psychological research literature for representing structure that may be inherent among a set of objects. Judging by the number of published substantive applications, whenever data are given in the form of a symmetric proximity matrix containing numerical relationship information between distinct object pairs, NMDS may have now become the default method of analysis. This routine use of NMDS, however, when faced with elucidating whatever pattern of relationships may underly a given set of proximities, does have interpretive implications and consequences. For one, there is an implicit choice made that whatever major generality will be allowed should reside in the particular proximities being fitted by the explicitly parameterized (Euclidean) spatial structure. Thus, an optimal (usually monotonic) transformation of the proximities is sought in conjunction with the construction of a spatial representation. Second, the parameterized spatial structure implicitly involves fitting the (transformed) proximities by some function of the differences in object placement along a set of coordinate axes that may be best suited for representing object variation that could, at least in theory, be allowed to vary continuously. For instance, in the common Euclidean model we use the square root of the sum of squared coordinate differences along a set of axes (although the particular axis system selected is open to some arbitrariness). The tacit implication is that if the structure underlying the proximities is more classificatory (and discrete) in nature, we may not do well in representing it by a spatial model that should do much better in the presence of more continuous variation (cf. Pruzansky, Tversky, and Carroll, 1982). In fact, in the limiting case where there exists a partition of the object set in which all proximities for object pairs within an object class are smaller than for object pairs between classes (and where proximities are keyed as dissimilarities so that larger values represent more dissimilar objects), NMDS will typically give a degenerate representation in which all objects within each class are located at the same spatial location and the optimally transformed proximities consist of just two values, one for the within-class proximities and one for the between-class proximities (cf. Shepard, 1974).

This part of the book concentrates on an alternative approach to understanding what a given proximity matrix may be depicting about the objects on which it was constructed, and one that does not require a prior commitment to the sole use of either some form of dimensional model (as in NMDS), or one that is strictly classificatory (as in the use of a partition hierarchy and the implicit fitting of an ultrametric that serves as the representational mechanism for the hierarchical clustering). The method of analysis is based on approximating a given proximity matrix additively by a sum of matrices, where each component in the sum is subject to specific patterning restrictions on its entries. The restrictions imposed on each component of the decomposition (to be referred to as matrices with anti-Robinson forms) are very general and encompass interpretations that might be dimensional, or classificatory, or some combination of both (e.g., through object classes that are themselves placed dimensionally in some space). Thus, as one special case, and particularly when an (optimal) transformation of the proximities is also permitted (as we will generally allow), proximity matrices that are well interpretable through NMDS should also be interpretable through an additive decomposition of the (transformed) proximity matrix. Alternatively, when classificatory structures of various kinds might underlie a set of proximities (and the direct use of NMDS could possibly lead to a degeneracy), additive decompositions may still provide an analysis strategy for elucidating the structure.

The algorithmic details of fitting to a given proximity matrix a sum of matrices each having the desired general patterning to its entries (or even more explicitly parameterized forms that may be of help in providing a detailed interpretation, such as those given by partition hierarchies or unidimensional scales) are available in a series of papers (i.e., Hubert and Arabie, 1994, 1995a,b; Hubert, Arabie, and Meulman, 1997, 1998). Thus, in this sequel we can merely refer to these sources for the actual mechanics of carrying out the various decompositions. More unique aspects that will be incorporated in the documentation to follow are (a) the possible integration of (optimal) transformations for use with the originally given proximities to be fitted by an additive matrix decomposition and (b) the fitting of more restrictive parameterized forms (such as in Parts I and II) to the various components of a decomposition in attempting to give a detailed substantive interpretation of what each separate matrix in the decomposition may be depicting. In this latter instance, one of our concerns might be directed toward the issue of whether a particular matrix as part of a decomposition is indicating primarily dimensional or classificatory aspects of the original proximities (or possibly, and what may be more typical, some combination of the two). In these latter cases, the M-files discussed as part of the documentation given in the earlier parts of this monograph for LUS and for the fitting of tree structures are particularly relevant.

Chapter 9

Anti-Robinson Matrices for Symmetric Proximity Data

Denoting an arbitrary symmetric $n \times n$ matrix by $\mathbf{A} = \{a_{ij}\}$, where the main diagonal entries are considered irrelevant and assumed to be zero (i.e., $a_{ii} = 0$ for $1 \le i \le n$), $\mathbf{A}$ is said to have an anti-Robinson (AR) form if after some reordering of the rows and columns of $\mathbf{A}$ the entries within each row and column have a distinctive pattern: moving away from the zero main diagonal entry within any row or any column, the entries never decrease. Generally, matrices having AR forms can appear both in spatial representations for a set of proximities as functions of the absolute differences in coordinate values along some axis or for classificatory structures that are characterized through an ultrametric.

To illustrate, we first let $\mathbf{P} = \{p_{ij}\}$ be a given $n \times n$ proximity (dissimilarity) matrix among the distinct pairs of n objects in a set $S = \{O_1, O_2, \ldots, O_n\}$ (where $p_{ii} = 0$ for $1 \le i \le n$). Then, suppose, for example, a two-dimensional Euclidean representation is possible for $\mathbf{P}$ and its entries are very well representable by the distances in this space, and thus

$$p_{ij} \approx \sqrt{(x_{1i} - x_{1j})^2 + (x_{2i} - x_{2j})^2} \, ,$$

where x_{ki} and x_{kj} are the coordinates on the kth axis (for $k = 1$ and 2) for objects O_i and O_j (and the symbol $\approx$ is used to indicate approximation). Here, a simple monotonic transformation (squaring) of the proximities should then be fitted well by the sum of two matrices both having AR forms, i.e.,

$$\{p_{ij}^2\} \approx \{(x_{1i} - x_{1j})^2\} + \{(x_{2i} - x_{2j})^2\}.$$

In a classificatory framework, if $\{p_{ij}\}$ were well representable, say, as a sum of two matrices, $\mathbf{A}_1 = \{a_{ij}^{(1)}\}$ and $\mathbf{A}_2 = \{a_{ij}^{(2)}\}$, each satisfying the ultrametric inequality, i.e., $a_{ij}^{(k)} \le \max\{a_{ih}^{(k)}, a_{hj}^{(k)}\}$ for $k = 1$ and 2, then

$$\{p_{ij}\} \approx \{a_{ij}^{(1)}\} + \{a_{ij}^{(2)}\},$$

and each of the constituent matrices can be reordered to display an AR form. As can be seen in Part II of this monograph, any matrix whose entries satisfy the ultrametric inequality can be represented by a sequence of partitions that are hierarchically related.

Given some proximity matrix $\mathbf{P}$, the task of approximating it as a sum of matrices each having an AR form is implemented through an iterative optimization strategy based on a least-squares loss criterion that is discussed in detail by Hubert and Arabie (1994). Given the manner in which the optimization process is carried out sequentially, *each successive AR matrix* in any decomposition generally accounts for less and less of the patterning of the original proximity information (which is very analogous to what is typically observed in a principal component decomposition of a covariance matrix). In fact, it has been found empirically that for the many data sets we have analyzed, only a very small number of such AR matrices are ever necessary to represent almost all of the patterning in the given proximities. A succinct summary that we could give to this empirical experience is that no more than three AR matrices are ever necessary, two are usually sufficient, and sometimes one will suffice.

The substantive challenge that remains, once a well-fitting decomposition is found for a given proximity matrix, is to interpret substantively what each term in the decomposition might be depicting. The strategy that could be followed would approximate each separate AR matrix by ones having a more restrictive form, usually those representing some type of unidimensional scale (a dimensional interpretation from Part I) or partition hierarchy (a classificatory interpretation from Part II).

9.0.1   Incorporating Transformations

One generalization that we will now allow to what has already been discussed in the literature for fitting sums of AR matrices to a proximity matrix $\mathbf{P}$ is the possible inclusion of an (optimal) transformation of the proximities. Thus, instead of just representing $\mathbf{P}$ as a sum of K matrices (and, generally, for K very small) that we might denote as $\mathbf{A}_1 + \cdots + \mathbf{A}_K$, where each $\mathbf{A}_k$, $1 \le k \le K$, has an AR form, an (optimally) transformed matrix $\tilde{\mathbf{P}} = \{\tilde{p}_{ij}\}$ will be fitted by such a sum, say, $\tilde{\mathbf{A}}_1 + \cdots + \tilde{\mathbf{A}}_K$, where the entries in $\tilde{\mathbf{P}}$ are monotonic with respect to those in $\mathbf{P}$, i.e., for all $O_i, O_j, O_k, O_l \in S$, $p_{ij} < p_{kl} \Rightarrow \tilde{p}_{ij} \le \tilde{p}_{kl}$. In what follows we will rely on the M-file proxmon.m, documented in Part I, which constructs optimal monotonic transformations by the same method of isotonic regression commonly used in NMDS (although using a different type of algorithm based on the Dykstra–Kaczmarz iterative projection strategy). The method is the primary approach of Kruskal (1964a,b) to tied proximities in $\mathbf{P}$ that are allowed to be untied after transformation. Such transformations, for example, form the default option in the implementation of NMDS in the program KYST-2A (Kruskal, Young, and Seery, 1977) and in SYSTAT (Wilkinson, 1988).

The process of finding $\tilde{\mathbf{P}}$ and $\tilde{\mathbf{A}}_1 + \cdots + \tilde{\mathbf{A}}_K$ proceeds iteratively, with the original proximity matrix $\mathbf{P}$ first fit by $\mathbf{A}_1 + \cdots + \mathbf{A}_K$; a subsequent optimal (monotonic) transformation of $\mathbf{P}$ (through a least-squares approximation to $\mathbf{A}_1 + \cdots + \mathbf{A}_K$) is identified, which is then refitted by the matrix sum. In many cases, this whole process can now be cycled through iteratively until convergence, i.e., a sequential fitting and refitting of the optimally transformed proximities and their representation as a sum of matrices each having an AR form.

In some contexts, however (particularly when fitting a single AR matrix (i.e., when $K = 1$)), it is probably best not to proceed to a complete convergence but instead to terminate the process after only a single optimal monotonic transformation of $\mathbf{P}$ is identified and then to refit by a matrix sum. This usage will be referred to as a single iteration optimal transformation (SIOT). If carried through to convergence, a perfect representation may be obtained but only at the expense of losing almost all the patterning contained within the original proximity matrix. For example, in fitting a single AR matrix, the optimal transformation identified after convergence might consist of just two values, with one corresponding to the smallest proximity in the original matrix and all others equal. Although technically permissible since this situation does reflect a perfect AR form, most of the detail present in the original proximity matrix is also lost. Difficulties with such so-called degeneracies have been pointed out by Carroll (1992), particularly when faced with fitting classificatory structures to a given proximity matrix.

9.0.2   Interpreting the Structure of an AR Matrix

In representing a proximity matrix $\mathbf{P}$ as a sum, $\mathbf{A}_1 + \cdots + \mathbf{A}_K$ (or an optimal transformation $\tilde{\mathbf{P}}$ as $\tilde{\mathbf{A}}_1 + \cdots + \tilde{\mathbf{A}}_K$), the interpretive task remains to explain substantively what each term of the decomposition might be depicting. We suggest four possible strategies below, with the first two attempting to understand the structure of an AR matrix directly and without much loss of detail; the last two require the imposition of strictly parameterized approximations in the form of either an ultrametric or a unidimensional scale. In the discussion below, $\mathbf{A} = \{a_{ij}\}$ will be assumed to have an AR form that is displayed by the given row and column order.

(A) Complete representation and reconstruction through a collection of subsets and associated subset diameters:

The entries in any AR matrix $\mathbf{A}$ can be reconstructed exactly through a collection of M subsets of the original object set $S = \{O_1, \ldots, O_n\}$, denoted by $S_1, \ldots, S_M$, and where M is determined by the particular pattern of tied entries, if any, in $\mathbf{A}$. These M subsets have the following characteristics:

(i) Each $S_m, 1 \le m \le M$, consists of a sequence of (two or more) consecutive integers so that $M \le n(n-1)/2$. (This bound holds because the number of different subsets having consecutive integers for any given fixed ordering is $n(n-1)/2$, and will be achieved if all the entries in the AR matrix $\mathbf{A}$ are distinct.)

(ii) Each $S_m, 1 \le m \le M$, has a diameter, denoted by $d(S_m)$, so that for all object pairs within S_m, the corresponding entries in $\mathbf{A}$ are less than or equal to the diameter. The subsets, $S_1, \ldots, S_M$, can be assumed ordered as $d(S_1) \le d(S_2) \le \cdots \le d(S_M)$, and if $S_m \subseteq S_{m'}, d(S_m) \le d(S_{m'})$.

(iii) Each entry in $\mathbf{A}$ can be reconstructed from $d(S_1), \ldots, d(S_M)$, i.e., for $1 \le i, j \le n$,

$$a_{ij} = \min_{1 \le m \le M} \{d(S_m) \mid O_i, O_j \in S_m\},$$

so that the minimum diameter for subsets containing an object pair $O_i, O_j \in S$ is equal to a_{ij}. Given $\mathbf{A}$, the collection of subsets $S_1, \ldots, S_M$ and their diameters can be identified by inspection through the use of an increasing threshold that starts from the smallest entry in $\mathbf{A}$ and by observing which subsets containing contiguous objects emerge from this process. The substantive interpretation of what $\mathbf{A}$ is depicting reduces to explaining why those subsets with the smallest diameters are so homogeneous. For convenience of reference, the subsets $S_1, \ldots, S_M$ will be referred to as the set of *AR reconstructive subsets*.

(B) Representation by a strongly anti-Robinson matrix:

If the matrix **A** has a somewhat more restrictive form than just being AR, and is also *strongly* anti-Robinson (SAR), a convenient graphical representation can be given to the collection of AR reconstructive subsets $S_1, \ldots, S_M$ and their diameters and how they can serve to retrieve **A**. Specifically, **A** is said to be SAR if (considering the above-diagonal entries of **A**) whenever two entries in adjacent columns are equal ($a_{ij} = a_{i(j+1)}$), those in the same two adjacent columns in the previous row are also equal ($a_{(i-1)j} = a_{(i-1)(j+1)}$ for $1 \leq i - 1 < j \leq n - 1$); also, whenever two entries in adjacent rows are equal ($a_{ij} = a_{(i+1)j}$), those in the same two adjacent rows in the succeeding column are also equal ($a_{i(j+1)} = a_{(i+1)(j+1)}$ for $2 \leq i + 1 < j \leq n - 1$).

When **A** is SAR, the collection of subsets, $S_1, \ldots, S_M$, and their diameters and how these serve to reconstruct **A** can be modeled graphically as we will see in Section 9.5. The internal nodes (represented by solid circles) in each of these figures are at a height equal to the diameter of the respective subset; the consecutive objects forming that subset are identifiable by downward paths from the internal nodes to the terminal nodes corresponding to the objects in $S = \{O_1, \ldots, O_n\}$ (represented by labeled open circles). An entry a_{ij} in **A** can be reconstructed as the minimum node height of a subset for which a path can be constructed from O_i up to that internal node and then back down to O_j. (To prevent undue graphical "clutter," only the most homogeneous subsets from $S_1, \ldots, S_M$ having the smallest diameters should actually be included in the graphical representation of an SAR matrix; each figure would explicitly show only how the smallest entries in **A** can be reconstructed, although each could be easily extended to include all of **A**. The calibrated vertical axis in such figures could routinely include the heights at which the additional internal nodes would have to be placed to effect such a complete reconstruction.)

Given an arbitrary AR matrix **A**, a least-squares SAR approximating matrix to **A** can be found using the heuristic optimization search strategy illustrated in Section 9.3 and developed in Hubert, Arabie, and Meulman (1998). This latter source also discusses in detail (through counterexample) why SAR conditions need to be imposed to obtain a consistent graphical representation.

(C) Representation by a unidimensional scale:

To obtain greater graphical simplicity for an eventual substantive interpretation than offered by an SAR matrix, one possibility is to use approximating unidimensional scales. To be explicit, one very simple form that an AR matrix **A** may assume is interpretable by a single dimension and through a unidimensional scale in which the entries have the parameterized form $\mathbf{A} = \{a_{ij}\} = \{\mid x_j - x_i \mid + c\}$, where the coordinates are ordered as $x_1 \leq x_2 \leq \cdots \leq x_n$, and c is an estimated constant. Given any proximity matrix, a least-squares approximating unidimensional scale can be obtained through the optimization strategies of Part I and would be one (dimensional) method that could be followed in attempting to interpret what a particular AR component of a decomposition might be revealing.

(D) Representation by an ultrametric:

A second simple form that an AR matrix **A** could have is strictly classificatory in which the entries in **A** satisfy the ultrametric condition $a_{ij} \leq \max\{a_{ik}, a_{jk}\}$ for all $O_i, O_j, O_k \in S$.

As a threshold is increased from the smallest entry in **A**, a sequence of partitions of S is identified in which each partition is constructed from the previous one by uniting pairs of subsets from the latter. A partition identified at a given threshold level has equal values in **A** between each given pair of subsets, and all the within-subset values are not greater than the between-subset values. The reconstructive subsets $S_1, \ldots, S_M$ that would represent the AR matrix **A** are now the new subsets that are formed in the sequence of partitions and have the property that if $d(S_m) \leq d(S_{m'})$, then $S_m \subseteq S_{m'}$ or $S_m \cap S_{m'} = \emptyset$. Given any proximity matrix, a least-squares approximating ultrametric can be constructed by the heuristic optimization routines developed in Part II and would be another (classificatory) strategy for interpreting what a particular AR component of a decomposition might be depicting. As might be noted, there are generally $n - 1$ subsets (each of size greater than one) in the collection of reconstructive subsets for any ultrametric, and thus $n - 1$ values need to be estimated in finding the least-squares approximation (which is the same number needed for a least-squares approximating unidimensional scale, based on obtaining the $n - 1$ nonnegative separation values between x_i and x_{i+1} for $1 \leq i \leq n - 1$).

9.1 Fitting a Given AR Matrix in the L_2-Norm

The function M-file arobfit.m fits an AR matrix using iterative projection to a symmetric proximity matrix in the L_2-norm. The usage syntax is of the form

```
[fit,vaf] = arobfit(prox,inperm)
```

where PROX is the input proximity matrix ($n \times n$ with a zero main diagonal and a dissimilarity interpretation); INPERM is a given permutation of the first n integers; FIT is the least-squares optimal matrix (with variance-accounted-for of VAF) to PROX having an AR form for the row and column object ordering given by INPERM. A recording of a MATLAB session using the number.dat data file and object ordering given by the identity permutation follows:

```
load number.dat
inperm = 1:10

inperm =

     1     2     3     4     5     6     7     8     9    10

[fit,vaf] = arobfit(number,inperm)

fit =

  Columns 1 through 6

        0    0.4210    0.5840    0.6965    0.6965    0.7960
   0.4210         0    0.2840    0.3460    0.6170    0.6170
   0.5840    0.2840         0    0.2753    0.2753    0.5460
   0.6965    0.3460    0.2753         0    0.2753    0.3844
   0.6965    0.6170    0.2753    0.2753         0    0.3844
```

```
     0.7960      0.6170      0.5460      0.3844      0.3844           0
     0.7960      0.6940      0.5460      0.3844      0.3844      0.3844
     0.8600      0.6940      0.5853      0.5853      0.5530      0.4000
     0.8600      0.7413      0.5853      0.5853      0.5530      0.5530
     0.8600      0.7413      0.7413      0.5853      0.5853      0.5853


  Columns  7 through 10


     0.7960      0.8600      0.8600      0.8600
     0.6940      0.6940      0.7413      0.7413
     0.5460      0.5853      0.5853      0.7413
     0.3844      0.5853      0.5853      0.5853
     0.3844      0.5530      0.5530      0.5853
     0.3844      0.4000      0.5530      0.5853
          0      0.3857      0.3857      0.3857
     0.3857           0      0.3857      0.3857
     0.3857      0.3857           0      0.3857
     0.3857      0.3857      0.3857           0
```

```
vaf =


     0.6979
```

9.1.1   Fitting the (In)equality Constraints Implied by a Given Matrix in the L_2-Norm

At times it may be useful to fit through iterative projection a given set of equality and inequality constraints (as represented by the equalities and inequalities present among the entries in a given target matrix) to a symmetric proximity matrix in the L_2-norm. Whenever the target matrix is AR in form already, the resulting fitted matrix would also be AR in form; more generally, however, the M-function targfit.m could be used with any chosen target matrix. The usage follows the form

```
[fit,vaf]  = targfit(prox,targ)
```

where, as usual, PROX is the input proximity matrix (with a zero main diagonal and a dissimilarity interpretation); TARG is a matrix of the same size as PROX; FIT is the least-squares optimal matrix (with variance-accounted-for of VAF) to PROX satisfying the equality and inequality constraints implicit among all the entries in TARG. An example follows in which the given target matrix is a distance matrix (having an AR form) between equally spaced object placements along a line; the resulting fitted matrix obviously has an AR form as well:

```
load number.dat
[fit,vaf] = targfit(number,targlin(10))
```

```
fit =

   Columns 1 through 6

           0      0.3714     0.3714     0.5363     0.5363     0.6548
      0.3714          0      0.3714     0.3714     0.5363     0.5363
      0.3714     0.3714          0      0.3714     0.3714     0.5363
      0.5363     0.3714     0.3714          0      0.3714     0.3714
      0.5363     0.5363     0.3714     0.3714          0      0.3714
      0.6548     0.5363     0.5363     0.3714     0.3714          0
      0.6548     0.6548     0.5363     0.5363     0.3714     0.3714
      0.7908     0.6548     0.6548     0.5363     0.5363     0.3714
      0.7908     0.7908     0.6548     0.6548     0.5363     0.5363
      0.8500     0.7908     0.7908     0.6548     0.6548     0.5363

   Columns 7 through 10

      0.6548     0.7908     0.7908     0.8500
      0.6548     0.6548     0.7908     0.7908
      0.5363     0.6548     0.6548     0.7908
      0.5363     0.5363     0.6548     0.6548
      0.3714     0.5363     0.5363     0.6548
      0.3714     0.3714     0.5363     0.5363
           0      0.3714     0.3714     0.5363
      0.3714          0      0.3714     0.3714
      0.3714     0.3714          0      0.3714
      0.5363     0.3714     0.3714          0


vaf =

      0.5105
```

9.2 Finding an AR Matrix in the L_2-Norm

The *fitting* of a given AR matrix by the M-function of Section 9.1, `arobfit.m`, requires the presence of an initial permutation to direct the optimization process. Thus, the *finding* of a best-fitting AR matrix reduces to the identification of an appropriate object permutation to use *ab initio*. We suggest the adoption of `order.m`, which carries out an iterative quadratic assignment (QA) maximization task using a given square $n \times n$ proximity matrix PROX (with a zero main diagonal and a dissimilarity interpretation) (see Section 1.2.1 and the references given there to the literature on QA). Three separate local operations are used to permute the rows and columns of the proximity matrix to maximize the cross-product index with respect to a given square target matrix TARG: (a) pairwise interchanges of objects in the permutation defining the row and column order of the square proximity matrix; (b) the insertion of from 1 to KBLOCK (which is less than or equal to $n - 1$) consecutive objects in the permutation defining the row and column order of the data matrix; and (c) the rotation of from 2 to KBLOCK (which is less than or equal to $n - 1$) consecutive objects in the permutation defining the row and column order of the data matrix. The usage syntax has the form

```
[outperm,rawindex,allperms,index] =  ...
    order(prox,targ,inperm,kblock)
```

where INPERM is the input beginning permutation (a permutation of the first n integers); OUTPERM is the final permutation of PROX with the cross-product index RAWINDEX with respect to TARG. The cell array ALLPERMS contains INDEX entries corresponding to all the permutations identified in the optimization from ALLPERMS$\{1\}$ = INPERM to ALLPERMS$\{$INDEX$\}$ = OUTPERM.

A recording of a MATLAB session using order.m is listed below with the beginning INPERM given as the identity permutation, TARG is given by an equally spaced object placement along a line, and KBLOCK = 3. Using the generated OUTPERM, arobfit.m is then invoked to fit an AR form having final VAF of .7782.

```
load number.dat
targlinear = targlin(10);
[outperm,rawindex,allperms,index] = ...
    order(number,targlinear,1:10,3);

outperm

outperm =

     1     2     3     5     4     6     7     9    10     8

rawindex

rawindex =

  206.4920

index

index =

     4

[fit, vaf] = arobfit(number, outperm)

fit =
```

```
Columns 1 through 6
```

0	0.4210	0.5840	0.6840	0.7090	0.7960
0.4210	0	0.2840	0.4960	0.4960	0.5880
0.5840	0.2840	0	0.0590	0.3835	0.4928
0.6840	0.4960	0.0590	0	0.3835	0.3985
0.7090	0.4960	0.3835	0.3835	0	0.3750
0.7960	0.5880	0.4928	0.3985	0.3750	0
0.7960	0.7357	0.4928	0.3985	0.3750	0.3750
0.8210	0.7357	0.4928	0.4928	0.4928	0.4928
0.8500	0.7357	0.7357	0.6830	0.4928	0.4928
0.9090	0.7357	0.7357	0.7357	0.5920	0.4928

```
Columns 7 through 10
```

0.7960	0.8210	0.8500	0.9090
0.7357	0.7357	0.7357	0.7357
0.4928	0.4928	0.7357	0.7357
0.3985	0.4928	0.6830	0.7357
0.3750	0.4928	0.4928	0.5920
0.3750	0.4928	0.4928	0.4928
0	0.3460	0.3460	0.4253
0.3460	0	0.3460	0.4253
0.3460	0.3460	0	0.4253
0.4253	0.4253	0.4253	0

```
vaf =

    0.7782
```

The M-file arobfnd.m is our preferred method for actually identifying a single AR form and incorporates an initial equally spaced target and uses the iterative QA routine of order.m to generate better permutations; the obtained AR forms are then used as new targets against which possibly even better permutations might be identified, until convergence (i.e., the identified permutations remain the same). The syntax is as follows:

```
[find, vaf, outperm] = arobfnd(prox, inperm, kblock)
```

where PROX is the input proximity matrix ($n \times n$ with a zero main diagonal and a dissimilarity interpretation); INPERM is a given starting permutation of the first n integers; FIND is the least-squares optimal matrix (with variance-accounted-for of VAF) to PROX having an AR form for the row and column object ordering given by the ending permutation OUTPERM; KBLOCK defines the block size in the use of the iterative QA routine.

   As seen from the example below, and starting from a random initial permutation, the same AR form is found as with just one application of order.m reported above.

```
[find, vaf, outperm] = arobfnd(number, randperm(10), 1);

vaf =

    0.7782


outperm =

    8    10     9     7     6     4     5     3     2     1
```

9.3   Fitting and Finding an SAR Matrix in the L_2-Norm

The M-functions sarobfit.m and sarobfnd.m are direct analogues of arobfit.m and arobfnd.m, respectively, but are concerned with fitting and finding SAR forms. The syntax for sarobfit.m, which fits an SAR matrix using iterative projection to a symmetric proximity matrix in the L_2-norm, is

```
[fit, vaf] = sarobfit(prox, inperm)
```

where, again, PROX is the input proximity matrix ($n \times n$ with a zero main diagonal and a dissimilarity interpretation); INPERM is a given permutation of the first n integers; FIT is the least-squares optimal matrix (with variance-accounted-for of VAF) to PROX having an SAR form for the row and column object ordering given by INPERM.

An example follows using the same identity permutation as was implemented in fitting an AR form with arobfit.m; as might be expected from using the more restrictive SAR form, the VAF drops to .6128 from .6979.

```
load number.dat
[fit,vaf] = sarobfit(number,1:10)

fit =

  Columns 1 through 6

         0    0.4210    0.5840    0.6965    0.6965    0.7960
    0.4210         0    0.2840    0.4815    0.4815    0.6555
    0.5840    0.2840         0    0.2753    0.2753    0.4652
    0.6965    0.4815    0.2753         0    0.2753    0.4652
    0.6965    0.4815    0.2753    0.2753         0    0.3844
    0.7960    0.6555    0.4652    0.4652    0.3844         0
    0.7960    0.6555    0.4652    0.4652    0.3844    0.3844
    0.8600    0.7256    0.6113    0.6113    0.5383    0.5383
    0.8600    0.7256    0.6113    0.6113    0.5383    0.5383
    0.8600    0.7256    0.6113    0.6113    0.5383    0.5383

  Columns 7 through 10
```

```
        0.7960      0.8600      0.8600      0.8600
        0.6555      0.7256      0.7256      0.7256
        0.4652      0.6113      0.6113      0.6113
        0.4652      0.6113      0.6113      0.6113
        0.3844      0.5383      0.5383      0.5383
        0.3844      0.5383      0.5383      0.5383
             0      0.3857      0.3857      0.3857
        0.3857           0      0.3857      0.3857
        0.3857      0.3857           0      0.3857
        0.3857      0.3857      0.3857           0
```

```
vaf =

    0.6076
```

The M-function sarobfnd.m finds and fits an SAR matrix using iterative projection to a symmetric proximity matrix in the L_2-norm based on a permutation identified through the use of iterative QA. The function has the expected syntax of

```
[find, vaf, outperm] = sarobfnd(prox, inperm, kblock)
```

where, again, PROX is the input proximity matrix ($n \times n$ with a zero main diagonal and a dissimilarity interpretation); INPERM is a given starting permutation of the first n integers; FIND is the least-squares optimal matrix (with variance-accounted-for of VAF) to PROX having an SAR form for the row and column object ordering given by the ending permutation OUTPERM. As usual, KBLOCK defines the block size in the use of the iterative QA routine.

In the MATLAB recording below, and starting from a random permutation, an SAR form is found with a VAF of .7210 (an expected drop from the value of .7782 for the AR form found using arobfnd.m).

```
[find,vaf,outperm] = sarobfnd(number,randperm(10),1)

find =

   Columns 1 through 6

         0      0.4210      0.5840      0.6965      0.6965      0.7960
    0.4210           0      0.2840      0.4960      0.4960      0.6619
    0.5840      0.2840           0      0.0590      0.3835      0.4456
    0.6965      0.4960      0.0590           0      0.3835      0.4456
    0.6965      0.4960      0.3835      0.3835           0      0.3750
    0.7960      0.6619      0.4456      0.4456      0.3750           0
    0.7960      0.6619      0.4456      0.4456      0.3750      0.3750
    0.8600      0.7357      0.5740      0.5740      0.5199      0.5199
    0.8600      0.7357      0.5740      0.5740      0.5199      0.5199
    0.8600      0.7357      0.6998      0.6998      0.5783      0.5783
```

```
Columns 7 through 10

    0.7960      0.8600      0.8600      0.8600
    0.6619      0.7357      0.7357      0.7357
    0.4456      0.5740      0.5740      0.6998
    0.4456      0.5740      0.5740      0.6998
    0.3750      0.5199      0.5199      0.5783
    0.3750      0.5199      0.5199      0.5783
         0      0.3460      0.3460      0.4253
    0.3460           0      0.3460      0.4253
    0.3460      0.3460           0      0.4253
    0.4253      0.4253      0.4253           0


vaf =

    0.6776


outperm =

     1     2     3     5     4     6     7     9    10     8
```

9.4　The Use of Optimal Transformations and the M-Function proxmon.m

As previously discussed in Part I, the function `proxmon.m` provides a monotonically transformed proximity matrix that is close in a least-squares sense to a given input matrix. The syntax is

```
[monproxpermut, vaf, diff] = proxmon(proxpermut,fitted)
```

where PROXPERMUT is the input proximity matrix (which may have been subjected to an initial row/column permutation, hence the suffix PERMUT) and FITTED is a given target matrix; the output matrix MONPROXPERMUT is closest to FITTED in a least-squares sense and obeys the order constraints obtained from each pair of entries in (the upper-triangular portion of) PROXPERMUT (and where the inequality constrained optimization is carried out using the Dykstra–Kaczmarz iterative projection strategy); VAF indicates how much variance in MONPROXPERMUT can be accounted for by FITTED; finally, DIFF is the value of the least-squares loss function and is (one-half) the sum of squared differences between the entries in MONPROXPERMUT and FITTED.

In the notation of the chapter introduction when fitting a given order, FITTED would correspond to the AR matrix $\mathbf{A} = \{a_{ij}\}$; the input PROXPERMUT would be $\{p_{\rho^0(i)\rho^0(j)}\}$; MONPROXPERMUT would be $\{f(p_{\rho^0(i)\rho^0(j)})\}$, where the function $f(\cdot)$ satisfies the monotonicity constraints; i.e., if $p_{\rho^0(i)\rho^0(j)} < p_{\rho^0(i')\rho^0(j')}$ for $1 \leq i < j \leq n$ and $1 \leq i' < j' \leq n$, then $f(p_{\rho^0(i)\rho^0(j)}) \leq f(p_{\rho^0(i')\rho^0(j')})$. The transformed proximity matrix $\{f(p_{\rho^0(i)\rho^0(j)})\}$ minimizes the least-squares criterion (DIFF) of

$$\sum_{i<j}(f(p_{\rho^0(i)\rho^0(j)}) - a_{ij})^2$$

over all functions $f(\cdot)$ that satisfy the monotonicity constraints. The VAF is a normalization of this loss value by the sum of squared deviations of the transformed proximities from their mean:

$$\text{VAF} = 1 - \frac{\sum_{i<j}(f(p_{\rho^0(i)\rho^0(j)}) - a_{ij})^2}{\sum_{i<j}(f(p_{\rho^0(i)\rho^0(j)}) - \bar{f})^2},$$

where $\bar{f}$ denotes the mean of the off-diagonal entries in $\{f(p_{\rho^0(i)\rho^0(j)})\}$.

The script M-file listed below gives an application of proxmon.m along with finding a best-fitting AR form for our number.dat matrix. First, arobfnd.m is invoked to obtain a best-fitting AR matrix (find); this is the same as found earlier based on the outperm of [1 2 3 5 4 6 7 9 10 8] and generating a VAF of .7782. The M-file proxmon.m is then used to generate the monotonically transformed proximity matrix (monproxpermut) with VAF of .8323. Given the SIOT discussed in the introduction to this chapter, it might now be best to fit once more an AR matrix to this now monotonically transformed proximity matrix but then stop. Otherwise, as seen in the output below, if the strategy is repeated cyclically (i.e., finding a fitted matrix based on the monotonically transformed proximity matrix, finding a new monotonically transformed matrix, and so on), a perfect VAF of 1.0 can be achieved at the expense of losing most of the detail in the transformed proximities; i.e., only five distinct values remain that correspond to the three largest and single smallest of the original proximities with *all* the remaining now tied at a value of .5467. (To avoid another type of degeneracy (where all matrices would converge to zeros), the sum of squares of the fitted matrix was maintained stationary; convergence is based on observing a minimal change (less than 1.0e-010) in the VAF.)

```
load number.dat
[find, vaf, outperm] = arobfnd(number,randperm(10),2)
[monproxpermut vaf diff] = ...
    proxmon(number(outperm,outperm),find)
sumfitsq = sum(sum(fit.^2));
prevvaf = 2;
while (abs(prevvaf-vaf) >= 1.0e-010)
   prevvaf = vaf;
   [fit vaf] = arobfit(monproxpermut,1:10);
   sumnewfitsq = sum(sum(fit.^2));
   find = sqrt(sumfitsq)*(fit/sqrt(sumnewfitsq));
    [monproxpermut, vaf, diff] = ...
      proxmon(number(outperm,outperm), find);
end

outperm
find
```

```
monproxpermut
vaf
diff

find =

   Columns 1 through 6

             0      0.4210      0.5840      0.6840      0.7090      0.7960
        0.4210           0      0.2840      0.4960      0.4960      0.5880
        0.5840      0.2840           0      0.0590      0.3835      0.4928
        0.6840      0.4960      0.0590           0      0.3835      0.3985
        0.7090      0.4960      0.3835      0.3835           0      0.3750
        0.7960      0.5880      0.4928      0.3985      0.3750           0
        0.7960      0.7357      0.4928      0.3985      0.3750      0.3750
        0.8210      0.7357      0.4928      0.4928      0.4928      0.4928
        0.8500      0.7357      0.7357      0.6830      0.4928      0.4928
        0.9090      0.7357      0.7357      0.7357      0.5920      0.4928

   Columns 7 through 10

        0.7960      0.8210      0.8500      0.9090
        0.7357      0.7357      0.7357      0.7357
        0.4928      0.4928      0.7357      0.7357
        0.3985      0.4928      0.6830      0.7357
        0.3750      0.4928      0.4928      0.5920
        0.3750      0.4928      0.4928      0.4928
             0      0.3460      0.3460      0.4253
        0.3460           0      0.3460      0.4253
        0.3460      0.3460           0      0.4253
        0.4253      0.4253      0.4253           0


vaf =

    0.7782


outperm =

     1     2     3     5     4     6     7     9    10     8


monproxpermut =
```

Columns 1 through 6

```
         0     0.4244     0.5549     0.6840     0.7058     0.7659
    0.4244          0     0.3981     0.5908     0.4054     0.5549
    0.5549     0.3981          0     0.0590     0.4054     0.5908
    0.6840     0.5908     0.0590          0     0.4244     0.4244
    0.7058     0.4054     0.4054     0.4244          0     0.4310
    0.7659     0.5549     0.5908     0.4244     0.4310          0
    0.7058     0.7058     0.4310     0.4054     0.3981     0.4054
    0.8210     0.7058     0.4054     0.3981     0.7058     0.5908
    0.8500     0.5908     0.7659     0.6830     0.3981     0.5549
    0.9090     0.5908     0.7058     0.7058     0.5908     0.4244
```

Columns 7 through 10

```
    0.7058     0.8210     0.8500     0.9090
    0.7058     0.7058     0.5908     0.5908
    0.4310     0.4054     0.7659     0.7058
    0.4054     0.3981     0.6830     0.7058
    0.3981     0.7058     0.3981     0.5908
    0.4054     0.5908     0.5549     0.4244
         0     0.4054     0.3981     0.4244
    0.4054          0     0.4054     0.4244
    0.3981     0.4054          0     0.4310
    0.4244     0.4244     0.4310          0
```

vaf =

    0.8323

diff =

    0.2075

outperm =

     1   2   3   5   4   6   7   9   10   8

find =

  Columns 1 through 6

```
       0    0.5467    0.5467    0.5467    0.5467    0.5467
  0.5467         0    0.5467    0.5467    0.5467    0.5467
  0.5467    0.5467         0    0.0609    0.5467    0.5467
  0.5467    0.5467    0.0609         0    0.5467    0.5467
  0.5467    0.5467    0.5467    0.5467         0    0.5467
  0.5467    0.5467    0.5467    0.5467    0.5467         0
  0.5467    0.5467    0.5467    0.5467    0.5467    0.5467
  0.8474    0.5467    0.5467    0.5467    0.5467    0.5467
  0.8774    0.5467    0.5467    0.5467    0.5467    0.5467
  0.9383    0.5467    0.5467    0.5467    0.5467    0.5467

Columns 7 through 10

  0.5467    0.8474    0.8774    0.9383
  0.5467    0.5467    0.5467    0.5467
  0.5467    0.5467    0.5467    0.5467
  0.5467    0.5467    0.5467    0.5467
  0.5467    0.5467    0.5467    0.5467
  0.5467    0.5467    0.5467    0.5467
       0    0.5467    0.5467    0.5467
  0.5467         0    0.5467    0.5467
  0.5467    0.5467         0    0.5467
  0.5467    0.5467    0.5467         0


monproxpermut =

Columns 1 through 6

       0    0.5467    0.5467    0.5467    0.5467    0.5467
  0.5467         0    0.5467    0.5467    0.5467    0.5467
  0.5467    0.5467         0    0.0609    0.5467    0.5467
  0.5467    0.5467    0.0609         0    0.5467    0.5467
  0.5467    0.5467    0.5467    0.5467         0    0.5467
  0.5467    0.5467    0.5467    0.5467    0.5467         0
  0.5467    0.5467    0.5467    0.5467    0.5467    0.5467
  0.8474    0.5467    0.5467    0.5467    0.5467    0.5467
  0.8774    0.5467    0.5467    0.5467    0.5467    0.5467
  0.9383    0.5467    0.5467    0.5467    0.5467    0.5467

Columns 7 through 10

  0.5467    0.8474    0.8774    0.9383
  0.5467    0.5467    0.5467    0.5467
  0.5467    0.5467    0.5467    0.5467
```

```
    0.5467      0.5467      0.5467      0.5467
    0.5467      0.5467      0.5467      0.5467
    0.5467      0.5467      0.5467      0.5467
         0      0.5467      0.5467      0.5467
    0.5467           0      0.5467      0.5467
    0.5467      0.5467           0      0.5467
    0.5467      0.5467      0.5467           0
```

vaf =

    1.0000

diff =

  8.3999e-011

9.5   Graphically Representing SAR Structures

The use of the very general form of representation offered by an AR matrix without the imposition of any further restrictions has one annoying interpretive difficulty. Specifically, it is usually necessary to interpret the fitted structures directly (and enumeratively) through a set of subsets or clusters that are all defined by objects contiguous in a specific object ordering; each such subset has an attached diameter that reflects its maximum within-class fitted value. More pointedly, it is generally *not* possible to use a more convenient graph-theoretic structure and the lengths of paths between objects in such a graph to represent visually a fitted AR matrix; this situation contrasts with opportunities resulting when the approximation matrix is more restricted and defined, say, by an ultrametric or an additive tree, or by a (linear or circular) unidimensional scaling (see Hubert, Arabie, and Meulman, 1997, or Parts I and II of this monograph).

As noted in the chapter introduction, the imposition of SAR conditions allows a representation of the fitted values in a (least-squares) SAR approximating matrix as lengths of paths in a graph, although this graph will not generally have the simplified form of a tree. A discussion of these latter SAR constraints is not new here, and several (theoretical) presentations of their usefulness exist in the literature (for example, see Critchley and Fichet, 1994; Critchley, 1994; Durand and Fichet, 1988; Mirkin, 1996, Chapter 7). Here, we give the example based on the number data from Hubert, Arabie, and Meulman (1998) for interpretative convenience. The latter data were transformed (in that reference) to a standard deviation of 1.0 and a mean of 4.0; thus, the numbers within the fitted matrices will differ from the examples given earlier. Approximating AR and SAR forms for the transformed number proximity data are given in the upper- and lower-triangular portions, respectively, of the matrix in Table 9.1. For convenience, below we will denote the upper-triangular AR matrix by $\mathbf{A}_{ut}$ and the lower-triangular SAR matrix by $\mathbf{A}_{lt}$.

Table 9.1. *Order-constrained least-squares approximations to the digit proximity data of Shepard, Kilpatric, and Cunningham* (1975); *the upper-triangular portion is AR and the lower-triangular portion is SAR.*

Digit	0	1	2	4	3	5	6	8	9	7
0	x	3.41	4.21	4.70	4.83	5.25	5.25	5.38	5.52	5.81
1	3.41	x	2.73	3.78	3.78	4.23	4.96	4.96	4.96	4.96
2	4.21	2.73	x	1.63	3.22	3.76	3.76	3.76	4.96	4.96
4	4.76	3.78	1.63	x	3.22	3.30	3.30	3.76	4.70	4.96
3	4.76	3.78	3.22	3.22	x	3.18	3.18	3.76	3.76	4.25
5	5.25	4.59	3.53	3.53	3.18	x	3.18	3.76	3.76	3.76
6	5.25	4.59	3.53	3.53	3.18	3.18	x	3.04	3.04	3.43
8	5.57	4.96	4.18	4.18	4.18	4.18	3.04	x	3.04	3.43
9	5.57	4.96	4.18	4.18	4.18	4.18	3.04	3.04	x	3.43
7	5.57	4.96	4.18	4.18	4.18	4.18	3.43	3.43	3.43	x

The $10(10 - 1)/2 = 45$ subsets defined by objects contiguous in the object ordering used to display the upper-triangular portion of Table 9.1 are listed in Table 9.2 according to increasing diameter values. For purposes of our later discussion, 22 of the subsets are given in italics to indicate that they are proper subsets of another listed subset having the same diameter. Substantively, the dominant patterning of the entries in A_{ut} appears to reflect (primarily) digit magnitude, except for the placement of digit 4 next to 2 and digit 7 being located in the last position. Both these latter deviations from an interpretation strictly according to digit magnitude show some of the salient structural properties of the digits. For example, the digit pair (2,4) has the absolute smallest dissimilarity in the data; besides being relatively close in magnitude, there are the possible (although redundant) similarity bases that $2 + 2 = 4$, $2 \times 2 = 4$, 4 is a power of 2, and both 2 and 4 are even numbers. Similarly, the placement of the digit 7 in the last position results from the salience of the triple $\{6, 8, 9\}$, which is the third to emerge according to its diameter. In addition to these three digits all being relatively close in magnitude, 6 and 8 are both even numbers, 6 and 9 are multiples of 3, and 8 is directly adjacent in size to 9. The three original dissimilarities within the set $\{6, 8, 9\}$ are all smaller than the dissimilarities digit 7 has to *any* other digit.

Given just the collection of subsets $S_1, \ldots, S_M$ listed in Table 9.2 and their associated diameters, it is possible (trivially) to reconstruct the original approximating matrix A_{ut} by identifying for each object pair the smallest diameter for a subset that contains that pair. (Explicitly, the smallest diameter for a subset that contains an object pair is equal to the value in A_{ut} associated with that pair, and the subset itself includes that object pair and all objects in between in the ordering that is used to display the AR form for A_{ut}.) This type of reconstruction is generally possible for any matrix that can be row/column reordered to an AR form through the collection of subsets $S_1, \ldots, S_M$ and their diameters identified by increasing a threshold variable from the smallest fitted value. In fact, even if all the italicized subsets were removed (that are proper subsets of another having the same diameter), exactly the same reconstruction could be carried out because the italicized subsets are redundant

Table 9.2. *The 45 subsets listed according to increasing diameter values that are contiguous in the object ordering used to display the upper-triangular portion of Table 9.1. The 22 subsets given in italics are redundant in the sense that they are proper subsets of another listed subset with the same diameter.*

Subset	Diameter
{2,4}	1.63
{1,2}	2.73
{6,8},{8,9},{6,8,9}	3.04
{3,5},{5,6},{3,5,6}	3.18
{4,3},{2,4,3}	3.22
{4,3,5},{4,3,5,6}	3.30
{0,1}	3.41
{9,7},{8,9,7},{6,8,9,7}	3.43
{5,6,8},{5,6,8,9},{5,6,8,9,7}	3.76
{3,5,6,8},{3,5,6,8,9}	3.76
{4,3,5,6,8},{2,4,3,5},{2,4,3,5,6},{2,4,3,5,6,8}	3.76
{1,2,4},{1,2,4,3}	3.78
{0,1,2}	4.21
{1,2,4,3,5}	4.23
{3,5,6,8,9,7}	4.25
{0,1,2,4},{4,3,5,6,8,9}	4.70
{0,1,2,4,3}	4.83
{1,2,4,3,5,6},{1,2,4,3,5,6,8}	4.96
{1,2,4,3,5,6,8,9},{2,4,3,5,6,8,9}	4.96
{2,4,3,5,6,8,9,7},{4,3,5,6,8,9,7}	4.96
{1,2,4,3,5,6,8,9,7}	4.96
{0,1,2,4,3,5},{0,1,2,4,3,5,6}	5.25
{0,1,2,4,3,5,6,8}	5.38
{0,1,2,4,3,5,6,8,9}	5.52
{0,1,2,4,3,5,6,8,9,7}	5.81

with respect to identifying for each object pair the smallest diameter for a subset that contains the pair.

Without imposing further restrictions on the approximating matrix other than just being AR, a more convenient representation using a graph and path lengths in such a graph is generally not possible. We will select two small (AR) submatrices from the upper-triangular portion of Table 9.1 to make this point more convincingly and in the process indicate by example how a graphical representation is to be constructed and why further restrictions on the approximating matrix may be necessary to carry out the task.

First, consider the fitted values for the first four placed digits, 0, 1, 2, and 4 in Figure 9.1(a), for which the desired type of graphical representation *is* possible without imposing any further constraints. This AR submatrix is given in Figure 9.1(a) along with

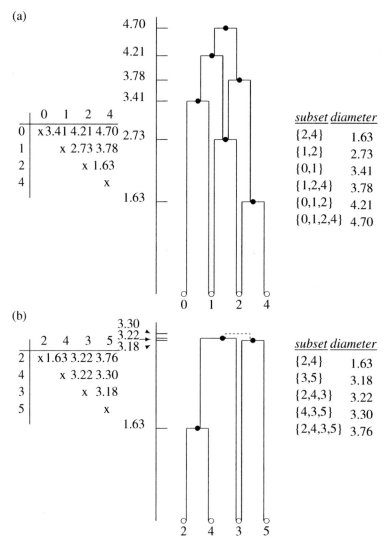

Figure 9.1. *Two 4 × 4 submatrices and the object subsets they induce, taken from the AR matrix in the upper-triangular portion of Table 9.1. For (a), a graphical representation of the fitted values is possible; for (b), the anomaly indicated by the dashed lines prevents a consistent graphical representation from being constructed.*

the six corresponding subsets of contiguous objects and their diameters and a graphical representation for the structure. The latter consists of four nodes corresponding to the original four objects that we represent by open circles (referred to as "terminal" nodes) plus six nodes represented by solid circles that denote the six subsets in the given listing (referred to as "internal" nodes). Based on this graph and the internal node heights provided by the calibrated scale on the left, a fitted value in the submatrix between any two terminal nodes can be obtained as one-half the length of the minimum path from one of the terminal nodes up to an internal node and back down to the other terminal node. All horizontal line segments are used here for display convenience only and are not actually assumed to contribute to the length of any path. Thus, if we changed the vertical scaling by a multiplier of 1/2, each of the fitted values in the submatrix would be exactly the length of the minimum path between two terminal nodes, which proceeded upward from one such node to an internal node and then back down to the other. We might also note that from the topmost internal node, all paths down to the terminal nodes have exactly the same length; i.e., there is an internal node equidistant from all terminal nodes.

Now, consider the fitted values for the four objects placed, respectively, at the third through sixth positions: 2, 4, 3, and 5, given in Figure 9.1(b) along with the corresponding subsets of contiguous objects and their diameters (excluding the redundant subset {4,3} which is a proper subset of {2,4,3} having the same diameter), and the beginnings of a graphical representation for its structure. There is a difficulty encountered, however, in defining a graph that would be completely consistent with all the fitted values in the 4×4 submatrix; we indicate this anomaly by the dashed vertical and horizontal lines. If an internal node were to be placed at the level of 3.30 to represent the cluster {4, 3, 5}, by implication the fitted value for the digit pair (2,5) should also be 3.30 (and not its current value of 3.76). Because digit 3 was "joined" to *both* 2 and 4 at the threshold level 3.22, and thus there are two fitted values tied at 3.22, a consistent graphical representation would be possible only if the fitted values for the pairs (2,5) and (4,5) were equal. *This last observation, that when some fitted values are tied in an approximating matrix* A_{ut} *others must also be tied to allow for the construction of a consistent graphical representation, is the motivating basis for considering an additional set of SAR constraints.*

When a graphical representation that permits their reconstruction through path lengths is desired for the collection of fitted values in an approximating matrix A, the small illustration just provided serves as justification for imposing a stricter collection of constraints on the approximating matrix than just being row/column reorderable to an AR form. In particular, the additional restriction will be imposed that the approximating matrix A is row/column reorderable to one that is SAR, which will eliminate the type of graphical anomaly present in Figure 9.1(b).

For the SAR approximation given in the lower-triangular portion of Table 9.1, there are now only fourteen (nonredundant) subsets identifiable by increasing a threshold variable from the smallest fitted value; these are listed in Table 9.3 along with their diameters.

Table 9.3. *The fourteen (nonredundant) subsets listed according to increasing diameter values are contiguous in the linear object ordering used to display the lower-triangular SAR portion of Table 9.1.*

Subset	Diameter	Subset	Diameter
{2,4}	1.63	{2,4,3,5,6}	3.53
{1,2}	2.73	{1,2,4,3}	3.78
{6,8,9}	3.04	{2,4,3,5,6,8,9,7}	4.18
{3,5,6}	3.18	{0,1,2}	4.21
{2,4,3}	3.22	{0,1,2,4,3}	4.76
{0,1}	3.41	{0,1,2,4,3,5,6}	5.25
{6,8,9,7}	3.43	{0,1,2,4,3,5,6,8,9,7}	5.57

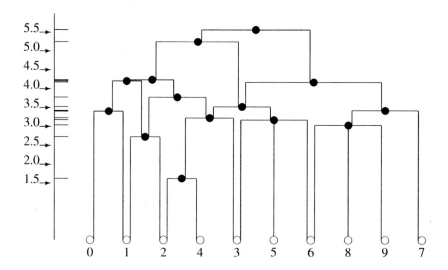

Figure 9.2. *A graphical representation for the fitted values given by the SAR matrix in the lower-triangular portion of Table 9.1.*

The imposition of the more restrictive SAR constraints allows the graphical representation given in Figure 9.2. Although we might not change our substantive comments about the approximating matrix (i.e., mostly digit magnitude with some structural characteristics for the subsets {2, 4} and {6, 8, 9}), a graphical representation makes these same observations visually clearer.

9.6   Representation Through Multiple (Strongly) AR Matrices

The representation of a proximity matrix by a single AR structure extends easily to the additive use of multiple matrices. The M-function `biarobfnd.m` fits the sum of two AR matrices using iterative projection to a symmetric proximity matrix in the L_2-norm based on permutations identified through the use of iterative QA. The usage syntax is

```
[find,vaf,targone,targtwo,outpermone,outpermtwo] = ...
biarobfnd(prox,inperm,kblock)
```

where, as before, PROX is the input proximity matrix ($n \times n$ with a zero main diagonal and a dissimilarity interpretation); INPERM is a given starting permutation of the first n integers; FIND is the least-squares optimal matrix (with variance-accounted-for of VAF) to PROX and is the sum of the two AR matrices TARGONE and TARGTWO based on the two row and column object orderings given by the ending permutations OUTPERMONE and OUTPERMTWO. As before, KBLOCK defines the block size in the use of the iterative QA routine.

In the example below, the two resulting AR forms are very clearly interpretable as number magnitude and digit structural properties; the VAF is, in effect, 100%.

```
load number.dat
[find,vaf,targone,targtwo,outpermone,outpermtwo] = ...
biarobfnd(number,1:10,1)


find =

  Columns 1 through 6

         0    0.4209    0.5840    0.7090    0.6840    0.8040
    0.4209         0    0.2840    0.3460    0.6460    0.5880
    0.5840    0.2840         0    0.3540    0.0588    0.6702
    0.7090    0.3460    0.3540         0    0.4130    0.4290
    0.6840    0.6460    0.0588    0.4130         0    0.4094
    0.8040    0.5880    0.6702    0.4290    0.4094         0
    0.7865    0.7568    0.4225    0.3000    0.3880    0.3960
    0.9107    0.6300    0.7960    0.5920    0.7420    0.4000
    0.8210    0.7975    0.3672    0.7975    0.2460    0.6714
    0.8500    0.6250    0.8080    0.2630    0.6829    0.5920

  Columns 7 through 10

    0.7865    0.9107    0.8210    0.8500
    0.7568    0.6300    0.7975    0.6250
    0.4225    0.7960    0.3672    0.8080
    0.3000    0.5920    0.7975    0.2630
    0.3880    0.7420    0.2460    0.6829
    0.3960    0.4000    0.6714    0.5920
         0    0.4169    0.3499    0.2960
    0.4169         0    0.4000    0.4587
    0.3499    0.4000         0    0.3922
    0.2960    0.4587    0.3922         0


vaf =

    0.9999


targone =

  Columns 1 through 6
```

0	0.3406	0.6710	0.6926	0.6956	0.6956
0.3406	0	0.2018	0.5421	0.5423	0.5880
0.6710	0.2018	0	0.3333	0.3680	0.4662
0.6926	0.5421	0.3333	0	0.3093	0.3206
0.6956	0.5423	0.3680	0.3093	0	0.2055
0.6956	0.5880	0.4662	0.3206	0.2055	0
0.8303	0.6764	0.4662	0.3779	0.3779	0.2876
0.8303	0.6764	0.6764	0.6764	0.6383	0.4675
0.8303	0.7511	0.7138	0.6764	0.6383	0.4745
0.8611	0.7943	0.7943	0.6764	0.6690	0.4836

Columns 7 through 10

0.8303	0.8303	0.8303	0.8611
0.6764	0.6764	0.7511	0.7943
0.4662	0.6764	0.7138	0.7943
0.3779	0.6764	0.6764	0.6764
0.3779	0.6383	0.6383	0.6690
0.2876	0.4675	0.4745	0.4836
0	0.3360	0.3366	0.3849
0.3360	0	0.2243	0.3783
0.3366	0.2243	0	0.3783
0.3849	0.3783	0.3783	0

targtwo =

Columns 1 through 6

0	-0.3923	-0.3092	-0.0093	0.0139	0.0139
-0.3923	0	-0.3092	-0.0116	0.0101	0.0139
-0.3092	-0.3092	0	-0.0870	-0.0438	0.0137
-0.0093	-0.0116	-0.0870	0	-0.0438	-0.0111
0.0139	0.0101	-0.0438	-0.0438	0	-0.0889
0.0139	0.0139	0.0137	-0.0111	-0.0889	0
0.1211	0.1037	0.0207	0.0164	-0.0779	-0.4134
0.1211	0.1037	0.0822	0.0804	0.0804	-0.1693
0.1757	0.1037	0.0822	0.0804	0.0804	0.0804
0.2039	0.2039	0.2039	0.1084	0.1084	0.1084

Columns 7 through 10

0.1211	0.1211	0.1757	0.2039
0.1037	0.1037	0.1037	0.2039
0.0207	0.0822	0.0822	0.2039
0.0164	0.0804	0.0804	0.1084

```
     -0.0779      0.0804      0.0804      0.1084
     -0.4134     -0.1693      0.0804      0.1084
           0     -0.1961     -0.0844      0.1084
     -0.1961           0     -0.1211           0
     -0.0844     -0.1211           0     -0.0745
      0.1084           0     -0.0745           0
```

```
outpermone =

    1     2     3     4     5     6     7     9     8    10
```

```
outpermtwo =

    9     5     3     1     7    10     4     2     8     6
```

For finding multiple SAR forms, bisarobfnd.m has usage syntax

```
[find,vaf,targone,targtwo,outpermone,outpermtwo] = ...
bisarobfnd(prox,inperm,kblock)
```

with all the various terms the same as for biarobfnd.m but now for SAR structures. The example below finds essentially the same representation as above (involving digit magnitude and structure) with a slight drop in the VAF to 99.06%.

```
[find,vaf,targone,targtwo,outpermone,outpermtwo] = ...
bisarobfnd(number,randperm(10),1)
```

```
find =

  Columns 1 through 6

          0      0.4210      0.5840      0.7095      0.6838      0.8519
     0.4210           0      0.2840      0.3460      0.6461      0.5892
     0.5840      0.2840           0      0.3541      0.0590      0.6090
     0.7095      0.3460      0.3541           0      0.4131      0.4278
     0.6838      0.6461      0.0590      0.4131           0      0.4090
     0.8519      0.5892      0.6090      0.4278      0.4090           0
     0.7260      0.7565      0.4830      0.3005      0.3882      0.3960
     0.8998      0.6153      0.8059      0.6067      0.7286      0.4000
     0.8208      0.8246      0.3670      0.7893      0.2460      0.6711
     0.8736      0.6250      0.7797      0.2630      0.6965      0.5920

  Columns 7 through 10

     0.7260      0.8998      0.8208      0.8736
     0.7565      0.6153      0.8246      0.6250
```

```
     0.4830      0.8059      0.3670      0.7797
     0.3005      0.6067      0.7893      0.2630
     0.3882      0.7286      0.2460      0.6965
     0.3960      0.4000      0.6711      0.5920
          0      0.4168      0.3502      0.2955
     0.4168           0      0.4000      0.4590
     0.3502      0.4000           0      0.3921
     0.2955      0.4590      0.3921           0
```

vaf =

```
     0.9906
```

targone =

  Columns 1 through 6

```
          0      0.3148      0.6038      0.6296      0.6296      0.7457
     0.3148           0      0.1778      0.5201      0.5201      0.6626
     0.6038      0.1778           0      0.2742      0.3230      0.5028
     0.6296      0.5201      0.2742           0      0.3192      0.5012
     0.6296      0.5201      0.3230      0.3192           0      0.2831
     0.7457      0.6626      0.5028      0.5012      0.2831           0
     0.7457      0.6626      0.5028      0.5012      0.3340      0.3021
     0.7936      0.7061      0.6997      0.6974      0.6027      0.5526
     0.7936      0.7061      0.6997      0.6974      0.6027      0.5526
     0.7936      0.7061      0.6997      0.6974      0.6027      0.5527
```

  Columns 7 through 10

```
     0.7457      0.7936      0.7936      0.7936
     0.6626      0.7061      0.7061      0.7061
     0.5028      0.6997      0.6997      0.6997
     0.5012      0.6974      0.6974      0.6974
     0.3340      0.6027      0.6027      0.6027
     0.3021      0.5526      0.5526      0.5527
          0      0.3229      0.3229      0.4963
     0.3229           0      0.2815      0.4197
     0.3229      0.2815           0      0.3001
     0.4963      0.4197      0.3001           0
```

targtwo =

Columns 1 through 6

```
        0    -0.3567    -0.2640     0.0542     0.0542     0.0938
  -0.3567          0    -0.3327     0.0272     0.0272     0.0919
  -0.2640    -0.3327          0    -0.0198    -0.0198     0.0799
   0.0542     0.0272    -0.0198          0    -0.0198     0.0799
   0.0542     0.0272    -0.0198    -0.0198          0    -0.2008
   0.0938     0.0919     0.0799     0.0799    -0.2008          0
   0.0938     0.0919     0.0799     0.0799    -0.2008    -0.4344
   0.1260     0.1185     0.1062     0.1062     0.0939    -0.0811
   0.1260     0.1185     0.1062     0.1062     0.0939     0.0393
   0.1260     0.1185     0.1062     0.1062     0.0939     0.0393
```

Columns 7 through 10

```
   0.0938     0.1260     0.1260     0.1260
   0.0919     0.1185     0.1185     0.1185
   0.0799     0.1062     0.1062     0.1062
   0.0799     0.1062     0.1062     0.1062
  -0.2008     0.0939     0.0939     0.0939
  -0.4344    -0.0811     0.0393     0.0393
        0    -0.1741    -0.0907    -0.0734
  -0.1741          0    -0.0907    -0.0734
  -0.0907    -0.0907          0    -0.1526
  -0.0734    -0.0734    -0.1526          0
```

outpermone =

```
    1     2     3     4     5     6     7     8     9    10
```

outpermtwo =

```
    5     9     3     1     7    10     4     2     8     6
```

Chapter 10

Circular Anti-Robinson Matrices for Symmetric Proximity Data

In the approximation of a proximity matrix $\mathbf{P}$ by one that is row/column reorderable to an AR form, the interpretation of the fitted matrix in general had to be carried out by identifying a set of subsets through an increasing threshold variable; each of the subsets contained objects that were contiguous with respect to a given *linear* ordering along a continuum and had a diameter defined by the maximum fitted value within the subset. To provide a further representation depicting the fitted values as lengths of paths in a graph, an approximation was sought that satisfied the additional constraints of an SAR matrix; still, the subsets thus identified had to contain objects contiguous with respect to a linear ordering. As one possible generalization of both the AR and SAR constraints, we can define what will be called circular anti-Robinson (CAR) and circular strongly anti-Robinson (CSAR) forms that allow the subsets identified from increasing a threshold variable to be contiguous with respect to a *circular* ordering of the objects around a closed continuum. Approximation matrices that are row/column reorderable to display an AR or SAR form, respectively, will also be (trivially) row/column reorderable to display what is formally characterized below as a CAR or a CSAR form but not conversely. (Historically, there is a large literature on the possibility of circular structures emerging from and being identifiable in a given proximity matrix. For a variety of references, the reader is referred to the American Psychological Association sponsored volume edited by Plutchik and Conte (1997), the discussion of metric circular unidimensional scaling (CUS) in Part I, Chapter 3, and in Hubert, Arabie, and Meulman (1997). The extension of CAR forms to those that are also CSAR, however, has apparently not been a topic discussed in the literature before the appearance of Hubert, Arabie, and Meulman (1998); this latter source forms the basis for much of the present chapter.)

To be explicit, an arbitrary symmetric matrix $\mathbf{Q} = \{q_{ij}\}$, where $q_{ii} = 0$ for $1 \leq i, j \leq n$, is said to be row/column reorderable to a CAR form (or, for short, $\mathbf{Q}$ is a CAR matrix) if there exists a permutation, $\rho(\cdot)$, on the first n integers such that the reordered matrix $\mathbf{Q}_\rho = \{q_{\rho(i)\rho(j)}\}$ satisfies the conditions given in (II):

(II): for $1 \leq i \leq n - 3$ and $i + 1 < j \leq n - 1$,

if $q_{\rho(i+1)\rho(j)} \leq q_{\rho(i)\rho(j+1)}$, then
$q_{\rho(i+1)\rho(j)} \leq q_{\rho(i)\rho(j)}$ and $q_{\rho(i+1)\rho(j)} \leq q_{\rho(i+1)\rho(j+1)}$;

143

if $q_{\rho(i+1)\rho(j)} \geq q_{\rho(i)\rho(j+1)}$, then
$q_{\rho(i)\rho(j)} \geq q_{\rho(i)\rho(j+1)}$ and $q_{\rho(i+1)\rho(j+1)} \geq q_{\rho(i)\rho(j+1)}$;
and, for $2 \leq i \leq n-2$,

if $q_{\rho(i+1)\rho(n)} \leq q_{\rho(i)\rho(1)}$, then
$q_{\rho(i+1)\rho(n)} \leq q_{\rho(i)\rho(n)}$ and $q_{\rho(i+1)\rho(n)} \leq q_{\rho(i+1)\rho(1)}$;
if $q_{\rho(i+1)\rho(n)} \geq q_{\rho(i)\rho(1)}$, then
$q_{\rho(i)\rho(n)} \geq q_{\rho(i)\rho(1)}$ and $q_{\rho(i+1)\rho(1)} \geq q_{\rho(i)\rho(1)}$.

Interpretatively, within each row of $\mathbf{Q}_\rho$ moving to the right from the main diagonal and then wrapping back around to reenter the same row from the left, the entries never decrease until a maximum is reached and then never increase moving away from the maximum until the main diagonal is again reached. Given the symmetry of $\mathbf{P}$, a similar pattern of entries would be present within each column as well. As noted above, any AR matrix is CAR but not conversely.

In analogy to the SAR conditions that permit graphical representation, a symmetric matrix $\mathbf{Q}$ is said to be row/column reorderable to a CSAR form (or, for short, $\mathbf{Q}$ is a CSAR matrix) if there exists a permutation, $\rho(\cdot)$, on the first n integers such that the reordered matrix $\mathbf{Q}_\rho = \{q_{\rho(i)\rho(j)}\}$ satisfies the conditions given by (II), *and*

for $1 \leq i \leq n-3$ and $i+1 < j \leq n-1$,

if $q_{\rho(i+1)\rho(j)} \leq q_{\rho(i)\rho(j+1)}$,
then $q_{\rho(i+1)\rho(j)} = q_{\rho(i)\rho(j)}$ implies $q_{\rho(i+1)\rho(j+1)} = q_{\rho(i)\rho(j+1)}$, and $q_{\rho(i+1)\rho(j)} = q_{\rho(i+1)\rho(j+1)}$ implies $q_{\rho(i)\rho(j)} = q_{\rho(i)\rho(j+1)}$;

if $q_{\rho(i+1)\rho(j)} \geq q_{\rho(i)\rho(j+1)}$,
then $q_{\rho(i)\rho(j+1)} = q_{\rho(i+1)\rho(j+1)}$ implies $q_{\rho(i)\rho(j)} = q_{\rho(i+1)\rho(j)}$, and $q_{\rho(i)\rho(j)} = q_{\rho(i)\rho(j+1)}$ implies $q_{\rho(i+1)\rho(j)} = q_{\rho(i+1)\rho(j+1)}$;

and for $2 \leq i \leq n-2$,

if $q_{\rho(i+1)\rho(n)} \leq q_{\rho(i)\rho(1)}$, then $q_{\rho(i+1)\rho(n)} = q_{\rho(i)\rho(n)}$ implies $q_{\rho(i+1)\rho(1)} = q_{\rho(i)\rho(1)}$, and $q_{\rho(i+1)\rho(n)} = q_{\rho(i+1)\rho(1)}$ implies $q_{\rho(i)\rho(n)} = q_{\rho(i)\rho(1)}$;

if $q_{\rho(i+1)\rho(n)} \geq q_{\rho(i)\rho(1)}$, then $q_{\rho(i)\rho(1)} = q_{\rho(i+1)\rho(1)}$ implies $q_{\rho(i)\rho(n)} = q_{\rho(i+1)\rho(n)}$, and $q_{\rho(i)\rho(n)} = q_{\rho(i)\rho(1)}$ implies $q_{\rho(i+1)\rho(n)} = q_{\rho(i+1)\rho(1)}$.

Again, the imposition of the stronger CSAR conditions avoids the type of graphical anomaly present in Figure 9.1(b) but now in the context of a CAR matrix—when two fitted values that are adjacent within a row are equal, the fitted values in the same two adjacent columns must also be equal for a row that is either its immediate predecessor (if $q_{\rho(i+1)\rho(j)} \leq q_{\rho(i)\rho(j+1)}$) or successor (if $q_{\rho(i+1)\rho(j)} \geq q_{\rho(i)\rho(j+1)}$); a similar condition is imposed when two fitted values that are adjacent within a column are equal. As noted, any SAR matrix is CSAR but not conversely.

The computational strategy we suggest for identifying a best-fitting CAR or CSAR approximation matrix is based on an initial CUS obtained through the optimization strategy developed by Hubert, Arabie, and Meulman (1997) that is reviewed in Part I, Chapter 3. Specifically, we first institute a combination of combinatorial search for good matrix reorderings and heuristic iterative projection to locate the points of inflection when minimum distance calculations change directionality around a closed circular structure. Approximation matrices to $\mathbf{P}$ are found through a least-squares loss criterion, and they have the parameterized form

$$\mathbf{Q}_\rho = \{\min(|\ x_{\rho(j)} - x_{\rho(i)}\ |,\ x_0 - |\ x_{\rho(j)} - x_{\rho(i)}\ |) + c\},$$

where c is an estimated additive constant, $x_{\rho(1)} \leq x_{\rho(2)} \leq \cdots \leq x_{\rho(n)} \leq x_0$, and the last coordinate, x_0, is the circumference of the circular structure. Based on the inequality constraints implied by such a collection of coordinates, a CAR approximation matrix can be fitted to **P** directly; then, beginning with this latter CAR approximation, the identification and imposition of CSAR constraints proceeds through the heuristic use of iterative projection, directly analogous to the way SAR constraints in the linear ordering context were identified and fitted, beginning with a best approximation matrix satisfying just the AR restrictions.

10.1 Fitting a Given CAR Matrix in the L_2-Norm

The function M-file `cirarobfit.m` fits a CAR matrix using iterative projection to a symmetric proximity matrix in the L_2-norm. Usage syntax is

```
[fit, vaf] = cirarobfit(prox,inperm,targ)
```

where PROX is the input proximity matrix ($n \times n$ with a zero main diagonal and a dissimilarity interpretation); INPERM is a given permutation of the first n integers (around a circle); TARG is a given $n \times n$ matrix having the CAR form that guides the direction in which distances are taken around the circle. The matrix FIT is the least-squares optimal approximation (with variance-accounted-for of VAF) to PROX having a CAR form for the row and column object ordering given by INPERM.

A recording of a MATLAB session follows that uses the `number.dat` data file, an equally spaced CAR matrix `targcircular` obtained from the utility M-file `targcir.m` first introduced in Part I, and the identity permutation for the objects around the circular structure. The fitted CAR matrix thus identified in this way has a VAF of 64.37%.

```
load number.dat
targcircular = targcir(10);
[fit vaf] = cirarobfit(number,1:10,targcircular)

fit =

  Columns 1 through 6

        0     0.4210    0.5840    0.6510    0.6835    0.8040
   0.4210         0    0.2840    0.3460    0.6170    0.6170
   0.5840    0.2840         0    0.2753    0.2753    0.5460
   0.6510    0.3460    0.2753         0    0.2753    0.3844
   0.6835    0.6170    0.2753    0.2753         0    0.3844
   0.8040    0.6170    0.5460    0.3844    0.3844         0
   0.7730    0.7730    0.5460    0.3844    0.3844    0.3844
   0.7695    0.7695    0.7960    0.5920    0.5530    0.4000
   0.6597    0.6597    0.6597    0.8040    0.5530    0.5530
```

```
   0.6510      0.6510      0.6510      0.6510      0.6835      0.5920

Columns 7 through 10

   0.7730      0.7695      0.6597      0.6510
   0.7730      0.7695      0.6597      0.6510
   0.5460      0.7960      0.6597      0.6510
   0.3844      0.5920      0.8040      0.6510
   0.3844      0.5530      0.5530      0.6835
   0.3844      0.4000      0.5530      0.5920
        0      0.3857      0.3857      0.3857
   0.3857           0      0.3857      0.3857
   0.3857      0.3857           0      0.3857
   0.3857      0.3857      0.3857           0
```

vaf =

```
   0.6437
```

10.2   Finding a CAR Matrix in the L_2-Norm

The M-file cirarobfnd.m is our suggested strategy for identifying a best-fitting CAR matrix for a symmetric proximity matrix in the L_2-norm based on a permutation that is initially identified through the use of iterative quadratic assignment (QA). Based on an equally spaced circular target matrix, order.m is first invoked to obtain a good (circular) permutation, which in turn is then used to construct a new circular target matrix with cirfit.m. (We will mention here but not illustrate with an example an alternative to the use of cirarobfnd.m called cirarobfnd_ac.m; the latter M-file has the same syntax as cirarobfnd.m but uses cirfitac.m rather than cirfit.m internally to obtain the new circular target matrices.) The final output is generated from cirarobfit.m that no better permutation can be identified using the newer circular target matrix. The usage syntax for cirarobfnd.m is as follows:

```
[find, vaf, outperm] = cirarobfnd(prox, inperm, kblock)
```

where PROX is the input proximity matrix ($n \times n$ with a zero main diagonal and a dissimilarity interpretation); INPERM is a given starting permutation (assumed to be around the circle) of the first n integers; FIND is the least-squares optimal matrix (with variance-accounted-for of VAF) to PROX having a CAR form for the row and column object ordering given by the concluding permutation OUTPERM. Again, KBLOCK defines the block size in the use of the iterative QA routine.

An example of the use of cirarobfnd.m is given below that seems to lead to a circular ordering best interpreted according to the structural properties of the digits. This solution is only one of several local optima identifiable by repeated application of the routine using other random starting permutations. In general, the different local optima observed differ in the way the odd digits, $\{3, 5, 7, 9\}$, and the even digits, $\{2, 4, 6, 8\}$, are ordered within these sets when moving clockwise around a circular structure. Explicitly, all local optima had a general structure of $\to 0 \to 1 \to \{3, 5, 7, 9\} \to \{2, 4, 6, 8\} \to$ but with some variation in order within the odd and even digits. For example, the CAR matrix given below uses the odd digits as $\to 3 \to 5 \to 9 \to 7 \to$ and the even digits as $\to 6 \to 8 \to 4 \to 2 \to$.

```
[find, vaf, outperm] = cirarobfnd(number, randperm(10), 3)

find =

   Columns 1 through 6

        0      0.3460    0.5315    0.5315    0.6069    0.8040
     0.3460       0      0.4210    0.4340    0.6069    0.7895
     0.5315    0.4210       0      0.4340    0.6069    0.7895
     0.5315    0.4340    0.4340       0      0.0590    0.3670
     0.6069    0.6069    0.6069    0.0590       0      0.2460
     0.8040    0.7895    0.7895    0.3670    0.2460       0
     0.4460    0.7895    0.7895    0.4210    0.3880    0.3500
     0.4460    0.6300    0.9090    0.7697    0.6069    0.3960
     0.4160    0.6250    0.8500    0.7698    0.6069    0.3960
     0.4160    0.5880    0.7698    0.7698    0.6069    0.6069

   Columns 7 through 10

     0.4460    0.4460    0.4160    0.4160
     0.7895    0.6300    0.6250    0.5880
     0.7895    0.9090    0.8500    0.7698
     0.4210    0.7697    0.7698    0.7698
     0.3880    0.6069    0.6069    0.6069
     0.3500    0.3960    0.3960    0.6069
        0      0.3907    0.3907    0.4160
     0.3907       0      0.3907    0.4160
     0.3907    0.3907       0      0.4160
     0.4160    0.4160    0.4160       0


vaf =

     0.8128


outperm =

     4     2     1     3     5     9     7     8    10     6
```

10.3   Finding a CSAR Matrix in the L_2-Norm

The two M-functions `cirsarobfit.m` and `cirsarobfnd.m` are direct analogues of `cirarobfit.m` and `cirarobfnd.m`, respectively but are concerned with fitting and finding *strongly* CAR forms (also, we mention but do not illustrate the M-file `cirsarobfnd_ac.m`, which uses `cirarobfnd_ac.m` to obtain the initial CAR matrix that is then strengthened into one that is CSAR). The syntax for `cirsarobfit.m`, which fits a CSAR matrix using iterative projection to a symmetric proximity matrix in the L_2-norm, is

```
[fit, vaf] = cirsarobfit(prox, inperm, targ)
```

where, again, PROX is the input proximity matrix ($n \times n$ with a zero main diagonal and a dissimilarity interpretation); INPERM is a given permutation of the first n integers; TARG is a given $n \times n$ matrix having the CAR form that guides the direction in which distances are taken around the circle. FIT is the least-squares optimal matrix (with variance-accounted-for of VAF) to PROX having a strongly CAR form for the row and column object ordering given by INPERM.

An example follows using the same identity permutation as in fitting a CAR form with `cirarobfit.m`; as might be expected from using the more restrictive CSAR form, the variance-accounted-for drops to .4501 from .6437.

```
[fit, vaf] = cirsarobfit(number,1:10,targcircular)

fit =

  Columns 1 through 6

         0      0.4210    0.5840    0.6505    0.6505    0.6505
    0.4210         0      0.2840    0.6505    0.6505    0.6505
    0.5840    0.2840         0      0.2753    0.2753    0.4306
    0.6505    0.6505    0.2753         0      0.2753    0.4306
    0.6505    0.6505    0.2753    0.2753         0      0.4306
    0.6505    0.6505    0.4306    0.4306    0.4306         0
    0.6505    0.6505    0.4306    0.4306    0.4306    0.4306
    0.6505    0.6505    0.6505    0.6505    0.6505    0.6505
    0.6505    0.6505    0.6505    0.6505    0.6505    0.6505
    0.6505    0.6505    0.6505    0.6505    0.6505    0.6505

  Columns 7 through 10

    0.6505    0.6505    0.6505    0.6505
    0.6505    0.6505    0.6505    0.6505
    0.4306    0.6505    0.6505    0.6505
    0.4306    0.6505    0.6505    0.6505
    0.4306    0.6505    0.6505    0.6505
    0.4306    0.6505    0.6505    0.6505
```

```
        0      0.3857    0.3857    0.3857
     0.3857       0      0.3857    0.3857
     0.3857    0.3857       0      0.3857
     0.3857    0.3857    0.3857       0
```

vaf =

    0.4501

The M-function `cirsarobfnd.m` finds and fits a CSAR matrix using iterative projection
to a symmetric proximity matrix in the L_2-norm based on a permutation identified through
the use of iterative QA. It has the expected syntax

```
[find, vaf, outperm] = cirsarobfnd(prox, inperm, kblock)
```

where, again, PROX is the input proximity matrix ($n \times n$ with a zero main diagonal and a
dissimilarity interpretation); INPERM is a given starting permutation of the first n integers;
FIND is the least-squares optimal matrix (with variance-accounted-for of VAF) to PROX
having a CSAR form for the row and column object ordering given by the ending permutation
OUTPERM. As usual, KBLOCK defines the block size in the use of the iterative QA routine.
(Analogous to the last section, and as noted above, an alternative to `cirsarobfnd.m`
is available, called `cirsarobfnd_ac.m`, that uses `cirfitac.m` to obtain the circular
target matrices.)

    In the MATLAB recording below, and starting from a random permutation, a CSAR
form was found with a VAF of .7296 (again, this represents an expected drop from the value
of .8119 for the CAR form—this result is also listed below).

```
[find, vaf, outperm] = cirsarobfnd(number,randperm(10), 2)
```

target =

    Columns 1 through 6

```
        0      0.4160    0.4160    0.4160    0.6262    0.6262
     0.4160       0      0.3907    0.3907    0.3960    0.6263
     0.4160    0.3907       0      0.3907    0.3960    0.6263
     0.4160    0.3907    0.3907       0      0.3500    0.3880
     0.6262    0.3960    0.3960    0.3500       0      0.2460
     0.6262    0.6263    0.6263    0.3880    0.2460       0
     0.7858    0.7858    0.7858    0.4210    0.3670    0.0590
     0.7858    0.7858    0.9090    0.7895    0.7895    0.5810
     0.5880    0.6250    0.6300    0.7895    0.7895    0.5810
     0.4160    0.4160    0.4460    0.4460    0.8040    0.5810
```

    Columns 7 through 10

```
     0.7858    0.7858    0.5880    0.4160
```

```
    0.7858       0.7858       0.6250       0.4160
    0.7858       0.9090       0.6300       0.4460
    0.4210       0.7895       0.7895       0.4460
    0.3670       0.7895       0.7895       0.8040
    0.0590       0.5810       0.5810       0.5810
         0       0.4340       0.4340       0.5315
    0.4340            0       0.4210       0.5315
    0.4340       0.4210            0       0.3460
    0.5315       0.5315       0.3460            0
```

vaf =

    0.8119

outperm =

     6   10   8   7   9   5   3   1   2   4

find =

  Columns 1 through 6

```
         0       0.4246       0.4246       0.4246       0.7304       0.7304
    0.4246            0       0.3907       0.3907       0.3960       0.7304
    0.4246       0.3907            0       0.3907       0.3960       0.7304
    0.4246       0.3907       0.3907            0       0.3500       0.3880
    0.7304       0.3960       0.3960       0.3500            0       0.2460
    0.7304       0.7304       0.7304       0.3880       0.2460            0
    0.7304       0.7304       0.7304       0.4210       0.3670       0.0590
    0.7304       0.7304       0.7304       0.7304       0.7304       0.5810
    0.7304       0.7304       0.7304       0.7304       0.7304       0.5810
    0.4246       0.4246       0.4246       0.4246       0.7304       0.5810
```

  Columns 7 through 10

```
    0.7304       0.7304       0.7304       0.4246
    0.7304       0.7304       0.7304       0.4246
    0.7304       0.7304       0.7304       0.4246
    0.4210       0.7304       0.7304       0.4246
    0.3670       0.7304       0.7304       0.7304
    0.0590       0.5810       0.5810       0.5810
         0       0.4340       0.4340       0.5315
    0.4340            0       0.4210       0.5315
```

```
    0.4340      0.4210           0      0.3460
    0.5315      0.5315      0.3460           0
```

vaf =

     0.7296

outperm =

     6   10   8   7   9   5   3   1   2   4

10.4   Graphically Representing CSAR Structures

As in the case of an AR or SAR matrix, the interpretation of the structure that may be represented by a CAR or CSAR matrix could proceed by first identifying those subsets and their diameters that emerge by increasing a threshold variable from the smallest fitted value. And in the case of a more restrictive CSAR matrix, this collection of subsets and their diameters can then be displayed by a graph where minimum length paths reconstruct the fitted values. To illustrate this graphical possibility on the transformed number.dat to mean 4.0 and variance 1.0 given in Hubert, Arabie, and Meulman (1998)—and used earlier to show the graphical representation of an SAR matrix—the fifteen (nonredundant) subsets identified from the CSAR matrix present in Table 10.2 are listed in Table 10.1 according to increasing diameter. Here, the structural properties of the digits are apparent (e.g., various subsets of the odd or even digits or those that are multiples or powers of 2 or 3), but some magnitude adjacencies can also be noted (e.g., {6, 7, 8, 9} or subsets of {0, 1, 2, 3}). The graph adhering to the CSAR restrictions is given in Figure 10.1, and again minimum path lengths (that proceed up from a terminal node to an internal node and then back down to the other terminal node) can be used to reconstruct the fitted values in **Q**.

In addition to searching for a best-fitting CSAR matrix directly, we might comment that the type of indirect approach mentioned in the chapter introduction for the case of SAR approximations could also be considered, although we will not go into the details here. For example, based on a best-fitting CAR matrix, the additional constraints of a circular unidimensional scale could be identified and then imposed (in fact, this is our starting place in first obtaining the CAR approximation); or those of an ultrametric (which would lead to an SAR matrix that is trivially CSAR as well); or possibly a collection of additive tree restrictions could be identified. In all cases, CSAR approximations would be automatically obtained.

10.5   Representation Through Multiple (Strongly) CAR Matrices

Just as we discussed in Section 9.6 on representing of proximity matrices through multiple (strongly) AR matrices, the analysis of a proximity matrix by a single (strongly)

Table 10.1. *The fifteen (nonredundant) subsets listed according to increasing diameter values are contiguous in the circular object ordering used to display the CSAR entries in Table 10.2.*

Subset	Diameter	Subset	Diameter
{4,2}	1.63	{6,8,4,2}	3.41
{8,4}	2.55	{0,1}	3.41
{1,3}	3.04	{3,5,9,7,6}	3.43
{6,8}	3.06	{2,0,1}	3.47
{8,4,2}	3.14	{2,0,1,3}	3.95
{6,8,4}	3.25	{4,2,0,1,3}	4.20
{9,7,6}	3.26	{0,1,3,5,9,7,6,8,4,2}	4.93
{9,7,6,8}	3.29		

Table 10.2. *A CSAR order-constrained least-squares approximation to the digit proximity data of Shepard, Kilpatric, and Cunningham (1975).*

Digit	0	1	3	5	9	7	6	8	4	2
0	x	3.41	3.95	4.93	4.93	4.93	4.93	4.93	4.20	3.47
1	3.41	x	3.04	4.93	4.93	4.93	4.93	4.93	4.20	3.47
3	3.95	3.04	x	3.43	3.43	3.43	3.43	4.93	4.20	3.95
5	4.93	4.93	3.43	x	3.43	3.43	3.43	4.93	4.93	4.93
9	4.93	4.93	3.43	3.43	x	3.26	3.26	3.29	4.93	4.93
7	4.93	4.93	3.43	3.43	3.26	x	3.26	3.29	4.93	4.93
6	4.93	4.93	3.43	3.43	3.26	3.26	x	3.06	3.25	3.41
8	4.93	4.93	4.93	4.93	3.29	3.29	3.06	x	2.55	3.14
4	4.20	4.20	4.20	4.93	4.93	4.93	3.25	2.55	x	1.63
2	3.47	3.47	3.95	4.93	4.93	4.93	3.41	3.14	1.63	x

CAR structure extends easily to the additive use of multiple matrices. The M-function `bicirarobfnd.m` fits the sum of two CAR matrices using iterative projection to a symmetric proximity matrix in the L_2-norm based on permutations identified through the use of iterative QA. The syntax usage is

```
[find,vaf,targone,targtwo,outpermone,outpermtwo] = ...
bicirarobfnd(prox,inperm,kblock)
```

where, as before, PROX is the input proximity matrix ($n \times n$ with a zero main diagonal and a dissimilarity interpretation); INPERM is a given initial permutation of the first n integers; FIND is the least-squares optimal matrix (with variance-accounted-for of VAF) to PROX and is the sum of the two CAR matrices TARGONE and TARGTWO based on the two row and column object orderings given by the final permutations OUTPERMONE and OUTPERMTWO.

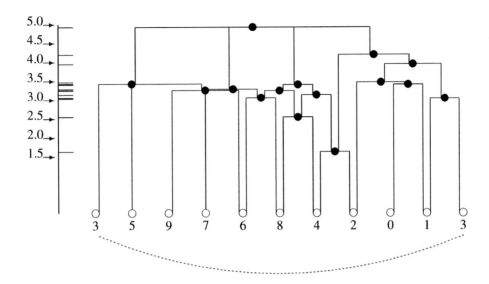

Figure 10.1. *A graphical representation for the fitted values given by the CSAR matrix in the lower-triangular portion of Table* 10.2 *(VAF = 72.96%). Note that digit 3 is placed both in the first and the last positions in the ordering of the objects with the implication that the sequence continues in a circular manner. This circularity is indicated by the curved dashed line.*

As before, KBLOCK defines the block size in the use of the iterative QA routine.

```
[find,vaf,targone,targtwo,outpermone,outpermtwo] = ...
bicirarobfnd(number,randperm(10),1)

find =

Columns 1 through 6

          0      0.4210     0.5632     0.7297     0.6840     0.8040
     0.4210          0     0.3048     0.3252     0.6460     0.5880
     0.5632     0.3048          0     0.3540     0.0380     0.6535
     0.7297     0.3252     0.3540          0     0.4340     0.4154
     0.6840     0.6460     0.0380     0.4340          0     0.4401
     0.8040     0.5880     0.6535     0.4154     0.4401          0
     0.7871     0.7580     0.4208     0.3317     0.3565     0.3963
     0.9090     0.6380     0.8131     0.5750     0.7418     0.4000
     0.8210     0.7926     0.3881     0.7841     0.2460     0.6710
     0.8521     0.6380     0.7841     0.2631     0.6830     0.5899

Columns 7 through 10
```

```
   0.7871      0.9090      0.8210      0.8521
   0.7580      0.6380      0.7926      0.6380
   0.4208      0.8131      0.3881      0.7841
   0.3317      0.5750      0.7841      0.2631
   0.3565      0.7418      0.2460      0.6830
   0.3963      0.4000      0.6710      0.5899
        0      0.4176      0.3500      0.2960
   0.4176           0      0.4000      0.4590
   0.3500      0.4000           0      0.3920
   0.2960      0.4590      0.3920           0
```

vaf =

   0.9955

targone =

  Columns 1 through 6

```
        0      0.0858      0.0858      0.3086      0.4576      0.4576
   0.0858           0      0.0096      0.2443      0.2443      0.3863
   0.0858      0.0096           0      0.2133      0.2391      0.2391
   0.3086      0.2443      0.2133           0      0.0994      0.1207
   0.4576      0.2443      0.2391      0.0994           0      0.1207
   0.4576      0.3863      0.2391      0.1207      0.1207           0
   0.4818      0.4818      0.3631      0.2195      0.2195      0.2195
   0.4818      0.4818      0.4818      0.2195      0.2195      0.2195
   0.3153      0.4902      0.4902      0.4902      0.4711      0.3356
   0.3153      0.4361      0.4628      0.4902      0.7370      0.7185
```

  Columns 7 through 10

```
   0.4818      0.4818      0.3153      0.3153
   0.4818      0.4818      0.4902      0.4361
   0.3631      0.4818      0.4902      0.4628
   0.2195      0.2195      0.4902      0.4902
   0.2195      0.2195      0.4711      0.7370
   0.2195      0.2195      0.3356      0.7185
        0     -0.0393      0.3356      0.4818
  -0.0393           0      0.3356      0.4818
   0.3356      0.3356           0      0.2371
   0.4818      0.4818      0.2371           0
```

```
targtwo =

  Columns 1 through 6

          0     0.0765     0.1367     0.2969     0.2969     0.2969
     0.0765          0     0.0289     0.2395     0.3704     0.3704
     0.1367     0.0289          0     0.1609     0.3582     0.4319
     0.2969     0.2395     0.1609          0     0.1905     0.2793
     0.2969     0.3704     0.3582     0.1905          0     0.0670
     0.2969     0.3704     0.4319     0.2793     0.0670          0
     0.2678     0.3024     0.3024     0.3024     0.1839     0.1169
     0.1122     0.3024     0.3024     0.3555     0.2480     0.1959
     0.1122     0.3024     0.3024     0.3555     0.2480     0.1959
     0.1122     0.2012     0.2364     0.3555     0.2480     0.1959

  Columns 7 through 10

     0.2678     0.1122     0.1122     0.1122
     0.3024     0.3024     0.3024     0.2012
     0.3024     0.3024     0.3024     0.2364
     0.3024     0.3555     0.3555     0.3555
     0.1839     0.2480     0.2480     0.2480
     0.1169     0.1959     0.1959     0.1959
          0    -0.0105    -0.0105     0.1558
    -0.0105          0    -0.1278    -0.0478
    -0.0105    -0.1278          0    -0.0478
     0.1558    -0.0478    -0.0478          0


outpermone =

     3     5     9     7     6     8    10     4     2     1


outpermtwo =

     7    10     9     8     1     6     2     3     4     5
```

For finding multiple CSAR forms, `bicirsarobfnd.m` has usage syntax

```
[find,vaf,targone,targtwo,outpermone,outpermtwo] = ...
bicirsarobfnd(prox,inperm,kblock)
```

with all the various terms the same as for `bicirarobfnd.m` but now for strongly CAR (CSAR) structures. The example below finds essentially the same representation as above (involving digit magnitude and structure) with a slight drop in the VAF from 99.55% for CAR to 91.06% for CSAR.

```
[find,vaf,targone,targtwo,outpermone,outpermtwo] = ...
bicirsarobfnd(number,randperm(10),1)

find =

  Columns 1 through 6
```

0	0.4212	0.6464	0.6464	0.6840	0.8040
0.4212	0	0.3284	0.3284	0.5122	0.6693
0.6464	0.3284	0	0.3273	0.0947	0.6682
0.6464	0.3284	0.3273	0	0.5111	0.3505
0.6840	0.5122	0.0947	0.5111	0	0.4090
0.8040	0.6693	0.6682	0.3505	0.4090	0
0.8420	0.7215	0.4802	0.4027	0.4493	0.3718
0.8420	0.7215	0.7215	0.6565	0.6906	0.4000
0.8420	0.7215	0.3041	0.7204	0.2732	0.6895
0.8420	0.7215	0.7204	0.2630	0.6895	0.5540

```
  Columns 7 through 10
```

0.8420	0.8420	0.8420	0.8420
0.7215	0.7215	0.7215	0.7215
0.4802	0.7215	0.3041	0.7204
0.4027	0.6565	0.7204	0.2630
0.4493	0.6906	0.2732	0.6895
0.3718	0.4000	0.6895	0.5540
0	0.4055	0.2292	0.3339
0.4055	0	0.4705	0.4055
0.2292	0.4705	0	0.4694
0.3339	0.4055	0.4694	0

```
vaf =

    0.9106


targone =

  Columns 1 through 6
```

0	0.3924	0.6326	0.6326	0.6326	0.6337
0.3924	0	0.3149	0.3149	0.4970	0.5686
0.6326	0.3149	0	0.3149	0.4970	0.5686
0.6326	0.3149	0.3149	0	0.1752	0.5686
0.6326	0.4970	0.4970	0.1752	0	0.5686

```
    0.6337      0.5686      0.5686      0.5686      0.5686           0
    0.6337      0.6337      0.6337      0.6337      0.6337      0.6337
    0.6337      0.6337      0.6337      0.6337      0.6337      0.6337
    0.2162      0.3924      0.6326      0.6326      0.6326      0.6337
    0.2162      0.3924      0.6326      0.6326      0.6326      0.6337
```

Columns 7 through 10

```
    0.6337      0.6337      0.2162      0.2162
    0.6337      0.6337      0.3924      0.3924
    0.6337      0.6337      0.6326      0.6326
    0.6337      0.6337      0.6326      0.6326
    0.6337      0.6337      0.6326      0.6326
    0.6337      0.6337      0.6337      0.6337
         0      0.4085      0.6337      0.6337
    0.4085           0      0.6337      0.6337
    0.6337      0.6337           0      0.2162
    0.6337      0.6337      0.2162           0
```

targtwo =

Columns 1 through 6

```
         0     -0.2236      0.0570      0.0570      0.0570      0.0570
   -0.2236           0     -0.1686      0.0570      0.0570      0.0570
    0.0570     -0.1686           0     -0.1632     -0.1632     -0.1632
    0.0570      0.0570     -0.1632           0     -0.1632     -0.1632
    0.0570      0.0570     -0.1632     -0.1632           0     -0.1632
    0.0570      0.0570     -0.1632     -0.1632     -0.1632           0
    0.0503      0.1703      0.2083      0.2083      0.2083      0.2083
   -0.1215      0.0356      0.0878      0.0878      0.0878      0.0878
   -0.1215      0.0356      0.0878      0.0878      0.0878      0.0878
   -0.1215      0.0356      0.0878      0.0878      0.0878      0.0878
```

Columns 7 through 10

```
    0.0503     -0.1215     -0.1215     -0.1215
    0.1703      0.0356      0.0356      0.0356
    0.2083      0.0878      0.0878      0.0878
    0.2083      0.0878      0.0878      0.0878
    0.2083      0.0878      0.0878      0.0878
    0.2083      0.0878      0.0878      0.0878
         0      0.0127      0.0127      0.0127
    0.0127           0     -0.3053     -0.3053
    0.0127     -0.3053           0     -0.3053
```

```
    0.0127    -0.3053    -0.3053           0
```

outpermone =

```
    5       7       6       4      10       8       2       1       9       3
```

outpermtwo =

```
    5       6       8       9      10       7       1       4       3       2
```

Chapter 11

Anti-Robinson Matrices for Two-Mode Proximity Data

In direct analogy to the extensions of linear unidimensional scaling (LUS) in Chapter 4, it is possible to find and fit (more general) anti-Robinson (AR) forms to two-mode proximity matrices. The same type of reordering strategy implemented in Section 4.1 by `ordertm.m` would be used, but the more general AR form would be fitted to the reordered square proximity matrix, $\mathbf{P}_{\rho_0}^{(tm)} = \{p_{\rho_0(i)\rho_0(j)}^{(tm)}\}$; the least-squares criterion

$$\sum_{i,j=1}^{n} w_{\rho_0(i)\rho_0(j)} (p_{\rho_0(i)\rho_0(j)}^{(tm)} - \hat{p}_{ij})^2$$

is minimized, where $w_{\rho_0(i)\rho_0(j)} = 0$ if $\rho_0(i)$ and $\rho_0(j)$ are both row or both column objects, and $= 1$ otherwise. The entries in the matrix $\{\hat{p}_{ij}\}$ fitted to $\mathbf{P}_{\rho_0}^{(tm)}$ are AR in form (and correspond to nonzero values of the weight function $w_{\rho_0(i)\rho_0(j)}$), and thus satisfy certain linear inequality constraints generated from how the row and column objects are intermixed by the given permutation $\rho_0(\cdot)$. We note here and discuss more completely in the section to follow that the patterning of entries in $\{\hat{p}_{ij}\}$ fitted to the original two-mode proximity matrix, with appropriate row and column permutations extracted from ρ_0, is called an anti-Q-form.

11.1 Fitting and Finding Two-Mode AR Matrices

The M-file `arobfittm.m` does a confirmatory two-mode AR fitting of a given ordering of the row and column objects of a two-mode proximity matrix using the Dykstra–Kaczmarz iterative projection least-squares method. The usage syntax has the form

```
[fit,vaf,rowperm,colperm] = arobfittm(proxtm,inperm)
```

where PROXTM is the input two-mode proximity matrix; INPERM is the given ordering of the row and column objects together; FIT is an $n_a \times n_b$ (number of rows by number of columns) matrix fitted to PROXTM(ROWPERM, COLPERM) with VAF being the variance-accounted-for based on the (least-squares criterion) sum of squared discrepancies between PROXTM(ROWPERM, COLMEAN) and FIT; ROWPERM and COLPERM are the row and column object orderings derived from INPERM.

The matrix given by `FIT` that is intended to approximate the row and column per-muted two-mode proximity matrix, `PROXTM(ROWPERM, COLPERM)`, displays a particu-larly important patterning of its entries called an anti-Q-form in the literature (see Hubert and Arabie, 1995a, for an extended discussion of this type of patterning for a two-mode matrix). Specifically, a matrix is said to have the anti-Q-form (for rows and columns) if within each row and column the entries are nonincreasing to a minimum and thereafter non-decreasing. *Matrices satisfying the anti-Q-form have a convenient interpretation presuming an underlying unidimensional scale that jointly represents both the row and column objects.* Explicitly, suppose a matrix has been appropriately row-ordered to display the anti-Q-form for columns. Any dichotomization of the entries within a column at some threshold value (using 0 for entries below the threshold and 1 for at or above) produces a matrix that has the consecutive zeros property within each column, that is, all zeros within a column occur consecutively, uninterrupted by intervening ones. In turn, any matrix with the consecutive zeros property for columns suggests the existence of a perfect scale (error-free), where row objects can be ordered along a continuum (using the same row order for the matrix that actually reflects the anti-Q-form for columns), and each column object is representable as an interval along the continuum (encompassing those consecutive row objects correspond-ing to zeros). Historically, the type of pattern represented by the anti-Q-form has played a major role in the literature of (unidimensional) unfolding and, for example, is the basis of the parallelogram structure from Coombs (1964, Chapter 4) for a two-mode proximity matrix. The reader is referred to Hubert (1974) for a review of some of these connections.

To provide an example of what an anti-Q-form looks like for our two-mode data matrix, `goldfish_receptor`, we will use `arobfndtm.m` both to find and fit an AR form using iterative projection to a two-mode proximity matrix in the L_2-norm based on a permutation identified through the use of iterative QA. The usage syntax is

```
[find, vaf, outperm, rowperm, colperm] = ...
 arobfndtm(proxtm, inperm, kblock)
```

where, again, `INPERM` is a given starting permutation of the first $n = n_a + n_b$ integers; `FIND` is the least-squares optimal matrix (with variance-accounted-for of `VAF`) displaying an anti-Q-form (because of the AR form constructed for the combined row and column object ordering given by the ending permutation `OUTPERM`). `KBLOCK` defines the block size in the use of the iterative QA routine. `ROWPERM` and `COLPERM` are the resulting row and column permutations for the objects. In the listing below, the `VAF` for the given fitted matrix is very high: .9667 (which can be compared to the alternative representations given earlier with values of .8072 (LUS), .6209 (ultrametric), and .8663 (additive tree)).

```
  load goldfish_receptor.dat
  [find,vaf,outperm,rowperm,colperm] = ...
arobfndtm(goldfish_receptor,randperm(20),2);
  find

find =

  Columns 1 through 6
```

```
 68.0000    54.5000    80.0000   138.0000   145.0000   162.8000
 71.5000    54.5000    64.0000   128.0000   144.0000   162.8000
 71.5000    47.0000    61.0000   117.5000   117.5000   145.0000
 80.0000    47.5000    47.5000    98.0000   116.0000   137.5000
155.0000   108.0000    63.0000    94.0000   103.0000   137.5000
174.0000   125.0000    84.0000    49.0000    47.6667    76.0000
200.0000   143.0000    91.0000    49.0000    47.6667    76.0000
200.0000   156.0000   107.0000    67.0000    47.6667    60.0000
200.0000   183.0000   177.0000   176.0000   168.0000   112.5000
200.0000   200.0000   200.0000   198.0000   186.0000   112.5000
200.0000   200.0000   200.0000   198.0000   188.0000   143.0000
```

```
Columns 7 through 9
```

```
162.8000   200.0000   200.0000
162.8000   162.8000   173.0000
145.0000   151.6667   158.0000
138.5000   151.6667   158.0000
138.5000   151.6667   158.0000
106.0000   134.5000   134.5000
106.0000   124.5000   124.5000
 78.0000   100.0000   100.0000
 82.5000    47.0000    46.0000
 82.5000    54.0000    47.5000
111.0000    54.0000    47.5000
```

```
vaf
```

```
vaf =
```

```
   0.9667
```

```
outperm
```

```
outperm =
```

```
Columns 1 through 10
```

```
   20    11    10    19     9    18     8     7    17    16
```

```
Columns 11 through 20
```

```
    6     5     4    15    14    13     3    12     2     1
```

```
rowperm'
```

```
ans =

  Columns 1 through 10

    11    10     9     8     7     6     5     4     3     2

  Column 11

     1

colperm'

ans =

     9     8     7     6     5     4     3     2     1
```

11.2   Multiple Two-Mode AR Reorderings and Fittings

The M-file `biarobfndtm.m` finds and fits the sum of two anti-Q-forms (extracted from fitting two AR matrices) using iterative projection to a two-mode proximity matrix in the L_2-norm based on permutations identified through the use of iterative QA. In the usage

```
[find,vaf,targone,targtwo,outpermone,outpermtwo, ...
     rowpermone,colpermone,rowpermtwo,colpermtwo] = ...
     biarobfndtm(proxtm,inpermone,inpermtwo,kblock)
```

PROXTM is the usual input two-mode proximity matrix ($n_a \times n_b$) with a dissimilarity interpretation, and FIND is the least-squares optimal matrix (with variance-accounted-for of VAF) to PROXTM. The latter matrix PROXTM is the sum of the two matrices TARGONE and TARGTWO based on the two row and column object orderings given by the ending permutations OUTPERMONE and OUTPERMTWO. The two ending permutations of OUTPERMONE and OUTPERMTWO contain the ending row and column object orderings of ROWPERMONE and ROWPERMTWO and COLPERMONE and COLPERMTWO. KBLOCK defines the block size in the use of the iterative QA routine; the input permutations are INPERMONE and INPERMTWO.

As can be seen in the example below, the sum of two anti-Q-forms fitted to the `goldfish_receptor` data provides an almost perfect reconstruction (with a VAF of .9995).

```
    [find,vaf,targone,targtwo,outpermone,outpermtwo, ...
rowpermone,colpermone,rowpermtwo,colpermtwo] = ...
biarobfndtm(goldfish_receptor,randperm(20),randperm(20),2);

find

find =
```

```
Columns 1 through 6

  47.3504    54.6226   111.0000   143.0000   188.0000   196.1177
  47.3504    54.6226    75.0000   100.0000   186.0000   199.8954
  46.0072    47.1738    90.0072   124.9856   167.9981   175.9981
  99.0098   101.1738    78.0098    59.9508    46.0000    66.9608
 122.0098   127.1738   115.0098    79.0098    48.9981    47.8673
 116.6197   152.0595    96.5053    72.7463    48.0000    52.0523
 198.0000   186.0000   154.0000   148.0000   103.0000    94.0000
 133.8750   156.0000   123.0000   126.7482   115.0000    98.0523
 141.0000   113.0000   142.0000   145.4795   115.0000   121.9575
 173.0000   140.0000   176.5991   176.4009   144.6719   128.6719
 200.2992   200.1738   160.7486   160.7486   145.0000   138.0000

Columns 7 through 9

 199.9608   200.0000   201.9327
 200.0000   199.9924   197.3046
 176.9981   182.9981   200.0135
 106.9608   156.0000   200.0000
  89.1327   142.9981   199.9981
  84.0000   124.9924   173.3897
  63.0000   108.0000   155.0000
  49.0000    46.0153    79.3897
  60.0425    47.0000    60.9419
  66.5870    56.6719    84.3973
  80.0000    53.0000    65.5700

vaf

vaf =

    0.9995

targone

targone =

Columns 1 through 6

  46.1875    46.1875   111.0900   143.0900   189.1858   197.1531
  46.1875    46.1875    83.7500   118.2801   187.1858   197.1531
  39.3017    38.7387    83.3017   118.2801   168.0431   176.0431
  96.3403    92.7387    75.3403    57.2813    57.2813    67.9962
 119.3403   118.7387   112.3403    76.3403    49.0431    49.7778
```

```
143.6244    143.6244    123.5100     80.9988     49.1858     49.3100
159.4691    147.4691    138.5000    135.0006    102.8519     94.0000
160.8797    151.8810    138.5000    135.0006    116.1858     95.3100
160.8797    153.7319    153.7319    153.7319    116.1858    113.2992
173.0000    166.2124    164.3730    164.1748    129.4690    113.4690
199.1362    191.7387    164.3730    164.3730    146.1858    138.0000
```

Columns 7 through 9

```
200.9962    203.4720    205.5571
200.0000    202.1911    205.5571
177.0431    183.0431    200.0585
107.9962    156.7769    200.0585
 91.0431    143.0431    200.0431
 84.0000    127.1911    181.6422
 63.0000    107.8519    154.8519
 48.2140     48.2140     87.6422
 51.3841     48.2140     69.1944
 51.3841     41.4690     69.1944
 80.0000     55.2081     69.1944
```

targtwo

targtwo =

  Columns 1 through 6

```
-26.2124           0     12.2261     12.2261     15.2029     15.2029
-40.7319    -19.8797    -11.7319     -8.2525     -8.2525     -1.2140
  4.1190    -27.0047    -15.5000     -8.2525     -8.2525     -2.1988
  8.4351    -27.0047    -27.0047     -8.2525     -8.2525     -2.1988
  8.4351      1.1630     -8.7500    -18.2801     -8.2525     -2.1988
  8.4351      1.1630     -3.6244     -3.6244     -3.6244     -2.2081
  8.4351      1.1630     -0.0900     -0.0900     -3.6244     -3.4720
  8.4351      2.6696      2.6696      2.6696     -0.0585     -0.7769
  8.4351      2.6696      2.6696      2.6696     -0.0450     -0.0450
  8.4351      6.7055      6.7055      6.7055     -0.0450     -0.0450
 38.5309     38.5309     15.5000     12.9994      0.1481      0.1481
```

  Columns 7 through 9

```
 15.2029     15.2029     15.2029
 -1.1858      8.6584      8.6584
 -1.1858      0.7860      2.7423
 -1.1858           0      2.7423
 -1.1858           0      2.7423
```

```
    -1.1858           0           0
    -1.1858     -1.0354     -1.0354
   -11.2813     -1.0354     -1.0354
    -0.0450     -1.9104     -1.9104
    -0.0450     -0.0450     -0.0450
     0.1481           0           0
```

outpermone

outpermone =

  Columns 1 through 10

     1   2   12   13   3   14   4   15   5   16

  Columns 11 through 20

     6   17   7   8   18   9   10   19   11   20

outpermtwo

outpermtwo =

  Columns 1 through 10

    10   13   9   12   8   14   6   15   2   20

  Columns 11 through 20

    11   1   19   16   4   5   18   17   3   7

rowpermone'

ans =

  Columns 1 through 10

     1   2   3   4   5   6   7   8   9   10

  Column 11

    11

colpermone'

ans =

```
      1       2       3       4       5       6       7       8       9

rowpermtwo'

ans =

  Columns 1 through 10

     10       9       8       6       2      11       1       4       5       3

  Column 11

      7

colpermtwo'

ans =

      2       1       3       4       9       8       5       7       6
```

Header Comments for the M-Files Mentioned in the Text and Given in Alphabetical Order

arobfit.m

```
function [fit, vaf] = arobfit(prox, inperm)

% AROBFIT fits an anti-Robinson matrix using iterative
% projection to a symmetric proximity matrix in the
% $L_{2}$-norm.
%
% syntax: [fit, vaf] = arobfit(prox, inperm)
%
% PROX is the input proximity matrix ($n \times n$ with
% a zero main diagonal and a dissimilarity
% interpretation); INPERM is a given permutation of the
% first $n$ integers;
% FIT is the least-squares optimal matrix (with variance-
% accounted-for of VAF) to PROX having an anti-Robinson
% form for the row and column object ordering given
% by INPERM.
```

arobfittm.m

```
function [fit,vaf,rowperm,colperm] = ...
    arobfittm(proxtm,inperm)

%  AROBFITTM does a confirmatory two-mode anti-Robinson
%  fitting of a given ordering of the row and column
%  objects of a two-mode proximity matrix PROXTM using
%  Dykstra's (Kaczmarz's) iterative projection
%  least-squares method.
%
```

```
%   syntax: [fit,vaf,rowperm,colperm] = ...
%       arobfittm(proxtm,inperm)
%
%   INPERM is the given ordering of the row and column
%   objects together; FIT is an nrow (number of rows)
%   by ncol (number of columns) matrix fitted to
%   PROXTM(ROWPERM,COLPERM) with VAF being the variance-
%   accounted-for and  based on the (least-squares
%   criterion) sum of squared discrepancies between FIT
%   and PROXTM(ROWPERM,COLMEAN); ROWPERM and COLPERM are
%   the row and column object orderings
%   derived from INPERM.
```

arobfnd.m

```
function [find,vaf,outperm] = arobfnd(prox,inperm,kblock)
```

```
% AROBFND finds and fits an anti-Robinson matrix using
% iterative projection to a symmetric proximity matrix
% in the $L_{2}$-norm based on a permutation identified
% through the use of iterative quadratic assignment.
%
% syntax: [find,vaf,outperm] = arobfnd(prox,inperm,kblock)
%
% PROX is the input proximity matrix ($n \times n$ with
% a zero main diagonal and a dissimilarity interpretation);
% INPERM is a given starting permutation of the first $n$
% integers; FIND is the least-squares optimal matrix (with
% variance-accounted-for of VAF) to PROX having an
% anti-Robinson form for the row and column object
% ordering given by the ending permutation OUTPERM.
% KBLOCK defines the block size in the use of the
% iterative quadratic assignment routine.
```

arobfndtm.m

```
function [find, vaf, outperm, rowperm, colperm] = ...
     arobfndtm(proxtm, inperm, kblock)
```

```
% AROBFNDTM finds and fits an anti-Robinson form using
% iterative projection to a two-mode proximity matrix
% in the $L_{2}$-norm based on a permutation identified
% through the use of iterative quadratic assignment.
%
% syntax: [find, vaf, outperm, rowperm, colperm] = ...
```

```
% arobfndtm(proxtm, inperm, kblock)
%
% PROXTM is the input two-mode proximity matrix
% ($n_{a} \times n_{b}$ with a dissimilarity
% interpretation);
% INPERM is a given starting permutation
% of the first $n = n_{a} + n_{b}$ integers;
% FIND is the least-squares optimal matrix (with
% variance-accounted-for of VAF) to PROXTM having the
% anti-Robinson form for the row and column
% object ordering given by the ending permutation
% OUTPERM. KBLOCK defines the block size in the use of
% the iterative quadratic assignment routine.
% ROWPERM and COLPERM are the resulting
% row and column permutations for the objects.
```

atreectul.m

```
function [find,vaf] = atreectul(prox,inperm)

% ATREECTUL finds and fits an additive tree by first
% fitting a centroid metric (using centfit.m) and
% secondly an ultrametric to the residual
% matrix (using ultrafnd.m).
%
% syntax: [find,vaf] = atreectul(prox,inperm)
%
% PROX is the input proximity matrix (with a zero main
% diagonal and a dissimilarity interpretation);
% INPERM is a permutation that determines the order
% in which the inequality constraints are considered;
% FIND is the found least-squares matrix (with
% variance-accounted-for of VAF) to PROX satisfying
% the additive tree constraints.
```

atreedec.m

```
function [ulmetric,ctmetric] = atreedec(prox,constant)

% ATREEDEC decomposes a given additive tree matrix into
% an ultrametric and a centroid metric matrix (where the
% root is halfway along the longest path).
%
% syntax: [ulmetric,ctmetric] = atreedec(prox,constant)
%
```

% PROX is the input proximity matrix (with a zero main
% diagonal and a dissimilarity interpretation);
% CONSTANT is a nonnegative number (less than or equal
% to the maximum proximity value) that controls the
% positivity of the constructed ultrametric values;
% ULMETRIC is the ultrametric component of the
% decomposition; CTMETRIC is the centroid metric
% component of the decomposition (given by values
% $g_{1},...,g_{n}$ for each of the objects,
% some of which may actually be negative depending on
% the input proximity matrix used).

atreefit.m

function [fit,vaf] = atreefit(prox,targ)

% ATREEFIT fits a given additive tree using iterative
% projection to a symmetric proximity matrix in the
% L_{2}-norm.
%
% syntax: [fit,vaf] = atreefit(prox,targ)
%
% PROX is the input proximity matrix (with a zero main
% diagonal and a dissimilarity interpretation);
% TARG is a matrix of the same size as PROX with
% entries satisfying the four-point additive tree
% constraints;
% FIT is the least-squares optimal matrix (with
% variance-accounted-for of VAF) to PROX satisfying the
% additive tree constraints implicit in TARG.

atreefnd.m

function [find,vaf] = atreefnd(prox,inperm)

% ATREEFND finds and fits an additive tree using iterative
% projection heuristically on a symmetric proximity matrix
% in the L_{2}-norm.
%
% syntax: [find,vaf] = atreefnd(prox,inperm)
%
% PROX is the input proximity matrix (with a zero main
% diagonal and a dissimilarity interpretation);
% INPERM is a permutation that determines the order in
% which the inequality constraints are considered;

```
% FIND is the found least-squares matrix (with
% variance-accounted-for of VAF) to PROX satisfying the
% additive tree constraints.
```

atreefndtm.m

```
function [find,vaf,ultra,lengths] = ...
     atreefndtm(proxtm,inpermrow,inpermcol)
```

```
% ATREEFNDTM finds and fits a two-mode additive tree;
% iterative projection is used
% heuristically to find a two-mode ultrametric component
% that is added to a two-mode centroid metric to
% produce the two-mode additive tree.
%
% syntax: [find,vaf,ultra,lengths] = ...
%      atreefndtm(proxtm,inpermrow,inpermcol)
%
% PROXTM is the input proximity matrix
% (with a dissimilarity interpretation);
% INPERMROW and INPERMCOL are permutations for the row
% and column objects that determine the order in which
% the inequality constraints are considered;
% FIND is the found least-squares matrix (with
% variance-accounted-for of VAF) to PROXTM satisfying
% the additive tree constraints;
% the vector LENGTHS contains the row followed by column
% values for the two-mode centroid metric component;
% ULTRA is the ultrametric component.
```

biarobfnd.m

```
function [find,vaf,targone,targtwo,outpermone,...
   outpermtwo] = biarobfnd(prox,inperm,kblock)
```

```
% BIAROBFND finds and fits the sum of two
% anti-Robinson matrices using iterative projection to
% a symmetric proximity matrix in the $L_{2}$-norm
% based on permutations identified through
% the use of iterative quadratic assignment.
%
% syntax: [find,vaf,targone,targtwo,outpermone, ...
% outpermtwo] = biarobfnd(prox,inperm,kblock)
%
% PROX is the input proximity matrix ($n \times n$ with
```

% a zero main diagonal and a dissimilarity
% interpretation); INPERM is a given starting
% permutation of the first n integers;
% FIND is the least-squares optimal matrix (with
% variance-accounted-for of VAF)
% to PROX and is the sum of the two anti-Robinson
% matrices TARGONE and TARGTWO based on the two row and
% column object orderings given by the ending
% permutations OUTPERMONE and OUTPERMTWO. KBLOCK defines
% the block size in the use of the iterative quadratic
% assignment routine.

biarobfndtm.m

```
function [find,vaf,targone,targtwo,outpermone,...
    outpermtwo,rowpermone,colpermone,rowpermtwo,...
    colpermtwo] = biarobfndtm(proxtm,inpermone,...
    inpermtwo,kblock)
```

% BIAROBFNDTM finds and fits the sum of
% two anti-Robinson matrices using iterative projection to
% a two-mode proximity matrix in the L_{2}-norm based on
% permutations identified through the use of
% iterative quadratic assignment.
%
% syntax: [find,vaf,targone,targtwo,outpermone,...
%   outpermtwo,rowpermone,colpermone,rowpermtwo,...
%   colpermtwo] = biarobfndtm(proxtm,inpermone,
%   inpermtwo,kblock)
%
%
% PROXTM is the input two-mode proximity matrix ($nrow
% \times ncol$) with a dissimilarity interpretation);
% FIND is the least-squares optimal matrix (with variance-
% accounted-for of VAF) to PROXTM and is the sum of the
% two matrices TARGONE and TARGTWO based on the two row
% and column object orderings given by the ending
% permutations OUTPERMONE and OUTPERMTWO,
% and in turn ROWPERMONE and ROWPERMTWO and
% COLPERMONE and COLPERMTWO. KBLOCK defines the block size
% in the use of the iterative quadratic assignment routine;
% the input permutations are INPERMONE and INPERMTWO.

biatreefnd.m

```
function [find,vaf,targone,targtwo] = ...
   biatreefnd(prox,inperm)
```

```
% BIATREEFND finds and fits the sum
% of two additive trees using iterative projection
% heuristically on a symmetric proximity matrix in the
% $L_{2}$-norm.
%
% syntax: [find,vaf,targone,targtwo] = ...
%    biatreefnd(prox,inperm)
%
% PROX is the input proximity matrix (with a zero main
% diagonal and a dissimilarity interpretation);
% INPERM is a permutation that determines the order
% in which the inequality constraints are considered;
% FIND is the found least-squares matrix (with
% variance-accounted-for of VAF) to PROX and is the sum
% of the two additive tree matrices TARGONE and TARGTWO.
```

bicirac.m

```
function [find,vaf,targone,targtwo,outpermone,...
   outpermtwo,addconone,addcontwo] = ...
   bicirac(prox,inperm,kblock)
```

```
% BICIRAC finds and fits the sum of two circular
% unidimensional scales using iterative projection to
% a symmetric proximity matrix in the $L_{2}$-norm based on
% permutations identified through the use
% of iterative quadratic assignment.
%
% syntax: [find,vaf,targone,targtwo,outpermone,...
%    outpermtwo,addconone,addcontwo] = ...
%    bicirac(prox,inperm,kblock)
%
% PROX is the input proximity matrix ($n \times n$ with
% a zero main diagonal and a dissimilarity
% interpretation); INPERM is a given starting permutation
% of the first $n$ integers;
% FIND is the least-squares optimal matrix (with variance-
% accounted-for of VAF) to PROX and is the sum of the two
% circular anti-Robinson matrices;
% TARGONE and TARGTWO are based on the two row and column
```

% object orderings given by the ending permutations
% OUTPERMONE and OUTPERMTWO.
% KBLOCK defines the block size in the use of the
% iterative quadratic assignment routine and ADDCONONE
% and ADDCONTWO are the two additive constants for the
% two model components.

bicirarobfnd.m

```
function [find,vaf,targone,targtwo,outpermone,...
    outpermtwo] = bicirarobfnd(prox,inperm,kblock)
```

% BICIRAROBFND finds and fits the sum of two circular
% anti-Robinson matrices using iterative projection to
% a symmetric proximity matrix in the L_{2}-norm
% based on permutations identified through the use of
% iterative quadratic assignment.
%
% syntax: [find,vaf,targone,targtwo,outpermone,...
%   outpermtwo] = bicirarobfnd(prox,inperm,kblock)
%
% PROX is the input proximity matrix ($n \times n$ with a
% zero main diagonal and a dissimilarity interpretation);
% INPERM is a given starting permutation of the first n
% integers; FIND is the least-squares optimal matrix (with
% variance-accounted-for of VAF) to PROX and is the sum of
% the two circular anti-Robinson matrices;
% TARGONE and TARGTWO are based on the two row and column
% object orderings given by the ending permutations
% OUTPERMONE and OUTPERMTWO.

bicirsarobfnd.m

```
function [find,vaf,targone,targtwo,outpermone,...
    outpermtwo] = bicirsarobfnd(prox,inperm,kblock)
```

% BICIRSAROBFND fits the sum of two strongly
% circular anti-Robinson matrices using iterative
% projection to a symmetric proximity
% matrix in the L_{2}-norm based on permutations
% identified through the use of iterative quadratic
% assignment.
%
% syntax: [find,vaf,targone,targtwo,outpermone,...
%   outpermtwo] = bicirsarobfnd(prox,inperm,kblock)

```
%
% PROX is the input proximity matrix ($n \times n$ with
% a zero main diagonal and a dissimilarity
% interpretation);
% INPERM is a given starting permutation of the first
% $n$ integers;
% FIND is the least-squares optimal matrix (with
% variance-accounted-for of VAF) to PROX and is the
% sum of the two strongly circular anti-Robinson matrices;
% TARGONE and TARGTWO are based on the two row and column
% object orderings given by the ending permutations
% OUTPERMONE and OUTPERMTWO. KBLOCK defines the block size
% in the use of the iterative quadratic assignment routine.
```

bimonscalqa.m

```
function [outpermone,outpermtwo,coordone,coordtwo,...
    fitone,fittwo,addconone,addcontwo,vaf,monprox] = ...
    bimonscalqa(prox,targone,targtwo,inpermone,...
    inpermtwo,kblock,nopt)
```

```
%   BIMONSCALQA carries out a bidimensional scaling of a
%   symmetric proximity matrix using iterative quadratic
%   assignment, plus it provides an optimal monotonic
%   transformation (MONPROX) of the original input
%   proximity matrix.
%
%   syntax: [outpermone,outpermtwo,coordone,coordtwo,...
%       fitone,fittwo,addconone,addcontwo,vaf,monprox] = ...
%       bimonscalqa(prox,targone,targtwo,inpermone,...
%       inpermtwo,kblock,nopt)
%
%   PROX is the input proximity matrix (with a zero main
%   diagonal and a dissimilarity interpretation);
%   TARGONE is the input target matrix for the
%   first dimension (usually with
%   a zero main diagonal and with a
%   dissimilarity interpretation representing
%   equally spaced locations along a continuum);
%   TARGTWO is the input target
%   matrix for the second dimension;
%   INPERMONE is the input beginning permutation for the
%   first dimension (a permutation of the first $n$
%   integers); INPERMTWO is the input beginning
%   permutation for the second dimension;
```

```
%   the insertion and rotation routines use from 1 to
%   KBLOCK   (which is less than or equal to $n-1$)
%   consecutive objects in the permutation defining the
%   row and column orders of the data
%   matrix; NOPT controls the confirmatory or exploratory
%   fitting of
%   the unidimensional scales; a value of NOPT = 0 will
%   fit in a
%   confirmatory manner the two scales indicated by
%   INPERMONE and INPERMTWO;
%   a value of NOPT = 1 uses iterative QA
%   to locate the better permutations to fit;
%   OUTPERMONE is the final object permutation for the
%   first
%   dimension; OUTPERMTWO is the final object
%   permutation for the second dimension;
%   COORDONE is the set of first dimension coordinates
%   in ascending order; COORDTWO is the set of second
%   dimension coordinates in ascending order;
%   ADDCONONE is the additive constant for the first
%   dimensional model; ADDCONTWO is the additive constant
%   for the second dimensional model; VAF is the
%   variance-accounted-for in MONPROX by the
%   bidimensional scaling.
```

bimonscaltmac.m

```
function [find,vaf,targone,targtwo,outpermone,outpermtwo,...
    rowpermone,colpermone,rowpermtwo,colpermtwo,addconone,...
    addcontwo,coordone,coordtwo,axes,monproxtm] = ...
  bimonscaltmac(proxtm,inpermone,inpermtwo,kblock,nopt)


% BIMONSCALTMAC finds and fits the sum of two linear
% unidimensional scales using iterative projection to
% a two-mode proximity matrix in the $L_{2}$-norm based on
% permutations identified through the use of iterative
% quadratic assignment.  It also provides an optimal
% monotonic transformation (MONPROX) of the original
% input proximity matrix.
%
% syntax: [find,vaf,targone,targtwo,outpermone,outpermtwo,...
%    rowpermone,colpermone,rowpermtwo,colpermtwo,addconone,...
%    addcontwo,coordone,coordtwo,axes,monproxtm] = ...
% bimonscaltmac(proxtm,inpermone,inpermtwo,kblock,nopt)
%
```

% PROXTM is the input two-mode proximity matrix ($nrow
% \times ncol$ with a dissimilarity interpretation);
% FIND is the least-squares optimal matrix (with variance-
% accounted-for of VAF) to the monotonic transformation
% MONPROXTM of the input proximity matrix and is the sum
% of the two matrices TARGONE and TARGTWO based on the two
% row and column object orderings given by the ending
% permutations OUTPERMONE and OUTPERMTWO,
% and in turn ROWPERMONE and ROWPERMTWO and
% COLPERMONE and COLPERMTWO. KBLOCK defines the block
% size in the use of the iterative quadratic assignment
% routine and ADDCONONE and ADDCONTWO are the two additive
% constants for the two model components;
% The n coordinates are in COORDONE and COORDTWO.
% The input permutations are INPERMONE and INPERMTWO. The
% $n \times 2$ matrix AXES gives the plotting coordinates
% for the combined row and column object set.
% NOPT controls the confirmatory or exploratory fitting of
% the unidimensional scales; a value of NOPT = 0 will fit
% in a confirmatory manner the two scales
% indicated by INPERMONE and INPERMTWO;
% a value of NOPT = 1 uses iterative QA
% to locate the better permutations to fit.

biplottm.m

```
function [] = biplottm(axes,nrow,ncol)
```

% BIPLOTTM plots the combined row and column object set
% using coordinates given in the $n \times 2$ matrix
% AXES; here the number of rows is NROW and the number
% of columns is NCOL, and n is the sum of NROW and NCOL.
%
% syntax: [] = biplottm(axes,nrow,ncol)
%
% The first NROW rows of AXES give the row object
% coordinates;
% the last NCOL rows of AXES give the column
% object coordinates.
% The plotting symbol for rows is a circle (o);
% for columns it is an asterisk (*).
% The labels for rows are from 1 to NROW;
% those for columns are from 1 to NCOL.

bisarobfnd.m

```
function [find,vaf,targone,targtwo,outpermone,...
    outpermtwo] = bisarobfnd(prox,inperm,kblock)
```

% BISAROBFND finds and fits the sum of two
% strongly anti-Robinson matrices using iterative
% projection to a symmetric proximity matrix in
% the L_{2}-norm based on permutations
% identified through the use of iterative quadratic
% assignment.
%
% syntax: [find,vaf,targone,targtwo,outpermone,...
%   outpermtwo] = bisarobfnd(prox,inperm,kblock)
%
% PROX is the input proximity matrix ($n \times n$ with a
% zero main diagonal and a dissimilarity interpretation);
% INPERM is a given starting permutation of the first n
% integers;
% FIND is the least-squares optimal matrix (with
% variance-accounted-for of VAF) to PROX and is the sum
% of the two strongly anti-Robinson matrices;
% TARGONE and TARGTWO are based on the two row and column
% object orderings given by the ending permutations
% OUTPERMONE and OUTPERMTWO.
% KBLOCK defines the block size in the use of the
% iterative quadratic assignment routine.

biscalqa.m

```
function [outpermone,outpermtwo,coordone,coordtwo,...
      fitone,fittwo,addconone,addcontwo,vaf] = ...
    biscalqa(prox,targone,targtwo,inpermone,inpermtwo,...
      kblock,nopt)
```

% BISCALQA carries out a bidimensional scaling of a
% symmetric proximity matrix using iterative
% quadratic assignment.
%
% syntax: [outpermone,outpermtwo,coordone,coordtwo,...
%   fitone,fittwo,addconone,addcontwo,vaf] = ...
%   biscalqa(prox,targone,targtwo,inpermone,inpermtwo,...
%   kblock,nopt)
%
% PROX is the input proximity matrix (with a zero main

```
%  diagonal and a dissimilarity interpretation);
%  TARGONE is the input target matrix for the first
%  dimension (usually with a zero main diagonal and a
%  dissimilarity interpretation representing
%  equally spaced locations along
%  a continuum); TARGTWO is the input target
%  matrix for the second dimension;
%  INPERMONE is the input beginning permutation for the
%  first  dimension (a permutation of the first $n$
%  integers);
%  INPERMTWO is the input beginning
%  permutation for the second dimension;
%  the insertion and rotation routines use from 1 to
%  KBLOCK (which is less than or equal to $n-1$)
%  consecutive objects in the permutation defining the
%  row and column orders of the data matrix.
%  NOPT controls the confirmatory or exploratory fitting
%  of the unidimensional scales; a value of NOPT = 0
%  will fit in a confirmatory manner the two scales
%  indicated by INPERMONE and INPERMTWO;
%  a value of NOPT = 1 uses iterative QA
%  to locate the better permutations to fit;
%  OUTPERMONE is the final object permutation for the
%  first dimension; OUTPERMTWO is the final object
%  permutation for the second dimension;
%  COORDONE is the set of first dimension coordinates
%  in ascending order; COORDTWO is the set of second
%  dimension coordinates in ascending order;
%  ADDCONONE is the additive constant for the first
%  dimensional model; ADDCONTWO is the additive constant
%  for the second dimensional model;
%  VAF is the variance-accounted-for in PROX by
%  the bidimensional scaling.
```

biscaltmac.m

```
function [find,vaf,targone,targtwo,outpermone,outpermtwo,...
   rowpermone,colpermone,rowpermtwo,colpermtwo,addconone,...
   addcontwo,coordone,coordtwo,axes] = ...
    biscaltmac(proxtm,inpermone,inpermtwo,kblock,nopt)


% BISCALTMAC finds and fits the sum of two linear
% unidimensional scales using iterative projection to
% a two-mode proximity matrix in the $L_{2}$-norm based on
% permutations identified through the use of iterative
```

```
% quadratic assignment.
%
% syntax: [find,vaf,targone,targtwo,outpermone,outpermtwo,...
%    rowpermone,colpermone,rowpermtwo,colpermtwo,addconone,...
%    addcontwo,coordone,coordtwo,axes] = ...
%      biscaltmac(proxtm,inpermone,inpermtwo,kblock,nopt)
%
% PROXTM is the input two-mode proximity matrix ($nrow
% \times ncol$ with a dissimilarity interpretation);
% FIND is the least-squares optimal matrix (with
% variance-accounted-for of VAF) to PROXTM and is
% the sum of the two matrices TARGONE and TARGTWO based
% on the two row and column object orderings given by the
% ending permutations OUTPERMONE and OUTPERMTWO,
% and in turn ROWPERMONE and ROWPERMTWO and
% COLPERMONE and COLPERMTWO. KBLOCK defines the block size
% in the use of the iterative quadratic assignment routine
% and ADDCONONE and ADDCONTWO are
% the two additive constants for the two model components;
% The $n$ coordinates are in COORDONE and COORDTWO.
% The input permutations are INPERMONE and INPERMTWO.
% The $n \times 2$ matrix AXES gives the
% plotting coordinates for the
% combined row and column object set.
% NOPT controls the confirmatory or
% exploratory fitting of the unidimensional
% scales; a value of NOPT = 0 will
% fit in a confirmatory manner the two scales
% indicated by INPERMONE and INPERMTWO;
% a value of NOPT = 1 uses iterative QA
% to locate the better permutations to fit.
```

biultrafnd.m

```
function [find,vaf,targone,targtwo] = ...
   biultrafnd(prox,inperm)


% BIULTRAFND finds and fits the sum
% of two ultrametrics using iterative projection
% heuristically on a symmetric proximity matrix in the
% $L_{2}$-norm.
%
% syntax: [find,vaf,targone,targtwo] = ...
%    biultrafnd(prox,inperm)
%
% PROX is the input proximity matrix (with a zero main
```

% diagonal and a dissimilarity interpretation);
% INPERM is a permutation that determines the order in
% which the inequality constraints are considered;
% FIND is the found least-squares matrix (with
% variance-accounted-for of VAF) to PROX and is the sum
% of the two ultrametric matrices TARGONE and TARGTWO.

centfit.m

```
function [fit,vaf,lengths] = centfit(prox)
```

% CENTFIT finds the least-squares fitted centroid metric
% (FIT) to PROX, the input proximity matrix (with a zero
% main diagonal and a dissimilarity interpretation).
%
% syntax: [fit,vaf,lengths] = centfit(prox)
%
% The n values that serve to define the approximating
% sums, $g_{i} + g_{j}$, are given in the vector LENGTHS
% of size $n \times 1$.

centfittm.m

```
function [fit,vaf,lengths] = centfittm(proxtm)
```

% CENTFITTM finds the least-squares fitted two-mode
% centroid metric (FIT) to PROXTM, the two-mode
% rectangular input proximity matrix (with a
% dissimilarity interpretation).
%
% syntax: [fit,vaf,lengths] = centfittm(proxtm)
%
% The n values (where n = number of rows + number
% of columns)% serve to define the approximating sums,
% $u_{i} + v_{j}$, where the u_{i} are for the rows
% and the v_{j} are for the columns;
% these are given in the vector LENGTHS of size
% $n \times 1$, with row values first followed by the
% column values.

cirarobfit.m

```
function [fit, vaf] = cirarobfit(prox,inperm,targ)
```

% CIRAROBFIT fits a circular anti-Robinson matrix using

```
% iterative projection to a symmetric proximity matrix
% in the $L_{2}$-norm.
%
% syntax: [fit, vaf] = cirarobfit(prox,inperm,targ)
%
% PROX is the input proximity matrix ($n \times n$ with
% a zero
% main diagonal and a dissimilarity interpretation);
% INPERM is a given permutation of the first $n$
% integers (around a circle); TARG is a given
% $n \times n$ matrix having the circular anti-Robinson
% form that guides the direction in which
% distances are taken around the circle.
% FIT is the least-squares optimal matrix (with
% variance-accounted-for of VAF) to PROX having
% a circular anti-Robinson form for the row and
% column object ordering given by INPERM.
```

cirarobfnd.m

```
function [find, vaf, outperm] = ...
    cirarobfnd(prox, inperm, kblock)

% CIRAROBFND finds and fits a circular
% anti-Robinson matrix using iterative projection to
% a symmetric proximity matrix in the $L_{2}$-norm based
% on a permutation identified through the use of
% iterative quadratic assignment.
%
% syntax: [find, vaf, outperm] = ...
%     cirarobfnd(prox, inperm, kblock)
%
% PROX is the input proximity matrix ($n \times n$
% with a zero main diagonal and a dissimilarity
% interpretation); INPERM is a given starting permutation
% (assumed to be around the circle) of the first
% $n$ integers; FIT is the least-squares optimal
% matrix (with variance-accounted-for of VAF) to PROX
% having a circular anti-Robinson form for the
% row and column object ordering given by the
% ending permutation OUTPERM.
% KBLOCK defines the block size in the use of the iterative
% quadratic assignment routine.
```

cirarobfnd_ac.m

```
function [find, vaf, outperm] = ...
    cirarobfnd_ac(prox, inperm, kblock)
```

```
% CIRAROBFND_AC fits a circular anti-Robinson matrix using
% iterative projection to a symmetric proximity matrix
% in the $L_{2}$-norm based on a permutation identified
% through the use of iterative quadratic assignment.
%
% syntax: [find, vaf, outperm] = ...
%    cirarobfnd_ac(prox, inperm, kblock)
%
% PROX is the input proximity matrix ($n \times n$
% with a zero main diagonal and a dissimilarity
% interpretation);
% INPERM is a given starting permutation (assumed
% to be around the circle) of the first $n$ integers;
% FIND is the least-squares optimal matrix (with
% variance-accounted-for of VAF) to PROX having a
% circular anti-Robinson form for the row and column
% object ordering given by the ending permutation
% OUTPERM. KBLOCK defines the block size in the use of
% the iterative quadratic assignment routine.
% In contrast to cirarobfnd.m, the circular target
% is constructed using cirfitac.m (as
% opposed to cirfit.m)
```

circularplot.m

```
function [circum,radius,coord,degrees,cumdegrees] = ...
    circularplot(circ,inperm)
```

```
% CIRCULARPLOT plots the object set using the
% coordinates around a circular structure derived
% from the $n \times n$ interpoint distance matrix
% around a circle given by CIRC.
% The positions are labeled by the order of objects
% given in INPERM.
%
% syntax: [circum,radius,coord,degrees,cumdegrees] = ...
%    circularplot(circ,inperm)
%
% The output consists of a plot, the circumference
% of the circle (CIRCUM) and radius (RADIUS),
```

```
% the coordinates of the plot positions (COORD),
% and the degrees and cumulative
% degrees induced between the plot positions
% (in DEGREES and CUMDEGREES).
% The positions around the circle are numbered from 1
% (at the ''noon'' position) to $n$, moving
% clockwise around the circular structure.
```

cirfit.m

```
function [fit, diff] = cirfit(prox,inperm)

%   CIRFIT does a confirmatory fitting of a given order
%   (assumed to reflect a circular ordering around a
%   closed  unidimensional structure) using Dykstra's
%   (Kaczmarz's) iterative projection least-squares
%    method.
%
%   syntax: [fit, diff] = cirfit(prox,inperm)
%
%   INPERM is the given order; FIT is an $n \times n$
%   matrix that is fitted to PROX(INPERM,INPERM)
%   with least-squares value DIFF.
```

cirfitac.m

```
function [fit, vaf, addcon] = cirfitac(prox,inperm)

%   CIRFITAC does a confirmatory fitting (including
%   the estimation of an additive constant) for a given
%   order(assumed to reflect a circular ordering around
%   a closed unidimensional structure) using the Dykstra--
%   Kaczmarz iterative projection least-squares method.
%
%   syntax: [fit, vaf, addcon] = cirfitac(prox,inperm)
%
%   INPERM is the given order; FIT is an $n \times n$
%   matrix that is fitted to PROX(INPERM,INPERM) with
%   variance-accounted-for of VAF; ADDCON is the
%   estimated additive constant.
```

cirfitac_ftarg.m

```
function [fit, vaf, addcon] = ...
    cirfitac_ftarg(prox,inperm,targ)
```

```
%   CIRFITAC_FTARG does a confirmatory fitting (including
%   the estimation of an additive constant) for a given
%   order (assumed to reflect a circular ordering
%   around a closed unidimensional structure) using the
%   Dykstra--Kaczmarz iterative projection least-squares
%   method.
%
%   syntax: [fit, vaf, addcon] = ...
%      cirfitac_ftarg(prox,inperm,targ)
%
%   The inflection points are implicitly given by TARG,
%   which is assumed to reflect a circular ordering of
%   the same size as PROX. INPERM is the given order;
%   FIT is an $n \times n$ matrix that is fitted to
%   PROX(INPERM,INPERM) with variance-accounted-for of VAF;
%   ADDCON is the estimated additive constant.
```

cirsarobfit.m

```
function [fit, vaf] = cirsarobfit(prox,inperm,target)
```

```
% CIRSAROBFIT fits a strongly circular anti-Robinson
% matrix using iterative projection to
% a symmetric proximity matrix in the $L_{2}$-norm.
%
% syntax: [fit, vaf] = cirsarobfit(prox,inperm,target)
%
% PROX is the input proximity matrix ($n \times n$ with
% a zero main diagonal and a dissimilarity
% interpretation);
% INPERM is a given permutation of the first $n$ integers
% (around a circle);
% TARGET is a given $n \times n$ matrix having the
% circular anti-Robinson form that guides the direction
% in which distances are taken around the circle.
% FIT is the least-squares optimal matrix (with
% variance-accounted-for of VAF) to PROX having
% a strongly circular anti-Robinson form for the
% row and column object ordering given by INPERM.
```

cirsarobfnd.m

```
function [find, vaf, outperm] = ...
    cirsarobfnd(prox, inperm, kblock)
```

```
% CIRSAROBFND finds and fits a strongly circular
% anti-Robinson matrix using iterative projection to
% a symmetric proximity matrix in the $L_{2}$-norm based
% on a permutation identified through the use of
% iterative quadratic assignment.
%
% syntax: [find, vaf, outperm] = ...
%    cirsarobfnd(prox, inperm, kblock)
%
% PROX is the input proximity matrix ($n \times n$ with a
% zero main diagonal and a dissimilarity interpretation);
% INPERM is a given starting permutation (assumed to be
% around the circle) of the first $n$ integers;
% FIT is the least-squares optimal matrix (with
% variance-accounted-for of VAF) to PROX having a strongly
% circular anti-Robinson form for the row and column
% object ordering given by the ending permutation OUTPERM.
% KBLOCK defines the block size in the use of the
% iterative quadratic assignment routine.
```

cirsarobfnd_ac.m

```
function [find, vaf, outperm] = ...
     cirsarobfnd_ac(prox, inperm, kblock)

% CIRSAROBFND_AC fits a strongly circular
% anti-Robinson matrix using iterative projection to
% a symmetric proximity matrix in the $L_{2}$-norm based
% on a permutation identified through the use of
% iterative quadratic assignment.
%
% syntax: [find, vaf, outperm] = ...
%     cirsarobfnd_ac(prox, inperm, kblock)
%
% PROX is the input proximity matrix ($n \times n$
% with a zero main diagonal
% and a dissimilarity interpretation);
% INPERM is a given starting permutation (assumed to be
% around the circle) of the first $n$ integers;
% FIND is the least-squares optimal matrix (with variance-
% accounted-for of VAF) to PROX having a strongly
% circular anti-Robinson form for the row and column
% object ordering given by the ending permutation
% OUTPERM. KBLOCK defines the block size in the use
```

```
% of the iterative quadratic assignment routine.
% In comparison to cirsarobfnd.m
% (which uses cirarobfnd.m internally), cirsarobfnd_ac
% uses cirarobfnd_ac to identify a circular target.
```

insertqa.m

```
function [outperm, rawindex, allperms, index] = ...
   insertqa(prox, targ, inperm, kblock)


% INSERTQA carries out an iterative
% quadratic assignment maximization task using the
% insertion of from 1 to KBLOCK
% (which is less than or equal to $n-1$) consecutive
% objects in the permutation defining the row and column
% order of the data matrix.
%
% syntax: [outperm, rawindex, allperms, index] = ...
%   insertqa(prox, targ, inperm, kblock)
%
% INPERM is the input beginning permutation
% (a permutation of the first $n$ integers).
% PROX is the $n \times n$ input proximity matrix.
% TARG is the $n \times n$ input target matrix.
% OUTPERM is the final permutation of PROX with the
% cross-product index RAWINDEX with respect to TARG.
% ALLPERMS is a cell array containing INDEX entries
% corresponding to all the permutations identified
% in the optimization from ALLPERMS{1} = INPERM to
% ALLPERMS{INDEX} = OUTPERM.
```

linfit.m

```
function [fit, diff, coord] = linfit(prox,inperm)


%   LINFIT does a confirmatory fitting of a given
%   unidimensional order using Dykstra's
%   (Kaczmarz's) iterative projection least-squares
%   method.
%
%   syntax: [fit, diff, coord] = linfit(prox,inperm)
%
%   INPERM is the given order;
%   FIT is an $n \times n$ matrix that is fitted to
%   PROX(INPERM,INPERM) with least-squares value DIFF;
```

```
%   COORD gives the ordered coordinates whose absolute
%   differences could be used to reconstruct FIT.
```

linfitac.m

```
function [fit,vaf,coord,addcon] = linfitac(prox,inperm)
```

```
%   LINFITAC does a confirmatory fitting of a given
%   unidimensional order using the Dykstra--Kaczmarz
%   iterative projection least-squares method
%   but differing from linfit.m in
%   including the estimation of an additive constant.
%
%   syntax: [fit,vaf,coord,addcon] = linfitac(prox,inperm)
%
%   INPERM is the given order;
%   FIT is an $n \times n$ matrix that is fitted to
%   PROX(INPERM,INPERM) with variance-accounted-for VAF;
%   COORD gives the ordered coordinates whose absolute
%   differences could be used to reconstruct FIT;
%   ADDCON is the estimated additive constant that
%   can be interpreted as being added to PROX.
```

linfittm.m

```
function [fit,diff,rowperm,colperm,coord] = ...
      linfittm(proxtm,inperm)
```

```
%   LINFITTM does a confirmatory two-mode fitting of a
%   given unidimensional ordering of the row and column
%   objects of a two-mode proximity matrix PROXTM
%   using Dykstra's (Kaczmarz's) iterative projection
%   least-squares method.
%
%   syntax: [fit,diff,rowperm,colperm,coord] = ...
%      linfittm(proxtm,inperm)
%
%   INPERM is the given ordering of the row and column
%   objects together;
%   FIT is an nrow (number of rows) by ncol (number
%   of columns) matrix of absolute coordinate differences
%   that is fitted to PROXTM(ROWPERM,COLPERM)
%   with DIFF being the (least-squares criterion) sum
%   of squared discrepancies between
%   FIT and PROXTM(ROWPERM,COLMEAN);
```

```
%   ROWPERM and COLPERM are the row and column object
%   orderings derived from INPERM.  The nrow + ncol
%   coordinates (ordered with the smallest
%   set at a value of zero) are given in COORD.
```

linfittmac.m

```
function [fit,vaf,rowperm,colperm,addcon,coord] = ...
  linfittmac(proxtm,inperm)
```

```
%   LINFITTMAC does a confirmatory two-mode fitting of a
%   given unidimensional ordering of the row and column
%   objects of a two-mode proximity matrix PROXTM using
%   Dykstra's (Kaczmarz's) iterative projection
%   least-squares method; it differs from linfittm.m
%   by including the estimation of an
%   additive constant.
%
%   syntax: [fit,vaf,rowperm,colperm,addcon,coord] = ...
%     linfittmac(proxtm,inperm)
%
%   INPERM is the given ordering of the row and column
%   objects together;
%   FIT is an nrow (number of rows) by ncol (number
%   of columns) matrix of absolute coordinate differences
%   that is fitted to PROXTM(ROWPERM,COLPERM) with VAF
%   being the variance-accounted-for.
%   ROWPERM and COLPERM are the row and
%   column object orderings derived from INPERM.
%   ADDCON is the estimated additive constant that
%   can be interpreted as being
%   added to PROXTM (or, alternatively, subtracted
%   from the fitted matrix FIT).
%   The nrow + ncol coordinates (ordered with the smallest
%   set at a value of zero) are given in COORD.
```

order.m

```
function [outperm,rawindex,allperms,index] =  ...
  order(prox,targ,inperm,kblock)
```

```
% ORDER carries out an iterative quadratic assignment
% maximization task using a given square ($n x n$)
% proximity matrix PROX (with a zero main diagonal
% and a dissimilarity interpretation).
```

```
%
% syntax: [outperm,rawindex,allperms,index] = ...
%   order(prox,targ,inperm,kblock)
%
% Three separate local operations are used to permute
% the rows and columns of the proximity matrix to
% maximize the cross-product index with respect to a
% given square target matrix TARG:
% pairwise interchanges of objects in the permutation
% defining the row and column order of the square
% proximity matrix;
% the insertion of from 1 to KBLOCK
% (which is less than or equal to $n-1$) consecutive
% objects in the permutation defining the row and column
% order of the data matrix;
% the rotation of from 2 to KBLOCK
% (which is less than or equal to $n-1$) consecutive
% objects in the permutation defining the row and
% column order of the data matrix.
% INPERM is the input beginning permutation (a
% permutation of the first $n$ integers).
% OUTPERM is the final permutation of PROX with the
% cross-product index RAWINDEX
% with respect to TARG. ALLPERMS is a cell array
% containing INDEX entries corresponding to all the
% permutations identified in the optimization from
% ALLPERMS{1} = INPERM to ALLPERMS{INDEX} = OUTPERM.
```

ordertm.m

```
function [outperm,rawindex,allperms,index, ...
   squareprox] = ordertm(proxtm,targ,inperm,kblock)

% ORDERTM carries out an iterative
% quadratic assignment maximization task using the
% two-mode proximity matrix PROXTM
% (with entries deviated from the mean proximity)
% in the upper-right- and lower-left-hand portions of
% a defined square ($n x n$) proximity matrix
% (called SQUAREPROX with a dissimilarity interpretation)
% with zeros placed elsewhere ($n$ = number of rows +
% number of columns of PROXTM = nrow + ncol).
%
% syntax: [outperm,rawindex,allperms,index,...
%    squareprox] = ordertm(proxtm, targ, inperm, kblock)
```

```
%
% Three separate local operations are used to permute
% the rows and columns of the square
% proximity matrix to maximize the cross-product
% index with respect to a square target matrix TARG:
% pairwise interchanges of objects in the
% permutation defining the row and column
% order of the square proximity matrix; the insertion of
% from 1 to KBLOCK (which is less than or equal to $n-1$)
% consecutive objects in the permutation defining the
% row and column order of the data matrix;
% the rotation of from 2 to KBLOCK (which is less than
% or equal to $n-1$) consecutive objects in
% the permutation defining the row and column order of
% the data matrix.
% INPERM is the input beginning permutation
% (a permutation of the first $n$ integers).
% PROXTM is the two-mode $nrow x ncol$ input
% proximity matrix.
% TARG is the $n x n$ input target matrix.
% OUTPERM is the final permutation of SQUAREPROX with the
% cross-product index RAWINDEX
% with respect to TARG. ALLPERMS is a cell array
% containing INDEX entries corresponding to all the
% permutations identified in the optimization from
% ALLPERMS{1} = INPERM to ALLPERMS{INDEX} = OUTPERM.
```

pairwiseqa.m

```
function [outperm, rawindex, allperms, index] = ...
   pairwiseqa(prox, targ, inperm)

% PAIRWISEQA carries out an iterative
% quadratic assignment maximization task using the
% pairwise interchanges of objects in the
% permutation defining the row and column
% order of the data matrix.
%
% syntax: [outperm, rawindex, allperms, index] = ...
%   pairwiseqa(prox, targ, inperm)
%
% INPERM is the input beginning permutation
% (a permutation of the first $n$ integers).
% PROX is the $n \times n$ input proximity matrix.
% TARG is the $n \times n$ input target matrix.
```

```
% OUTPERM is the final permutation of
% PROX with the cross-product index RAWINDEX
% with respect to TARG.
% ALLPERMS is a cell array containing INDEX entries
% corresponding to all the permutations identified
% in the optimization from ALLPERMS{1} = INPERM to
% ALLPERMS{INDEX} = OUTPERM.
```

proxmon.m

```
function [monproxpermut, vaf, diff] = ...
    proxmon(proxpermut, fitted)


%   PROXMON produces a monotonically transformed
%   proximity matrix (MONPROXPERMUT) from the order
%   constraints obtained from each  pair of entries
%   in the input proximity matrix PROXPERMUT
%   (symmetric with a zero main diagonal and a
%   dissimilarity  interpretation).
%
%   syntax: [monproxpermut, vaf, diff] = ...
%       proxmon(proxpermut, fitted)
%
%   MONPROXPERMUT is close to the
%   $n \times n$ matrix FITTED in the least-squares
%   sense;
%   the variance-accounted-for (VAF) is how
%   much variance in MONPROXPERMUT can be accounted
%   for by FITTED;
%   DIFF is the value of the least-squares criterion.
```

proxmontm.m

```
function [monproxpermuttm, vaf, diff] = ...
     proxmontm(proxpermuttm, fittedtm)


%   PROXMONTM produces a monotonically transformed
%   two-mode proximity matrix (MONPROXPERMUTTM)
%   from the order constraints obtained
%   from each pair of entries in the input two-mode
%   proximity matrix PROXPERMUTTM (with a dissimilarity
%   interpretation).
%
%   syntax: [monproxpermuttm, vaf, diff] = ...
%       proxmontm(proxpermuttm, fittedtm)
```

```
%
%   MONPROXPERMUTTM is close to the $nrow \times ncol$
%   matrix FITTEDTM in the least-squares sense;
%   the variance-accounted-for (VAF) is how much variance
%   in MONPROXPERMUTTM can be accounted for by FITTEDTM;
%   DIFF is the value of the least-squares criterion.
```

proxrand.m

```
function [randprox] = proxrand(prox)

%   PROXRAND produces a symmetric proximity matrix
%   RANDPROX with a zero main diagonal having
%   entries that are a random permutation of those
%   in the symmetric input proximity
%   matrix PROX.
%
%   syntax: [randprox] = proxrand(prox)
```

proxrandtm.m

```
function [randproxtm] = proxrandtm(proxtm)


%   PROXRANDTM produces a two-mode proximity matrix
%   (RANDPROXTM) having entries that are a random
%   permutation of those in the two-mode input
%   proximity matrix PROXTM.
%
%   syntax: [randproxtm] = proxrandtm(proxtm)
```

proxstd.m

```
function [stanprox, stanproxmult] = proxstd(prox,mean)

%   PROXSTD produces a standardized proximity matrix
%   (STANPROX) from the input $n \times n$ proximity
%   matrix (PROX) with zero main diagonal and a
%   dissimilarity interpretation.
%
%   syntax: [stanprox, stanproxmult] = proxstd(prox,mean)
%
%   STANPROX entries have unit variance (standard
%   deviation of one) with a mean of MEAN given as an
```

```
%    input number;
%    STANPROXMULT (upper-triangular) entries have a sum of
%    squares equal to $n(n-1)/2$.
```

proxstdtm.m

```
function [stanproxtm, stanproxmulttm] = ...
    proxstdtm(proxtm,mean)


%    PROXSTDTM produces a standardized two-mode
%    proximity matrix (STANPROXTM) from the input
%    $nrow \times ncol$ two-mode proximity matrix (PROXTM)
%    with a dissimilarity interpretation.
%
%    syntax: [stanproxtm, stanproxmulttm] = ...
%       proxstdtm(proxtm,mean)
%
%    STANPROXTM entries have unit variance (standard
%    deviation of one) with a mean of MEAN given as an
%    input number;
%    STANPROXMULTTM entries have a sum of squares equal to
%    $nrow*rcol$.
```

randprox.m

```
function [prox] = randprox(n)


%    RANDPROX produces a random symmetric proximity matrix
%    (PROX) of size $n \times n$,
%    with a zero main diagonal and entries uniform
%    between 0 and 1.
%
%    syntax: [prox] = randprox(n)
```

rotateqa.m

```
function [outperm, rawindex, allperms, index] = ...
    rotateqa (prox, targ, inperm, kblock)


% ROTATEQA carries out an iterative
% quadratic assignment maximization task using the
% rotation of from 2 to KBLOCK (which is less than or
% equal to $n-1$) consecutive objects in
% the permutation defining the row and column order of
```

```
% the data matrix.
%
% syntax: [outperm, rawindex, allperms, index] = ...
%    rotateqa (prox, targ, inperm, kblock)
%
% INPERM is the input beginning permutation
% (a permutation of the first $n$ integers).
% PROX is the $n \times n$ input proximity matrix.
% TARG is the $n \times n$ input target matrix.
% OUTPERM is the final permutation of PROX with the
% cross-product index RAWINDEX with respect to TARG.
% ALLPERMS is a cell array containing INDEX entries
% corresponding to all the permutations identified
% in the optimization from
% ALLPERMS{1} = INPERM to ALLPERMS{INDEX} = OUTPERM.
```

sarobfit.m

```
function [fit, vaf] = sarobfit(prox, inperm)

% SAROBFIT fits a strongly anti-Robinson matrix using
% iterative projection to a symmetric proximity matrix
% in the $L_{2}$-norm.
% PROX is the input proximity matrix ($n \times n$ with a
% zero main diagonal and a dissimilarity interpretation).
%
% syntax: [fit, vaf] = sarobfit(prox, inperm)
%
% INPERM is a given permutation of the first $n$
% integers;
% FIT is the least-squares optimal matrix (with
% variance-accounted-for of VAF) to PROX having
% a strongly anti-Robinson form for the row and column
% object ordering given by INPERM.
```

sarobfnd.m

```
function [find,vaf,outperm] = ...
    sarobfnd(prox,inperm,kblock)

% SAROBFND finds and fits a strongly
% anti-Robinson matrix using iterative projection to
% a symmetric proximity matrix in the $L_{2}$-norm based
% on a permutation identified through the use of
% iterative quadratic assignment.
```

```
%
% syntax: [find,vaf,outperm] = ...
%    sarobfnd(prox,inperm,kblock)
%
% PROX is the input proximity matrix ($n \times n$ with a
% zero main diagonal and a dissimilarity interpretation);
% INPERM is a given starting permutation of the first $n$
% integers; FIND is the least-squares optimal matrix
% (with variance-accounted-for of VAF) to PROX having a
% strongly anti-Robinson form for the row and column
% object ordering given by the ending permutation OUTPERM.
% KBLOCK defines the block size in the use of the iterative
% quadratic assignment routine.
```

targcir.m

```
function [targcircular] = targcir(n)

%   TARGCIR produces a symmetric proximity matrix of size
%   $n \times n$, containing distances
%   between equally and unit-spaced positions
%   around a circle: targcircular(i,j) =
%   min(abs(i-j),n-abs(i-j)).
%
%   syntax: [targcircular] = targcir(n)
```

targfit.m

```
function [fit, vaf] = targfit(prox,targ)

% TARGFIT fits through iterative projection a given set
% of equality and inequality constraints (as represented
% by the equalities and inequalities present among the
% entries in a target matrix TARG) to a symmetric
% proximity matrix in the $L_{2}$-norm.
%
% syntax: [fit, vaf] = targfit(prox,targ)
%
% PROX is the input proximity matrix (with a zero
% main diagonal and a dissimilarity interpretation);
% TARG is a matrix of the same size as PROX;
% FIT is the least-squares optimal matrix (with
% variance-accounted-for of VAF) to PROX satisfying the
% equality and inequality constraints implicit in TARG.
```

targlin.m

```
function [targlinear] = targlin(n)

%   TARGLIN produces a symmetric proximity matrix of size
%   $n \times n$, containing distances
%   between equally and unit-spaced positions
%   along a line: targlinear(i,j) = abs(i-j).
%
%   syntax: [targlinear] = targlin(n)
```

trimonscalqa.m

```
function [outpermone,outpermtwo,outpermthree,coordone, ...
     coordtwo,coordthree,fitone,fittwo,fitthree, ...
         addconone,addcontwo,addconthree,vaf,monprox] = ...
  trimonscalqa(prox,targone,targtwo,targthree,inpermone,...
     inpermtwo,inpermthree,kblock,nopt)

%   TRIMONSCALQA carries out a tridimensional scaling of a
%   symmetric proximity matrix using iterative
%   quadratic assignment, plus it provides an optimal
%   monotonic transformation (MONPROX) of the
%   original input proximity matrix.
%
%   syntax: [outpermone,outpermtwo,outpermthree,coordone, ...
%      coordtwo,coordthree,fitone,fittwo,fitthree, ...
%          addconone,addcontwo,addconthree,vaf,monprox] = ...
%   trimonscalqa(prox,targone,targtwo,targthree,inpermone,...
%      inpermtwo,inpermthree,kblock,nopt)
%
%   PROX is the input proximity matrix (with a zero main
%   diagonal and a dissimilarity interpretation);
%   TARGONE is the input target matrix for the first
%   dimension (usually with a zero main diagonal
%   and with a dissimilarity interpretation representing
%   equally spaced locations along a continuum);
%   TARGTWO is the input target matrix for
%   the second dimension; TARGTHREE is the input target
%   matrix for the third dimension;
%   INPERMONE is the input beginning permutation for the
%   first dimension (a permutation of the first $n$
%   integers);
%   INPERMTWO is the input beginning
%   permutation for the second dimension; INPERMTHREE
```

```
%    is the input beginning permutation for the third
%    dimension;
%    the insertion and rotation routines use from 1
%    to KBLOCK (which is less than or equal to $n-1$)
%    consecutive objects in the permutation defining the
%    row and column orders of the data matrix;
%    NOPT controls the confirmatory or exploratory fitting
%    of the unidimensional scales; a value of NOPT = 0 will
%    fit in a confirmatory manner the two scales
%    indicated by INPERMONE and INPERMTWO; a value of
%    NOPT = 1 uses iterative QA to locate the better
%    permutations to fit;
%    OUTPERMONE is the final object permutation for the
%    first dimension;
%    OUTPERMTWO is the final object permutation
%    for the second dimension; OUTPERMTHREE is the final
%    object permutation for the third dimension;
%    COORDONE is the set of first dimension coordinates
%    in ascending order; COORDTWO is the set of second
%    dimension coordinates in ascending order;
%    COORDTHREE is the set of
%    second dimension coordinates in ascending order;
%    ADDCONONE is the additive constant for the first
%    dimensional model; ADDCONTWO is the additive constant
%    for the second dimensional model; ADDCONTHREE is the
%    additive constant for the third dimensional model;
%    VAF is the variance-accounted-for in MONPROX by
%    the tridimensional scaling.
```

triscalqa.m

```
function [outpermone,outpermtwo,outpermthree,coordone,...
 coordtwo,coordthree,fitone,fittwo,fitthree,addconone,...
 addcontwo,addconthree,vaf] =...
   triscalqa(prox,targone,targtwo,targthree,inpermone,...
    inpermtwo,inpermthree,kblock,nopt)

%   TRISCALQA carries out a tridimensional scaling
%   of a symmetric proximity matrix using iterative
%   quadratic assignment.
%
%   syntax: [outpermone,outpermtwo,outpermthree,coordone,...
%   coordtwo,coordthree,fitone,fittwo,fitthree,addconone,...
%    addcontwo,addconthree,vaf] =...
%     triscalqa(prox,targone,targtwo,targthree,inpermone,...
```

```
%     inpermtwo,inpermthree,kblock,nopt)
%
% PROX is the input proximity matrix (with a zero main
% diagonal and a dissimilarity interpretation);
% TARGONE is the input target matrix for the first
% dimension (usually with a zero main diagonal and
% with a dissimilarity interpretation representing
% equally spaced locations along
% a continuum); TARGTWO is the input target
% matrix for the second dimension; TARGTHREE is the input
% target matrix for the third dimension;
% INPERMONE is the input beginning permutation for the
% first dimension (a permutation of the first
% $n$ integers);
% INPERMTWO is the input beginning permutation for the
% second dimension; INPERMTHREE is the input beginning
% permutation for the third dimension;
% the insertion and rotation routines use from 1 to
% KBLOCK (which is less than or equal to $n-1$)
% consecutive objects in the permutation defining the
% row and column orders of the data
% matrix; NOPT controls the confirmatory or exploratory
% fitting of the unidimensional scales;
% a value of NOPT = 0 will fit in
% a confirmatory manner the three scales
% indicated by INPERMONE and INPERMTWO;
% a value of NOPT = 1 uses iterative QA
% to locate the better permutations to fit.
% OUTPERMONE is the final object permutation for
% the first dimension; OUTPERMTWO is the final object
% permutation for the second dimension;
% OUTPERMTHREE is the final object
% permutation for the third dimension;
% COORDONE is the set of
% first dimension coordinates in ascending order;
% COORDTWO is the set of second dimension coordinates
% in ascending order;
% COORDTHREE is the set of third dimension coordinates
% in ascending order; ADDCONONE is the additive constant
% for the first dimensional model;
% ADDCONTWO is the additive constant
% for the second dimensional model;
% ADDCONTHREE is the additive
% constant for the third dimensional model;
% VAF is the variance-accounted-for in PROX by the
% bidimensional scaling.
```

ultracomptm.m

```
function [ultracomp] = ultracomptm(ultraproxtm)
```

```
% ULTRACOMPTM provides a completion of a given two-mode
% ultrametric matrix to a symmetric proximity matrix
% satisfying the usual ultrametric constraints.
%
% syntax: [ultracomp] = ultracomptm(ultraproxtm)
%
% ULTRAPROXTM is the $nrow \times ncol$ two-mode
% ultrametric matrix;
% ULTRACOMP is the completed symmetric
% $n \times n$ proximity matrix having the usual
% ultrametric pattern for $n = nrow + ncol$.
```

ultrafit.m

```
function [fit,vaf] = ultrafit(prox,targ)
```

```
% ULTRAFIT fits a given ultrametric using iterative
% projection to a symmetric proximity matrix in the
% $L_{2}$-norm.
%
% syntax: [fit,vaf] = ultrafit(prox,targ)
%
% PROX is the input proximity matrix (with a zero main
% diagonal and a dissimilarity interpretation);
% TARG is an ultrametric matrix of the same size as PROX;
% FIT is the least-squares optimal matrix (with
% variance-accounted-for of VAF) to PROX satisfying the
% ultrametric constraints implicit in TARG.
```

ultrafittm.m

```
function [fit,vaf] = ultrafittm(proxtm,targ)
```

```
% ULTRAFITTM fits a given (two-mode) ultrametric using
% iterative projection to a two-mode (rectangular)
% proximity matrix in the $L_{2}$-norm.
%
% syntax: [fit,vaf] = ultrafittm(proxtm,targ)
%
% PROXTM is the input proximity matrix (with a
% dissimilarity interpretation);
```

```
% TARG is an ultrametric matrix of the same size
% as PROXTM; FIT is the least-squares optimal matrix
% (with variance-accounted-for of VAF) to PROXTM
% satisfying the ultrametric constraints implicit in TARG.
```

ultrafnd.m

```
function [find,vaf] = ultrafnd(prox,inperm)
```

```
% ULTRAFND finds and fits an ultrametric using iterative
% projection heuristically on a symmetric proximity
% matrix in the $L_{2}$-norm.
%
% syntax: [find,vaf] = ultrafnd(prox,inperm)
%
% PROX is the input proximity matrix (with a zero main
% diagonal and a dissimilarity interpretation);
% INPERM is a permutation that determines the order
% in which the inequality constraints are considered;
% FIND is the found least-squares matrix
% (with variance-accounted-for of VAF) to PROX
% satisfying the ultrametric constraints.
```

ultrafndtm.m

```
function [find,vaf] = ...
    ultrafndtm(proxtm,inpermrow,inpermcol)
```

```
% ULTRAFNDTM finds and fits a two-mode ultrametric using
% iterative projection heuristically on a rectangular
% proximity matrix in the $L_{2}$-norm.
%
% syntax: [find,vaf] = ...
%    ultrafndtm(proxtm,inpermrow,inpermcol)
%
% PROXTM is the input proximity matrix (with a
% dissimilarity interpretation);
% INPERMROW and INPERMCOL are permutations for the row
% and column objects that determine the order in which
% the inequality constraints are considered;
% FIND is the found least-squares matrix (with
% variance-accounted-for of VAF) to PROXTM satisfying
% the ultrametric constraints.
```

ultraorder.m

```
function [orderprox,orderperm] = ultraorder(prox)
```

% ULTRAORDER finds for the input proximity matrix PROX
% (assumed to be ultrametric with a zero main diagonal)
% a permutation ORDERPERM that displays the anti-
% Robinson form in the reordered proximity matrix
% ORDERPROX; thus, prox(orderperm,orderperm) = orderprox.
%
% syntax: [orderprox,orderperm] = ultraorder(prox)

ultraplot.m

```
function [] = ultraplot(ultra)
```

% ULTRAPLOT gives a dendrogram plot for the input
% ultrametric dissimilarity matrix ULTRA.
%
% syntax: [] = ultraplot(ultra)

unicirac.m

```
function [find, vaf, outperm, addcon] = ...
    unicirac(prox, inperm, kblock)
```

% UNICIRAC finds and fits a circular
% unidimensional scale using iterative projection to
% a symmetric proximity matrix in the L_{2}-norm based
% on a permutation identified through the use of
% iterative quadratic assignment.
%
% syntax: [find, vaf, outperm, addcon] = ...
%   unicirac(prox, inperm, kblock)
%
% PROX is the input proximity matrix ($n \times n$ with a
% zero main diagonal and a dissimilarity interpretation);
% INPERM is a given starting permutation (assumed to be
% around the circle) of the first n integers;
% FIND is the least-squares optimal matrix (with
% variance-accounted-for of VAF) to PROX having a circular
% anti-Robinson form for the row and column
% object ordering given by the ending permutation OUTPERM.
% The spacings among the objects are given by the diagonal
% entries in FIND (and the extreme (1,n) entry in FIND).

```
% KBLOCK defines the block size in the use of
% the iterative quadratic assignment routine.
% The additive constant for the model is
% given by ADDCON.
```

uniscalqa.m

```
function [outperm,rawindex,allperms,index,coord,...
    diff] = uniscalqa(prox, targ, inperm, kblock)

%   UNISCALQA carries out a unidimensional scaling of a
%   symmetric proximity matrix using iterative
%   quadratic assignment.
%
%   syntax: [outperm,rawindex,allperms,index,coord,...
%      diff] = uniscalqa(prox, targ, inperm, kblock)
%
%   PROX is the input proximity matrix (with a zero main
%   diagonal and a dissimilarity interpretation);
%   TARG is the input target matrix (usually with a zero
%   main diagonal and a dissimilarity interpretation
%   representing equally spaced locations along a
%   continuum);
%   INPERM is the input beginning permutation
%   (a permutation of the first $n$ integers).
%   OUTPERM is the final permutation of PROX
%   with the cross-product index RAWINDEX
%   with respect to TARG redefined as
%   $ = \{abs(coord(i) - coord(j))\}$;
%   ALLPERMS is a cell array containing INDEX entries
%   corresponding to all the permutations identified
%   in the optimization from
%   ALLPERMS{1} = INPERM to ALLPERMS{INDEX} = OUTPERM.
%   The insertion and rotation routines use from 1 to
%   KBLOCK (which is less than or equal to $n-1$)
%   consecutive objects in the permutation defining
%   the row and column order of the data
%   matrix.  COORD is the set of coordinates of
%   the unidimensional scaling in ascending order;
%   DIFF is the value of the least-squares loss
%   function for the coordinates and object permutation.
```

uniscaltmac.m

```
function [find,vaf,outperm,rowperm,colperm,addcon, ...
  coord] = uniscaltmac(proxtm,inperm,kblock)
```

```
% UNISCALTMAC finds and fits a linear
% unidimensional scale using iterative projection to
% a two-mode proximity matrix in the $L_{2}$-norm based
% on a permutation identified through the use of iterative
% quadratic assignment.
%
% syntax: [find,vaf,outperm,rowperm,colperm,addcon,...
%    coord] = uniscaltmac(proxtm,inperm,kblock)
%
% PROXTM is the input two-mode proximity matrix
% ($n_{a} \times n_{b}$ with a zero main diagonal
% and a dissimilarity interpretation);
% INPERM is a given starting permutation of the
% first $n = n_{a} + n_{b}$ integers;
% FIND is the least-squares optimal matrix (with
% variance-accounted-for of VAF) to PROXTM having a
% linear unidimensional form for the row and column
% object ordering given by the ending permutation OUTPERM.
% The spacings among the objects are given by the entries
% in FIND.
% KBLOCK defines the block size in the use of the
% iterative quadratic assignment routine.
% The additive constant for the model is given by ADDCON.
% ROWPERM and COLPERM are the resulting row and column
% permutations for the objects.  The nrow + ncol
% coordinates (ordered with the smallest set at a
% value of zero) are given in COORD.
```

Bibliography

Arabie, P. (1991). Was Euclid an unnecessarily sophisticated psychologist? *Psychometrika*, *56*, 567–587.

Arabie, P., Carroll, J. D., & DeSarbo, W. S. (1987). *Three-way scaling and clustering.* Newbury Park, CA: Sage. (Translated into Japanese by A. Okada & T. Imaizumi, 1990. Tokyo: Kyoritsu Shuppan.)

Barthélemy, J.-P., & Guénoche, A. (1991). *Trees and proximity representations.* Chichester: Wiley.

Bodewig, E. (1956). *Matrix calculus.* Amsterdam: North–Holland.

Brossier, G. (1987). Étude des matrices de proximité rectangulaires en vue de la classification [A study of rectangular proximity matrices from the point of view of classification]. *Revue de Statistiques Appliquées, 35(4)*, 43–68.

Brusco, M. J. (2001). A simulated annealing heuristic for unidimensional and multidimensional (city-block) scaling of symmetric proximity matrices. *Journal of Classification, 18*, 3–33.

Brusco, M. J., & Stahl, S. (2005). Optimal least-squares unidimensional scaling: Improved branch-and-bound procedures and comparison to dynamic programming. *Psychometrika, 70*, 253–270.

Busing, F. M. T. A., Commandeur, J. J. F., & Heiser, W. J. (1997). PROXSCAL: A multidimensional scaling program for individual differences scaling with constraints. In W. Bandilla & F. Faulbaum (Eds.), *Softstat '97: Advances in statistical software, Vol. 6* (pp. 67–74). Stuttgart: Lucius & Lucius.

Carroll, J. D. (1976). Spatial, non-spatial and hybrid models for scaling. *Psychometrika, 41*, 439–463.

Carroll, J. D. (1992). Metric, nonmetric, and quasi-nonmetric analysis of psychological data. Division 5 Presidential Address, American Psychological Association, Washington, DC, August, 1992 (published in *Score*, Newsletter of Division 5, October, 1992, pp. 4–5).

Carroll, J. D., & Arabie, P. (1998). Multidimensional scaling. In M. H. Birnbaum (Ed.), *Handbook of perception and cognition, Vol. 3* (pp. 179–250). San Diego: Academic Press.

Carroll, J. D., & Chang, J. J. (1970). Analysis of individual differences in multidimensional scaling via an N-way generalization of "Eckhart-Young" decomposition. *Psychometrika*, *35*, 283–319.

Carroll, J. D., Clark, L. A., & DeSarbo, W. S. (1984). The representation of three-way proximity data by single and multiple tree structure models. *Journal of Classification*, *1*, 25–75.

Carroll, J. D., & Pruzansky, S. (1975). Fitting of hierarchical tree structure (HTS) models, mixtures of HTS models, and hybrid models, via mathematical programming and alternating least squares. *Proceedings of the U.S.-Japan Seminar on Multidimensional Scaling*, 9–19.

Carroll, J. D., & Pruzansky, S. (1980). Discrete and hybrid scaling models. In E. D. Lantermann & H. Feger (Eds.), *Similarity and choice* (pp. 108–139). Bern: Hans Huber.

Cheney, W., & Goldstein, A. (1959). Proximity maps for convex sets. *Proceedings of the American Mathematical Society*, *10*, 448–450.

Coombs, C. H. (1964). *A theory of data.* New York: Wiley.

Critchley, F. (1994). On exchangeability-based equivalence relations induced by strongly Robinson and, in particular, by quadripolar Robinson dissimilarity matrices. In B. van Cutsem (Ed.), *Classification and dissimilarity analysis*, Lecture Notes in Statistics (pp. 173–199). New York: Springer-Verlag.

Critchley, F., & Fichet, B. (1994). The partial order by inclusion of the principal classes of dissimilarity on a finite set, and some of their basic properties. In B. van Cutsem (Ed.), *Classification and dissimilarity analysis*, Lecture Notes in Statistics (pp. 5–65). New York: Springer-Verlag.

Day, W. H. E. (1987). Computational complexity of inferring phylogenies from dissimilarity matrices. *Bulletin of Mathematical Biology*, *49*, 461–467.

Day, W. H. E. (1996). Complexity theory: An introduction for practitioners of classification. In P. Arabie, L. J. Hubert, & G. De Soete (Eds.), *Clustering and classification* (pp. 199–233). River Edge, NJ: World Scientific.

Defays, D. (1978). A short note on a method of seriation. *British Journal of Mathematical and Statistical Psychology*, *3*, 49–53.

de Leeuw, J., & Heiser, W. J. (1977). Convergence of correction-matrix algorithms for multidimensional scaling. In J. C. Lingoes, E. E. Roskam, & I. Borg (Eds.), *Geometric representations of relational data* (pp. 735–752). Ann Arbor, MI: Mathesis Press.

De Soete, G. (1983). A least squares algorithm for fitting additive trees to proximity data. *Psychometrika*, *48*, 621–626.

De Soete, G. (1984a). A least squares algorithm for fitting an ultrametric tree to a dissimilarity matrix. *Pattern Recognition Letters*, *2*, 133–137.

De Soete, G. (1984b). Ultrametric tree representations of incomplete dissimilarity data. *Journal of Classification, 1*, 235–242.

De Soete, G. (1984c). Additive tree representations of incomplete dissimilarity data. *Quality and Quantity, 18*, 387–393.

De Soete, G., Carroll, J. D., & DeSarbo, W. S. (1987). Least squares algorithms for constructing constrained ultrametric and additive tree representations of symmetric proximity data. *Journal of Classification, 4*, 155–173.

De Soete, G., DeSarbo, W. S., Furnas, G. W., & Carroll, J. D. (1984). The estimation of ultrametric and path length trees from rectangular proximity data. *Psychometrika, 49*, 289–310.

Durand, C., & Fichet, B. (1988). One-to-one correspondences in pyramidal representations: A unified approach. In H. H. Bock (Ed.), *Classification and related methods of data analysis* (pp. 85–90). Amsterdam: North–Holland.

Dykstra, R. L. (1983). An algorithm for restricted least squares regression. *Journal of the American Statistical Association, 78*, 837–842.

Francis, R. L., & White, J. A. (1974). *Facility layout and location: An analytical approach.* Englewood Cliffs, NJ: Prentice–Hall.

Furnas, G. W. (1980). *Objects and their features: The metric representation of two class data.* Unpublished doctoral dissertation. Stanford, CA: Stanford University.

Groenen, P. J. F., Heiser, W. J., & Meulman, J. J. (1999). Global optimization in least-squares multidimensional scaling by distance smoothing. *Journal of Classification, 16*, 225–254.

Guttman, L. (1968). A general nonmetric technique for finding the smallest coordinate space for a configuration of points. *Psychometrika, 33*, 469–506.

Hubert, L. J. (1974). Problems of seriation using a subject by item response matrix. *Psychological Bulletin, 81*, 976–983.

Hubert, L. J., & Arabie, P. (1986). Unidimensional scaling and combinatorial optimization. In J. de Leeuw, W. J. Heiser, J. J. Meulman, & F. Critchley (Eds.), *Multidimensional data analysis* (pp. 181–196). Leiden, The Netherlands: DSWO Press.

Hubert, L. J., & Arabie, P. (1994). The analysis of proximity matrices through sums of matrices having (anti-)Robinson forms. *British Journal of Mathematical and Statistical Psychology, 47*, 1–40.

Hubert, L. J., & Arabie, P. (1995a). The approximation of two-mode proximity matrices by sums of order-constrained matrices. *Psychometrika, 60*, 573–605.

Hubert, L. J., & Arabie, P. (1995b). Iterative projection strategies for the least-squares fitting of tree structures to proximity data. *British Journal of Mathematical and Statistical Psychology, 48*, 281–317.

Hubert, L. J., Arabie, P., & Hesson-McInnis, M. (1992). Multidimensional scaling in the city-block metric: A combinatorial approach. *Journal of Classification, 9*, 211–236.

Hubert, L. J., Arabie, P., & Meulman, J. J. (1997). Linear and circular unidimensional scaling for symmetric proximity matrices. *British Journal of Mathematical and Statistical Psychology, 50*, 253–284.

Hubert, L. J., Arabie, P., & Meulman, J. J. (1998) Graph-theoretic representations for proximity matrices through strongly-anti-Robinson or circular strongly-anti-Robinson matrices. *Psychometrika, 63*, 341–358.

Hubert, L. J., Arabie, P., & Meulman, J. J. (2001). *Combinatorial data analysis: Optimization by dynamic programming.* Philadelphia: SIAM.

Hubert, L. J., Arabie, P., & Meulman, J. J. (2002). Linear unidimensional scaling in the L_2-norm: Basic optimization methods using MATLAB. *Journal of Classification, 19*, 303–328.

Hubert, L. J., & Schultz, J. W. (1976). Quadratic assignment as a general data analysis strategy. *British Journal of Mathematical and Statistical Psychology, 29*, 190–241.

Hutchinson, J. W. (1989). NETSCAL: A network scaling algorithm for nonsymmetric proximity data. *Psychometrika, 54*, 25–51.

Johnson, R. A., & Wichern, D. W. (2002). *Applied multivariate statistical analysis.* Fifth Edition. Upper Saddle River, NJ: Prentice–Hall.

Kaczmarz, S. (1937). Angenäherte Auflösung von Systemen linearer Gleichungen. *Bulletin of the Polish Academy of Sciences, A35*, 355–357.

Klauer, K. C., & Carroll, J. D. (1989). A mathematical programming approach to fitting general graphs. *Journal of Classification, 6*, 247–270.

Klauer, K. C., & Carroll, J. D. (1991). A comparison of two approaches to fitting directed graphs to nonsymmetric proximity measures. *Journal of Classification, 8*, 251–268.

Křivánek, M. (1986). On the computational complexity of clustering. In E. Diday, Y. Escoufier, L. Lebart, J. P. Pagès, Y. Schektman, & R. Tomassone (Eds.), *Data analysis and informatics, IV*(pp. 89–96). Amsterdam: North–Holland.

Křivánek, M., & Morávek, J. (1986). NP-hard problems in hierarchical-tree clustering. *Acta Informatica, 23*, 311–323.

Kruskal, J. B. (1964a). Multidimensional scaling by optimizing goodness of fit to a nonmetric hypothesis. *Psychometrika, 29*, 1–27.

Kruskal, J. B. (1964b). Nonmetric multidimensional scaling: A numerical method. *Psychometrika, 29*, 115–129.

Kruskal, J. B., & Wish, M. (1978). *Multidimensional scaling.* Newbury Park, CA: Sage.

Kruskal, J. B., Young, F. W., & Seery, J. B. (1977). *How to use KYST2, a very flexible program to do multidimensional scaling and unfolding.* Murray Hill, NJ: AT&T Bell Laboratories.

Lawler, E. L. (1975). The quadratic assignment problem: A brief review. In B. Roy (Ed.), *Combinatorial programming: Methods and applications* (pp. 351–360). Dordrecht, The Netherlands: Reidel.

Mardia, K. V., Kent, J. T., & Bibby, J. M. (1979). *Multivariate analysis.* New York: Academic Press.

Marks, W. B. (1965). *Difference spectra of the visual pigments in single goldfish cones.* Unpublished doctoral dissertation. Baltimore, MD: The Johns Hopkins University.

Mirkin, B. (1996). *Mathematical classification and clustering.* Dordrecht, The Netherlands: Kluwer.

Pardalos, P. M., & Wolkowicz, H. (Eds.). (1994). *Quadratic assignment and related problems.* DIMACS Series on Discrete Mathematics and Theoretical Computer Science. Providence, RI: American Mathematical Society.

Plutchik, R. & Conte, H. R. (Eds.). (1997). *Circumplex models of personality and emotions.* Washington, DC: American Psychological Association.

Pruzansky, S., Tversky, A., & Carroll, J. D. (1982). Spatial versus tree representations of proximity data. *Psychometrika, 47,* 3–24.

Rothkopf, E. Z. (1957). A measure of stimulus similarity and errors in some paired-associate learning tasks. *Journal of Experimental Psychology, 53,* 94–101.

Schiffman, H., & Falkenberg, P. (1968). The organization of stimuli and sensory neurons. *Physiology and Behavior, 3,* 197–201.

Schiffman, S. S., Reynolds, M. L., & Young, F. W. (1981). *Introduction to multidimensional scaling.* New York: Academic Press.

Shepard, R. N. (1962a). Analysis of proximities: Multidimensional scaling with an unknown distance function I. *Psychometrika, 27,* 125–140.

Shepard, R. N. (1962b). Analysis of proximities: Multidimensional scaling with an unknown distance function II. *Psychometrika, 27,* 219–246.

Shepard, R. N. (1963). Analysis of proximities as a technique for the study of information processing in man. *Human Factors, 5,* 33–48.

Shepard, R. N. (1974). Representation of structure in similarity data: Problems and prospects. *Psychometrika, 39,* 373–421.

Shepard, R. N., Kilpatric, D. W., & Cunningham, J. P. (1975). The internal representation of numbers. *Cognitive Psychology, 7,* 82–138.

Späth, H. (1991). *Mathematical algorithms for linear regression.* San Diego: Academic Press.

Wilkinson, L. (1988). *SYSTAT: The system for statistics.* Evanston, IL: SYSTAT, Inc.

Author Index

Subject Index